T0211045

Communications
in Computer and Information Science   1598

More information about this series at https://link.springer.com/bookseries/7899

Mirjana Ivanovic · Marite Kirikova ·
Laila Niedrite (Eds.)

Digital Business and Intelligent Systems

15th International Baltic Conference, Baltic DB&IS 2022
Riga, Latvia, July 4–6, 2022
Proceedings

 Springer

Editors
Mirjana Ivanovic ⓘ
University of Novi Sad
Novi Sad, Serbia

Marite Kirikova ⓘ
Riga Technical University
Riga, Latvia

Laila Niedrite ⓘ
University of Latvia
Riga, Latvia

ISSN 1865-0929   ISSN 1865-0937 (electronic)
Communications in Computer and Information Science
ISBN 978-3-031-09849-9   ISBN 978-3-031-09850-5 (eBook)
https://doi.org/10.1007/978-3-031-09850-5

This Springer imprint is published by the registered company Springer Nature Switzerland AG
The registered company address is: Gewerbestrasse 11, 6330 Cham, Switzerland

Preface

This volume contains a selection of papers presented at the 15th International Baltic Conference on Digital Business and Intelligent Systems (DB&IS 2022). The conference was held during July 4–6, 2022, in Riga, Latvia.

The 15th International Baltic Conference on Digital Business and Intelligent Systems is a continuation of the biennial International Baltic Conference on Databases and Information Systems (Baltic DB&IS) held since 1994 in Trakai, Tallinn (1996, 2002, 2008, 2014, 2020), Riga (1998, 2004, 2010, 2016), and Vilnius (2000, 2006, 2012, 2018). After the 14th International Baltic Conference on Databases and Information Systems (Tallinn, 2020) the conference steering committee decided to extend the conference with more contemporary research topics and to decipher the acronym Baltic DB&IS as Digital Business and Intelligent Systems. Although the conference has grown out of the Baltics region, the conference name still carries it as a reference to its origins and long history.

Inheriting the scope of the previous editions of the conference series, the Baltic DB&IS 2022 conference focused on the advances of computer science in digital business and intelligent systems and provided a rich environment for exchanging research findings and ideas among scientists, practitioners, and doctoral students from the Baltic region and Europe but also the rest of the world.

Baltic DB&IS 2022 was organized by the Faculty of Computing of the University of Latvia together with Riga Technical University, Tallinn University of Technology, Vilnius University, Vilnius Gediminas Technical University, and the University of Tartu. The International Program Committee consisted of 82 researchers and representatives from 36 countries all over the world. This year, 42 submissions from authors in 16 countries were received. At least three reviewers evaluated each conference paper by applying the single-blind type of peer review. As a result, 16 papers were accepted as full papers and one paper was accepted as a short paper for publication in the present volume. The conference program was enriched with several keynote talks on challenging and emerging research topics. The conference was also accompanied by a Forum and a Doctoral Consortium.

The selected papers span a wide spectrum of topics related to digital business and intelligent systems, which have been grouped into five sections. The first, and largest, section addresses Computer Science Models, Methods, Algorithms, and Tools for Digital Business. The second section concerns Knowledge and Knowledge Technologies for Digital Business and Intelligent Systems. The third section proposes and describes approaches useful in IT Support for Digital Transformation. The fourth section concerns different perspectives on Artificial Agents and Smart Systems for Digital Business. Finally, the fifth section goes under the umbrella topic heading of Data, Data Science, and Computing for Digital Business and Intelligent Systems, proposing novel methods, algorithms, and architectures in the data science area.

We would like to express our warmest thanks to all authors who contributed to the 15th International Baltic Conference on Digital Business and Intelligent Systems 2022. Our special thanks go to the keynote speakers, Marlon Dumas, Alvis Brazma,

Robert E. Tarjan, and Talal G. Shamoon, for sharing their knowledge with the conference participants.

We are very grateful to the members of the international Program Committee and additional referees for their reviews and useful comments that helped authors to improve their original submitted papers. We are grateful to the presenters, session chairs, and conference participants for their time and effort that made DB&IS 2022 successful.

We also wish to express our thanks to the conference organizing team, the University of Latvia, and other supporters for their contributions.

Finally, we would like to thank Springer for their excellent cooperation during the publication of this volume.

July 2022

Mirjana Ivanovic
Marite Kirikova
Laila Niedrite

Organization

General Chair

Juris Borzovs   University of Latvia, Latvia

Program Committee Co-chairs

Mirjana Ivanovic   University of Novi Sad, Serbia
Marite Kirikova   Riga Technical University, Latvia
Laila Niedrite   University of Latvia, Latvia

Steering Committee

Janis Bubenko (1935–2022)   Royal Institute of Technology and Stockholm
 (Honorary Member)   University, Sweden
Arne Sølvberg (Honorary   Norwegian University of Science and Technology,
 Member)   Norway
Guntis Arnicāns   University of Latvia, Latvia
Juris Borzovs   University of Latvia, Latvia
Gintautas Dzemyda   Vilnius University, Lithuania
Jānis Grundspeņķis   Riga Technical University, Latvia
Hele-Mai Haav   Tallinn University of Technology, Estonia
Diana Kalibatiene   Vilnius Gediminas Technical University,
           Lithuania
Mārīte Kirikova   Riga Technical University, Latvia
Innar Liiv   Tallinn University of Technology, Estonia
Audronė Lupeikienė   Vilnius University, Lithuania
Raimundas Matulevičius   University of Tartu, Estonia
Tarmo Robal   Tallinn University of Technology, Estonia
Olegas Vasilecas   Vilnius Gediminas Technical University,
           Lithuania

Program Committee

Guntis Arnicans   University of Latvia, Latvia
Liz Bacon   Abertay University, UK
Stefano Bonnini   University of Ferrara, Italy
Dominik Bork   TU Wien, Austria
Juris Borzovs   University of Latvia, Latvia

Additional Reviewers

Andrej Bugaev
Eike Schallehn
Viktoras Chadyšas
Panagiotis Dimitrakopoulos
Iason-Ioannis Panagos
Gabriel Campero Durand
Mari Seeba
Abrar Alhasan

Contents

Artificial Agents and Smart Systems for Digital Business

**Data, Data Science, and Computing for Digital Business and
Intelligent Systems**

Computer Science Models, Methods, Algorithms, and Tools for Digital Business

Elevator Passenger In-Cabin Behaviour – A Study on Smart-Elevator Platform

Kevin Basov, Tarmo Robal$^{(\boxtimes)}$ ⓘ, Uljana Reinsalu ⓘ, and Mairo Leier ⓘ

Tallinn University of Technology, 12618 Tallinn, Estonia
{kevbas,tarmo.robal,uljana.reinsalu,mairo.leier}@taltech.ee

Abstract. Modern elevators became into wide use some 150 years ago. With the advancement of technology, the main task of elevators has remained the same – transport people and goods in between floors – yet elevators have become more sophisticated with a trend towards smart elevators. Have you ever wondered why some people always stand in the same place, or what is your favourite sport to stand in an elevator? In this study, we use an existing smart elevator platform to explore passengers' in-cabin behaviour while travelling from one floor to another as a part of human behavioural patterns. For this, we establish a location analysis model, evaluation method, and analyse real elevator passengers' data. We show that while travelling alone, passengers tend to choose their favourite position inside the cabin.

Keywords: Smart elevator · Human behaviour · Socio-Cyber-Physical Systems

1 Introduction

The history of modern elevators for transporting humans exclusively goes back to the beginning of 1800s when steam and hydraulic power were introduced for lifting. The first passenger elevator powered by a steam engine was installed in 1857 but received a cold reception from passengers with refusal to accept it [3]. Today, elevators are a norm for modern commercial and residential buildings, especially in high-rise buildings equipped with several elevators, providing an easy way for people to move between floors. In Estonia (since 2019) new buildings with five or more floors must be fitted with an elevator, as required by the law.

The ever-increasing computerization has also shaped the development of elevators, and today we can address these as Cyber Physical (Social) Systems (CPSS) [7,9,17,35] having a high impact on our daily lives. Further, with the emerge of smart cities, the social aspect is becoming even more important and future elevators can be addressed as Socio-Cyber-Physical Systems (SCPS) [6], driving the necessity to model and understand human involvement and behaviour within such systems, and allow engineers to reason about the latter.

A lot of research is available on CPSS, yet smart elevators as SCPS have still received little attention with focus on reducing waiting time and energy

M. Ivanovic et al. (Eds.): Baltic DB&IS 2022, CCIS 1598, pp. 3–18, 2022.
https://doi.org/10.1007/978-3-031-09850-5_1

consumption [2, 4, 8, 10, 11, 33] and thereby carbon footprint, optimal parking in group elevator control [5], use of floor sensors and RFID technology for elevator scheduling [16], and the use of mobiles phones to improve flow of people [32]. A thorough overview of elevator control systems is provided in [10, 12], and passenger behavioral patterns while using elevators discussed in [19].

In this paper we focus on elevator passengers' movement behaviour inside the elevator cabin during travelling from one floor to another. We take advantage of the existing smart elevator infrastructure and study human location preferences and movement behaviour, and the dependencies on cabin occupancy. The results can be later used in various fields, such as passenger movement behaviour prediction using machine learning, better layout of sensorics in smart elevator environment, and enabling personalization for future smart elevators. To the best of our knowledge, human movement behaviour inside an elevator car has not yet been studied in the context of and using the equipment of a smart elevator.

For the study we use the smart elevator system [18, 22, 23] set up at TalTech (Tallinn University of Technology), located in the ICT-building in the university campus. This is a single shaft single car elevator in a typical eight-floor office building, equipped with many smart devices such as cameras, speakers, microphones, and various sensors to collect a variety of data. The system also facilitates passenger identification and profiles. In this study we use and model real passengers' travel data to answer the following three research questions:

RQ1: *What are the most preferred standing positions of passengers in an elevator cabin while travelling alone, or in a crowded elevator?* We hypothesize that with single occupancy passengers prefer to stand near the doors or in the middle of the elevator, whereas in a crowded elevator distance is kept.

RQ2: *How likely is an elevator passenger to choose the same standing location for successive travels?* The hypothesis is that each traveller tends to have a preferred location(s) to stand in the elevator cabin.

RQ3: *What are the in-cabin movement path patterns passengers follow during their travels, if any?* We hypothesize that each passenger has certain path (s)he follows in the elevator cabin environment while entering and exiting.

The results indicate that passengers favour to stand in the middle of the elevator cabin, within the reach of the floor buttons while travelling alone, and tend to choose the same spot to stand in the elevator for successive travels.

The rest of the paper is organized as follows. Section 2 is dedicated to related works, while Sect. 3 presents the Smart Elevator System (SES) used for the study. Section 4 discusses the location analysis model and the experiments, Sect. 5 answers the research questions, and in Sect. 6 we draw conclusions.

2   Related Works

The research on human behaviour regarding elevators has mainly focused on passenger arrival at elevator lobbies [29, 30], passenger flow influence on lift control systems [20], finding patterns in usage [19], or exploring evacuation models [14, 25]. Sorsa et al. [29, 30] rejected the assumption that passengers arrive at the elevator lobbies separately, showing that in multi-storey office, hotel and residential buildings people tend to arrive in batches of variable size depending on the time of day. Considering batch arrival helped to improve elevator group performance by reducing car loading, round-trip time and passenger waiting times by 30–40%. Liang et al. [19] gathered real-world traces of human behaviour data from 12 elevators in an 18-story office building, showing that elevator usage patterns vary depending on the layout of the building (e.g., proximity of stairs to elevators), and the function of the building (e.g., in hospitals and hotels most of the vertical movement is done using elevators). They also claim that high-rise buildings with multiple elevators benefit more than low-rise buildings from human behavioural patterns on elevator usages since waiting time is minimal in smaller buildings. While [19] studied human behavioural patterns in the context of elevator exploitation through indicators such as load factor, number of floors travelled and doors-opened events to describe general behavioural patterns of office-building inhabitants, using the data (logs) generated by the elevator system itself, we in contrary focus not on the external events caused by the passengers but the passengers' behaviour in traveling situation inside the elevator cabin, and for this advantage from special equipment to collect such data on passengers.

Ronchi and Nilsson [25] focused on investigating the capabilities of evacuation models in high-rise buildings, and showed that the use of elevators can reduce the evacuation time in a non-fire emergency, while for fire events the elevator was less valuable due to the layout of the particular building used in the study. Heyes and Spearpoint [14] explored evacuation behaviour of building residents in case of a fire. The intention was to develop parameters that could be used for designing an evacuation system that uses elevators. The results of their study show that the number of building occupants that are likely to use the elevator as an evacuation method was increasingly dependent on the floor level. The primary factor whether to choose stairs or elevator is the prediction of how much time it takes to reach the ground level via each evacuation route.

Our previous work has focused on using the existing smart elevator platform [18] to profile passengers for travel behaviour characterization and floor prediction [22,23] for enhanced travel experience in smart elevators. Here we continue our work on this track and contribute to fill the gap in the existing literature for social research in the context of elevators by providing a method to study and evaluate passengers' behaviour during their travels, and applying the method in real-life scenario using real-world data.

3   Smart Elevator System

A smart elevator system can be considered as a CPSS and SCPS advantaging of data mining, Artificial Intelligence (AI) [27], for instance facial image recognition [24,28,31,34] and human speech recognition [1,13,15,26]. Our passenger in-cabin movement behaviour study is carried out using the smart elevator system (SES) [18] developed and installed at TalTech ICT building. The building has two KONE elevators, out of which one is equipped with additional hard- and software to deliver the features of the smart elevator – a RGB camera (Basler acA2040-25gc) for facial recognition, four depth cameras (Intel Real Sense D435) to detect passengers' location within the cabin, a speakerphone (Senheiser SP20) enabling voice commands, and a mini-PC (Intel NUC Mini PC NUC5i7RYB) for processing sensor data – as shown on Fig. 1 together with the coordinates system used by the SES positioning service. The smart elevator is operating between all the eight floors of the ICT-building. The main passengers of the elevator are the employees of the university and the companies having offices in the building, and students accessing classrooms and working-places.

For our study, we use the four depth cameras located over the elevator ceiling (Fig. 1) to capture passenger movement data in the cabin. The known passengers are identified by SES using the Basler RGB camera and matched to existing profiles (anonymous), no facial data as photos/video is stored, neither any personal data. In the scope of this study we use passenger profiles just as numerical ID's to distinguish between known travellers while addressing RQ2 and RQ3.

We proceed with defining some terms. A *travel* is defined as a ride of an elevator passenger between departure and destination floors, such that it starts with a passenger entering the elevator cabin and ends with exiting the cabin. Each travel is assigned a new travel identification number (travel ID) in the SES stored alongside with track data. A *track* is the location of the passenger inside the elevator cabin attributed with travel ID, position coordinates (x, y), and timestamp. *Single travel* is a travel with only one passenger occupying the elevator cabin, whereas *crowded travel* with at least two passengers in the cabin.

The passenger position data is gathered using the SES positioning service, which allows to collect position data individually for each passenger by tracking and retrieving sensor data from the four depth sensors located in the ceiling of the elevator cabin. Detection of traveller is done using an image processing algorithm. The algorithm delimits the heads of passengers in the elevator cabin regardless of their height. The system starts to locate heads at the height of

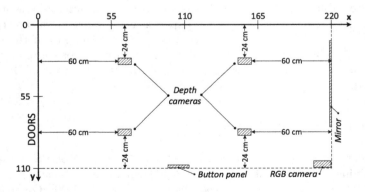

Fig. 1. Elevator cabin context and the coordinates system of the SES positioning service.

120 cm and by every iteration increasing the detection height by 5 cm. Every height layer is run through until the ceiling height is reached. All the detected heads' movement will be monitored throughout the travel and track data stored periodically (every 200 ms). Whenever a passenger with an existing profile (the passenger has travelled previously) is identified, the track is associated with profile ID in the SES. The coordinates in the SES positioning service are expressed in the metric system using centimetres as the unit (Fig. 1). The numerical values of coordinates for the x-axis are in a range from 0 to 220 cm and for the y-axis from 0 to 110 cm, reflecting the central position of the detected object position at 120 cm or higher above the floor.

4   Study Setup and Experiments

Our study is based on the location data of real elevator passengers captured by the smart elevator system (SES) positioning service. Therefore, to be able to properly interpret the data, we carried out a ground truth study consisting of a series of validation experiments, based on the passenger location analysis model.

4.1   Passenger Location Analysis Model

To analyse the passenger's travel data and answer the research questions, we developed a model for passenger location interpretation. The model divides the elevator floor area into eight equal square-sized sections with an additional section of the same size overlaying the sections in the middle of the cabin (Fig. 2). Each of the 9 sections identifies a potential location of an elevator passenger.

The division into the given nine sections was carried by a hypothesis that a passenger takes a space with a diameter of approximately 50 cm (together with space between other passengers) in a two-dimensional room. A study by Randall et al. [21] for Army Air Force reports that 95% of cadets have shoulder-width (biacromial) of 42.90 cm. Considering the latter, the division of the elevator floor into nine equal sections, where the width of each section is 55 cm, is justified, and gives passengers enough individual space, taking into account that not every passenger might be in the ideal shape of a 'cadet'. Thus, the centre point of a passenger is at ca 22 cm according to the passenger's shoulder width, which correlates with the centre point of the location model sections (27.5 cm). As usually passengers do not stand against the wall, there is a high probability that the passenger centre point aligns well with the section centre point in the model. For a crowded travel situation the elevator producer KONE has limited the maximum number of people for this elevator type to 13. Figure 2 outlines the location model with 9 sections, and the context of the elevator cabin environment, i.e., the position of doors sliding open from left-to-right while standing in the cabin and facing the doors, location of the floor buttons, back-wall mirror, and the Basler RGB camera used for face recognition by the SES.

We use this zoned location model to validate the SES passenger positioning service, and in further to analyse passenger in-cabin location behaviour based on real travel data captured to answer RQ1–RQ3.

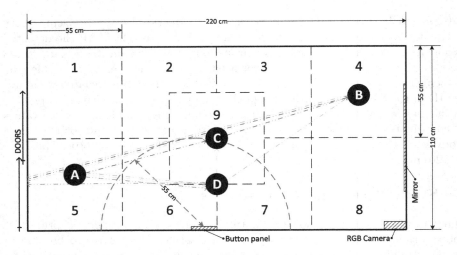

Fig. 2. The model for passenger location analysis with nine sections (1–9), and the context of the elevator cabin environment. Letters *A–D* mark the stand-location points used in the ground truth study. Dash-dot-dot coloured lines mark the movement path for the continuous location detection study: Route#1 – blue, Route#2 – green, Route#3 – orange, and Route#4 – magenta. (Color figure online)

4.2   Ground Truth Study

On 6 April 2021 late evening (after 20:00) a ground truth study was carried out by a single test passenger to evaluate the technical setup and its precision in detecting a passengers' location in the smart elevator cabin according to the location analysis model (Sect. 4.1). We chose a late hour to have minimum disturbance for other potential travellers, as well as for the continuity of the experiments. During the study, the performance and accuracy of the SES positioning service was validated whereas the test passenger location inside the elevator cabin was known in advance. Multiple locations inside the elevator cabin were selected with the goal to determine the accuracy of passenger position detection in a given section according to the location analysis model, and to identify the variability of detection within the model. The study assumed that the test subject was always standing in the middle of the designated zone of the location analysis model. For the experiments a grid was marked down on the elevator floor with paint tape (Fig. 3).

Two different experiment series: (i) *static stand positions*, and (ii) *continuous position detection for path* were carried out. Although the total number of planned test travels was 60–10 for each static stand position, and 5 for every continuous position detection experiment – the actual number of travels captured was 61 (due to miscount). Four additional travel records appeared in the captured data as other passengers entered the cabin mid experiment. These travels were removed from the analysis data, leaving thereby a dataset of 59 travel and location tracks data of 37,044 coordinate pairs. The collected data was analysed

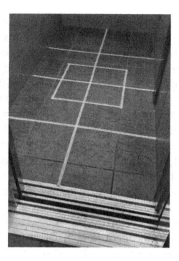

Fig. 3. Marking of the elevator floor area into sections of the location analysis model.

using general-purpose programming language Python (ver. 3.7) with *Psycopg*[1] PostgreSQL database adapter, and *XlsxWriter*[2], *DateTime*[3], *numpy*[4] and *Matplotlib*[5] packages.

4.3 Static Stand Positions

First, a static stand-still study to validate the SES positioning service against the location analysis model was carried out with four different purposefully selected stand-positions A–D (Fig. 2) in the elevator cabin. The position A represents a zone right in front of the elevator doors on the opening side (doors open in the direction from Section 5 to 1). Position B in Section 4 marks the back corner of the elevator cabin in front of the mirror, while C (Section 9) the middle of the elevator, and D on the border of Sects. 6 and 7 an ambiguous multi-section area in front of the elevator floor buttons, which can be reached for pressing from Sections 6, 7 or 9 in an approximate reach radius of 55 cm (Fig. 2).

Each position A–D was tested with a series of ten travels (except C for which 1 series appeared invalid and was removed) between two floor levels (e.g., floor 3 to 5), with a travel lasting about 20 s. The top-ceiling depth camera system setup captures passenger position tracks with a sample rate of 200 ms – roughly 100 position data points for each travel in the experiment. The collected data indicated 104 tracks in average per experiment travel (min 88 and max 112).

---

[1] https://pypi.org/project/psycopg2/.
[2] https://pypi.org/project/XlsxWriter/.
[3] https://pypi.org/project/DateTime/.
[4] https://pypi.org/project/numpy/.
[5] https://pypi.org/project/matplotlib/.

For the sake of data completeness, for each travel a new elevator call was made. In addition, the test passenger was required to follow the same route when entering the elevator and to stand in the centre of the agreed position (A, B, C, or D), and turn around to face the doors once reaching the position.

Standing in each position A–D was analysed separately. To evaluate the accuracy of measuring the static stand location, the data coordinates describing the movement into the required position A–D were filtered out as follows: first, any coordinate outside of the planned stand position section was deemed as movement into the section and thus eliminated; and further, the movement points from the section edge to the centre of the planned stand position section were additionally removed until five consecutive points (ca 1 s) were captured at the planned stand position section to assure a safe margin for reaching a stand position. Similar filtering action was carried out for data describing exiting a section and the elevator. Figure 4 visualises the experiment data before and after filtering for position C located in Section 9.

Table 1 outlines the results of the static stand positions experiment series. On average 210 location points for each series were deemed to describe moving to location and thus removed from the analysis – more for positions further away from the doors (e.g., position B). We noted that for position B the deviation for determining the x-coordinate differs from all other findings, which could be the misalignment of the positioning service or also the effect of the back-wall mirror. In further analysis, this blind-spot area has been accounted for.

The results of static stand position experiments indicate that the coordinates captured by the elevator positioning system are slightly off centred on the x-axis, while the y-coordinates are rather accurate. The misalignment may have been caused by several reasons, one of which could be the test passenger's posture, but also an alignment shift in the SES positioning service. Overall, the system is able to locate the passenger in a section center with a deviation of 8 cm on x-axis and 3 cm on the y-axis, which considering the technical setup is satisfactory. With this study, besides validating the positioning service, we also determined the viewing range of the four depth cameras and confirmed the elevator coordinate

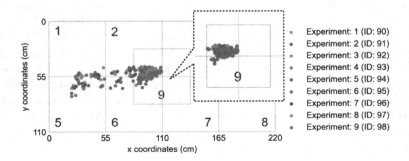

Fig. 4. Captured location data visualisation before and after (callout with a dashed line) data filtering for location point C in Section 9 of the location analysis model.

Table 1. Experiment results for the static stand position study.

Position	# Track coordinates		$M_{x,y}$* [cm]		$E_{x,y}$** [cm]		Average deviation	
	Experiments	Filtered	x	y	x	y	x	y
A	983	893	27.5	82.5	32	76.5	4.9 ± 4.4	-7.3 ± 4.2
B	1156	759	192.5	27.5	170.4	28.5	-21.3 ± 4.8	1.4 ± 3.3
C	962	778	110	55	100.9	52.6	-9.4 ± 2.9	-2.8 ± 1.5
D	1042	873	110	82.5	103.9	80.9	-7.1 ± 4.5	-2.8 ± 4.9
Avg	1036	826	n/a	n/a	n/a	n/a	-8.2 ± 4.2	-2.9 ± 3.5
Sum	4143	3303	n/a	n/a	n/a	n/a	n/a	n/a

* Central section coordinates in the model.
** Median central coordinates of section in experiments.

system in SES. The experiment forms a benchmark for interpreting the travel track dataset of real passengers, used for *RQ*1 and *RQ*2.

4.4 Continuous Position Detection for a Path

To validate the detection of passenger movement path inside the elevator cabin using the SES positioning service, we planned four different routes starting and ending at the cabin doors in between the positions *A–D* (Fig. 2):

- Route#1: $A \rightarrow C \rightarrow B \rightarrow A$, as a scenario when a passenger enters the elevator, moves to the middle, reaches the floor buttons, and proceeds to move to the back corner of the cabin for the duration of travel.
- Route#2: $A \rightarrow D \rightarrow B \rightarrow A$, a scenario similar to Route#1, except the floor buttons are reached right in front of these at the position *D*.
- Route#3: $A \rightarrow D \rightarrow C \rightarrow A$, where after pressing the floor buttons the passenger proceeds to stand in the middle of the elevator at the position *C*.
- Route#4: $A \rightarrow D \rightarrow A$, where the passenger reaches the button panel and then immediately steps back to the closest position to doors on opening side.

The test passenger followed each route for five times during the experiments. Each travel was through four floor levels (e.g., floor 1 to 5) with an average travel duration of 25 s, during which in average 112 track points for each travel were captured by SES. At each point (*A–D*) the test passenger made a short stop, yet keeping the movement as natural as possible. While exiting, the shortest path through the opening side of the doors (position *A*) was taken.

For the analysis the captured test passenger's location data was filtered and compressed as follows: a section and location coordinates were added to the movement path whenever five consecutive points were captured by SES in the same section (at rate of 200 ms), provided that the section was a neighbouring section (in the analysis model) to the previous one in the movement route list. The path was constructed as a sequence of sections (identified by the coordinates) passed by the passenger, where each section is sequentially counted only once, forming for example a path $5 - 6 - 9 - 6 - 5$. Figure 5 exemplifies the path detection according to these rules for Route#2 in the experiments.

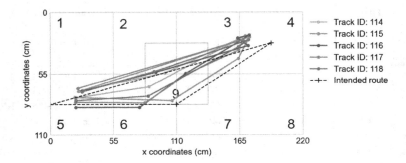

Fig. 5. Movement path construction with applied data filtering for Route#2 in the experiments. The dashed black line indicates the planned route for the experiment.

From this study we also notice that there is a certain blind-spot area of approximately 15 cm from the wall into which no coordinates fall. First of all, the SES positioning service estimates the centre point of the passenger, and second, even if a passenger stands against the wall, the detected centre point of the person would still be ca 15 cm away from it.

The continuous location detection experiment confirmed that the SES positioning service can sufficiently track the passenger movement inside the elevator cabin throughout the travel, and can be successfully matched against the established location analysis model using the noise removal and data point reduction technique described. The results will be applied to answer *RQ3*.

5   Behaviour Analysis

In this section we apply the knowledge gained from the ground truth study to answer the three research questions about passenger movement behaviour in elevator cabin. For this, we use the track data of real passengers collected through 61 days (2 months, April – May 2021) and consisting of 11,731 travels, out of which 67.9% of travels were made by a single passenger, and in 32.1% of cases there were multiple passengers in the cabin. The period of data collection matches with the enforced COVID-19 restrictions (2+2 rule and facial mask mandate), which affects the available number of travels as well as the ability of the SES to differentiate between known travellers through facial recognition (no data used in this study is personalized). In addition, the ICT-building was partially closed for students due to the pandemics, and we also noticed that people preferred stairs over elevator. Travels performed by the test passenger for the ground truth study have been excluded. Table 2 characterizes the used data.

5.1   RQ1: Preferred Standing Positions

The first question to consider is the most preferred standing location while travelling alone or in a crowded elevator cabin. To answer *RQ1* we look at all track

Table 2. Smart elevator passenger data used for the behaviour analysis.

	# Travels	# Tracks	ntp_{avg}*	d_{avg}**
Total (count)	11,731	1,414,740	120	24
Travelling alone in cabin (count)	7,790	1,034,162	130	26
Travelling in a crowded cabin (count)	3,761	380,578	101	20

* Avg. tracks per travel per passenger. ** Avg. travel duration per passenger [s].

data on passengers' position in two groups: travels with one passenger in the cabin (*single*), and travels with more than one passenger in the cabin (*crowded*), in two categories: (i) *coordinate-based positioning* into sections of the analysis model for the whole travel, and (ii) *travel-based standing position*, i.e., the most occupied section is deemed the standing position of the travel. The analysis for *RQ1* is based on all the available data for all the passengers during the study period regardless whether they had an existing profile or not. The data is analysed according to the location analysis model and the method described in Sect. 4, according to which for each track coordinate a section (1–9) is identified.

The analysis (Fig. 6) reveals that for single travels in most cases passengers tend to stand in the middle of the elevator (Section 9). Whenever there are fellow passengers in the elevator, distance is kept and the central location is chosen only in fifth of the cases, having a dramatic drop of two times compared to single travel. The least desirable position to stand is in front of the facial recognition camera (Section 8). The passengers are four times more likely to stand next to the door on the closing side (Section 1) when travelling in a crowded elevator than travelling alone. There is almost no difference in standing in front of the doors on the opening side (Section 5). Also, we notice that passengers prefer to stand on the opposite side to the button panel and level indicator above it (compare Sections 2 & 3 to Sections 6 & 7). We believe this is due to have a better view over the travel status from the floor indicator but also not to block the (de-)boarding passengers. Figure 7 presents the location density maps for passenger locations in the category of coordinate-based positioning through all track data.

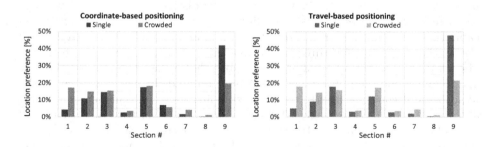

Fig. 6. Preferred standing positions according to the section model for single and crowded cabin travel situation: based on all coordinates of a travel (left), the most occupied section during a travel (right).

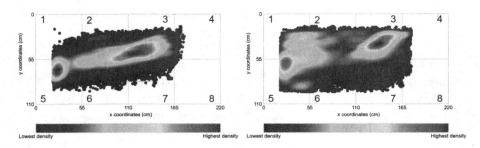

Fig. 7. Density maps for elevator passengers positions in cabin trough travels: single passenger in cabin (left), multiple passengers in cabin (right).

We acknowledge that these findings apply to this particular elevator cabin type with the floor buttons located in the middle of one of the sidewalls. However, in many larger elevators the buttons are doubled on both sides of the elevator doors, and doors open to both sides, which is likely to change the favourable standing positions layout. It would be interesting to carry out this experiment on different elevator layouts, equipment permitting, to explore whether the general findings, e.g., for single travel the centre of elevator is preferred, hold or not.

5.2   RQ2: Preferred Standing Position for Successive Travels

The second question we consider is the likelihood of a passenger to choose the same standing location in the elevator cabin for re-occurring travels, i.e., do passengers have their favourite spots to stand in the elevator cabin. To answer $RQ2$, we analyse only the track data of known (profiled) passengers by their travels. These profiles are created and identified by the smart elevator system automatically using the implemented face recognition system [18,23] with an identification success rate 98.2%. Unfortunately, during the study Covid-19 restrictions (including mask mandate) were effective, which significantly reduced the travel data available for profiled passengers – the SES was unable to recognise all known passengers. We obtain only 793 travels with 305 distinct profiles, which we once again separate into two groups: travelling alone (single: 30.0%) or in a crowded cabin (two passengers: 42.1%, three: 21.7%, four and more: 5.9%). We reject any profile that has less than three travels associated. Further, we organize travels of each profile in chronological order and split the set into two and use the first 2/3 to determine the preferred standing position, and the last 1/3 to verify the hypothesis of choosing mostly the same standing location. This leaves us with 361 travels (46%), 83 as single, and 278 as crowded cabin travels, with 17 and 60 profiles correspondingly. To determine the preferred location we apply the same approach as for RQ1 based on the location analysis model, determining the preferred standing position as one of the nine sections. For each passenger we find over her travels a list of standing positions (Section 1–9) in a decreasing order, and use the top two items as the most likely standing positions as *Top 1* and *Top 2* of this list. We then compare these to the remaining 1/3 of data

(Table 3). Based on the little data we have, we see that while travelling alone in the cabin, passengers tend to choose the same standing locations as previously, while in the situation of crowded cabin, no favourable position is chosen, and a random open spot is occupied.

Table 3. Probability of choosing the same standing position for re-occurring travels.

Cabin situation group	# Profiles	# Travels	Top 1	Top 2	Top 1 or Top 2
Single travel	17	83	60%	31%	91%
Crowded travel	60	278	26%	9%	35%

5.3   RQ3: Recurring Movement Flow Patterns

The last question we address when studying passenger in-cabin behaviour is whether passengers tend to follow the same movement path through the cabin during their travels. To answer *RQ3* we analyse the successive travels of profiled passengers (single travel only) and use the same dataset as for RQ2. From RQ2 we already know that passengers tend to choose the same standing location in 60% of cases when travelling alone. We decide not to analyse movement routes while travelling in a crowded elevator as the route would greatly depend on the occupancy of the elevator cabin and locations of the other passengers.

For each travel associated with a profile, we construct a movement path based on the sections the traveller has been found to be present in (passing or standing) using the method described in Sect. 4.4, producing a path (e.g., $5 - 6 - 9 - 1 - 5$) for each travel of a profiled passenger. Table 4 characterises the movement paths for the 83 single travels available for 17 profiled passengers.

Based on the small sample of data we were able to collect, we do not find that passengers would in an identifiable way follow the same movement path when entering, standing, and exiting the elevator for travelling in between floors. The average path consists of four to eight sections of movement with a maximum of 11 sections. The same path is followed only in 13% of travels observed. However, for two profiled travellers we notice the exact path match to be 75% and 67%. Analysing the first three positions of a path, we interestingly find that the same

Table 4. Characterisation of constructed movement paths and re-occurrence match.

	# Travels/profile	L_{path}*	$L_{pax-path}$**	M*** [%]	$M_{partial}$**** [%]
Avg	5 ± 2	6	$6,4 \pm 1,0$	13%	62,3%
Min	3	3	$5,2 \pm 1,3$	75%	100,0%
Max	12	11	$7,8 \pm 1,4$	0%	0%

* Path length over all travels. ** Avg. path length per passenger.
*** Exact path match rate. **** Partial path match rate on the first three positions.

passenger who had the exact match rate at 75% had a movement path match by first three positions at 100%, whereas the general rate for all single-travelling profiled passengers was at 62%. This is somewhat expected, as passengers usually enter from Section 5, move to Section 6 to press a floor button, and then to Section 9 to stand in the middle of the elevator cabin. With a larger set of data available and for a longer duration, there might be some interesting findings in the future.

6   Conclusions

With the advancement of technology, smart elevators as CP(S)S are increasingly becoming a reality. These smart elevators provide an excellent platform to study passengers behaviour – once used to be possible only with surveillance cameras and manual work – to improve elevator systems, quality of provided service and passenger experience, and further enhance the concept of a smart elevators.

In this paper we established an elevator passenger location analysis model, formulated a method to evaluate passengers movement behaviour, benchmarked it against the smart elevator positioning service, and investigated elevator passenger in-cabin behaviour using an existing smart elevator platform. Although our study was only limited to one type of an elevator cabin, the established zone-based location analysis model and method could be applied to any other elevator type able to carry more than 10 persons at a time and being therefore large enough by floor area. Such elevators are typically found in large commercial buildings, shopping malls, hotels, hospitals etc. With the model, method and experiments we also fill the gap in existing literature regarding studies of human behavioural patterns in the context of elevator travels. The results can be used for (smart) elevator cabin layout design, including sensors, but also improving the quality of service by knowing how the passengers take advantage of the existing elevator in real-life situations – all in all, little things matter!

As for the movement behaviour studies, we first explored whether there are favourable standing places for elevator passengers in general. The study showed that passengers tend to prefer to stand in the middle of the elevator while being the only occupant of the elevator cabin, which is not the case for crowded cabin situation, where a random open spot is occupied. Further, we advantaged from the smart elevator system profiling capabilities to identify repeatedly travelling passengers to investigate whether passengers tend to have personal preferred standing locations and if they follow certain movement path in the cabin. The analysis revealed that passengers tend to choose the same standing location quite often (60%) in case they are the only occupant of the cabin. We however failed to find confident results that passengers would always follow the same movement path while entering, travelling and exiting the elevator. The small sample of data we collected due to covid-restrictions intervening our study was not sufficient to draw any confirmatory conclusions. Thereby, once the situation normalizes and all the technical capabilities of the smart elevator can again be efficiently used, we plan for a larger long-term study on passenger in-cabin behaviour.

References

1. Allen, J.: Speech Recognition and Synthesis, pp. 1664–1667. John Wiley and Sons Ltd., GBR (2003)
2. Bamunuarachchi, D.T., Ranasinghe, D.N.: Elevator group optimization in a smart building. In: 2015 IEEE 10th International Conference on Industrial and Information Systems (ICIIS), pp. 71–76 (2015)
3. Bernard, A.: Lifted: A Cultural History of the Elevator. NYU Press, New York (2014)
4. Bharti, H., Saxena, R.K., Sukhija, S., Yadav, V.: Cognitive model for smarter dispatch system/elevator. In: 2017 IEEE International Conference on Cloud Computing in Emerging Markets (CCEM), pp. 21–28 (2017)
5. Brand, M., Nikovski, D.: Optimal parking in group elevator control. In: Proceedings of IEEE International Conference on Robotics and Automation, ICRA 2004, vol. 1, pp. 1002–1008, April 2004
6. Calinescu, R., Cámara, J., Paterson, C.: Socio-cyber-physical systems: models, opportunities, open challenges. In: 2019 IEEE/ACM 5th Intl Workshop on Software Engineering for Smart Cyber-Physical Systems (SEsCPS), pp. 2–6 (2019)
7. Cassandras, C.G.: Smart cities as cyber-physical social systems. Engineering 2(2), 156–158 (2016)
8. Chou, S., Budhi, D.A., Dewabharata, A., Zulvia, F.E.: Improving elevator dynamic control policies based on energy and demand visibility. In: 2018 3rd International Conference on Intelligent Green Building and Smart Grid (IGBSG), pp. 1–4 (2018)
9. Dressler, F.: Cyber physical social systems: towards deeply integrated hybridized systems. In: 2018 International Conference on Computing, Networking and Communications (ICNC), pp. 420–424 (2018)
10. Fernandez, J.R., Cortes, P.: A survey of elevator group control systems for vertical transportation: a look at recent literature. IEEE Control Syst. Mag. 35(4), 38–55 (2015)
11. Fujimura, T., Ueno, S., Tsuji, H., Miwa, H.: Control algorithm for multi-car elevators with high transportation flexibility. In: 2013 IEEE 2nd Global Conference on Consumer Electronics (GCCE), pp. 544–545 (2013)
12. Ge, H., Hamada, T., Sumitomo, T., Koshizuka, N.: Intellevator: a context-aware elevator system for assisting passengers. In: 2018 IEEE 16th International Conference on Embedded and Ubiquitous Computing (EUC), pp. 81–88 (2018)
13. Goetsu, S., Sakai, T.: Voice input interface failures and frustration: Developer and user perspectives. In: The Adjunct Publication of the 32nd Annual ACM Symposium on User Interface Software and Technology, UIST 2019, pp. 24–26. Association for Computing Machinery, New York (2019)
14. Heyes, E., Spearpoint, M.: Lifts for evacuation - human behaviour considerations. Fire Mater. 36(4), 297–308 (2012)
15. Ketkar, S.S., Mukherjee, M.: Speech recognition system. In: Proceedings of the International Conference and Workshop on Emerging Trends in Technology, ICWET 2011, pp. 1234–1237. Association for Computing Machinery, New York (2011)
16. Kwon, O., Lee, E., Bahn, H.: Sensor-aware elevator scheduling for smart building environments. Build. Environ. 72, 332–342 (2014)
17. Lee, E.A., Seshia, S.A.: Introduction to Embedded Systems: A Cyber-Physical Systems Approach, 2nd edn. The MIT Press, Cambridge (2016)
18. Leier, M., et al.: Smart elevator with unsupervised learning for visitor profiling and personalised destination prediction. In: 2021 IEEE Conference on Cognitive and Computational Aspects of Situation Management (CogSIMA), pp. 9–16 (2021)

19. Liang, C.J.M., Tang, J., Zhang, L., Zhao, F., Munir, S., Stankovic, J.A.: On human behavioral patterns in elevator usages. In: Proceedings of the 5th ACM Workshop on Embedded Systems For Energy-Efficient Buildings, BuildSys 2013, pp. 1–2. Association for Computing Machinery, New York (2013)
20. Lin, K.K., Lupin, S., Vagapov, Y.: Analysis of lift control system strategies under uneven flow of passengers. In: Camarinha-Matos, L.M., Falcão, A.J., Vafaei, N., Najdi, S. (eds.) DoCEIS 2016. IAICT, vol. 470, pp. 217–225. Springer, Cham (2016). https://doi.org/10.1007/978-3-319-31165-4_22
21. Randall, F.E., Damon, A., Benton, R.S., Patt, D.I.: Human body size in military aircraft and personal equipment (1946)
22. Reinsalu, U., Robal, T., Leier, M.: Floor selection proposal for automated travel with smart elevator. In: Robal, T., Haav, H.-M., Penjam, J., Matulevičius, R. (eds.) DB&IS 2020. CCIS, vol. 1243, pp. 38–51. Springer, Cham (2020). https://doi.org/10.1007/978-3-030-57672-1_4
23. Robal, T., Reinsalu, U., Leier, M.: Towards personalized elevator travel with smart elevator system. Baltic J. Mod. Comput. 8(4), 675–697 (2020). https://doi.org/10.22364/bjmc.2020.8.4.12
24. Robal, T., Zhao, Y., Lofi, C., Hauff, C.: Webcam-based attention tracking in online learning: a feasibility study. In: 23rd International Conference on Intelligent User Interfaces, IUI 2018, pp. 189–197. ACM, New York (2018)
25. Ronchi, E., Nilsson, D.: Fire evacuation in high-rise buildings: a review of human behaviour and modelling research. Fire Sci. Rev. 2(1), 1–21 (2013). https://doi.org/10.1186/2193-0414-2-7
26. Ross, S., Brownholtz, E., Armes, R.: Voice user interface principles for a conversational agent. In: Proceedings of the 9th International Conference on Intelligent User Interfaces, IUI 2004, pp. 364–365. Association for Computing Machinery, New York (2004)
27. Russell, S., Norvig, P.: Artificial Intelligence: A Modern Approach, 3rd edn. Prentice Hall Press, New York (2009)
28. Silva, E.M., Boaventura, M., Boaventura, I.A.G., Contreras, R.C.: Face recognition using local mapped pattern and genetic algorithms. In: Proceedings of the International Conference on Pattern Recognition and Artificial Intelligence, PRAI 2018, pp. 11–17. Association for Computing Machinery, New York (2018)
29. Sorsa, J., Kuusinen, J.M., Siikonen, M.L.: Passenger batch arrivals at elevator lobbies. Elevator World 61(1), 108–120 (2013)
30. Sorsa, J., Siikonen, M.L., Kuusinen, J.M., Hakonen, H.: A field study and analysis of passengers arriving at lift lobbies in social groups in multi-storey office, hotel and residential buildings. Build. Serv. Eng. Res. Technol. 42(2), 197–210 (2021)
31. Stark, L.: Facial recognition is the plutonium of AI. XRDS 25(3), 50–55 (2019)
32. Turunen, M., et al.: Mobile interaction with elevators: improving people flow in complex buildings. In: Proceedings of Intl Conference on Making Sense of Converging Media, AcademicMindTrek 2013, pp. 43–50. ACM, New York (2013)
33. Wang, F., Tang, J., Zong, Q.: Energy-consumption-related robust optimization scheduling strategy for elevator group control system. In: 2011 IEEE 5th Intl Conference on Cybernetics and Intelligent Systems (CIS), pp. 30–35, September 2011
34. Zhao, W., Chellappa, R., Phillips, P.J., Rosenfeld, A.: Face recognition: a literature survey. ACM Comput. Surv. 35(4), 399–458 (2003)
35. Zhuge, H.: Cyber-physical society-the science and engineering for future society. Futur. Gener. Comput. Syst. 32, 180–186 (2014)

Efficient Access Control to Parking Space for Different Customer Segments

Thomas Müller[1](✉) (iD), Gunther Piller[2] (iD), and Franz Rothlauf[3] (iD)

[1] Mainz University of Applied Sciences, Lucy-Hillebrand-Straße 2, 55128 Mainz, Germany
thomas.mueller@hs-mainz.de
[2] Ludwigshafen University of Business and Society, Ernst-Boehe-Str. 4, 67059 Ludwigshafen, Germany
[3] Johannes Gutenberg University Mainz, Saarstr. 21, 55122 Mainz, Germany

Abstract. In urban areas, the number of parking spaces is limited and takes up valuable space that is also needed for other purposes. Demand-driven and systematic utilisation of parking spaces can help to gain the most out of available space. We propose a probability-based approach to control access to off-street parking lots. Our approach takes into account distinct offerings for different customer segments. Registered customers, who pay a monthly fee and have a guarantee of a free parking space at all times, and public customers, who pay according to their parking time. The latter is more profitable and needs to be maximized. We test our approach in a case study with a historic dataset and compare our results with the original control of access. Over two months, we could release on critical periods approximately 22% more parking spaces for public customers.

Keywords: Parking management · Demand forecast · Smart city

1 Introduction

In densely populated urban areas, space is a valuable asset and is in high demand for multiple purposes such as housing, retail, business, and infrastructure. A significant part of land use in cities is due to parking. Manville and Shoup [1] state, that car parking space accounts for 23% of the total land in Munich; in Frankfurt am Main it even amounts to as much as 38%. These numbers emphasise that parking takes up a large part of the limited space in urban areas.

Urban land used for parking must be managed efficiently. A private parking space can increase the housing prices in urban areas by 6 to 13% [2]. This could be reduced, by better utilisation of existing parking lots. For example, Cai et al. [3] proposed to make unused parking space of public buildings available to private persons. A similar initiative is underway to utilise unused parking lots of companies [4]. Furthermore, some cities are striving to reduce traffic and the number of cars in inner cities [5]. This often comes with a planned reduction and deconstruction of car parks [6]. The remaining parking space must then be managed all the better.

© The Author(s), under exclusive license to Springer Nature Switzerland AG 2022
M. Ivanovic et al. (Eds.): Baltic DB&IS 2022, CCIS 1598, pp. 19–30, 2022.
https://doi.org/10.1007/978-3-031-09850-5_2

Predicting the availability and occupancy of parking spaces is an important instrument for doing so. It enables efficient management of valuable urban space. In addition, the search for free parking spaces, which typically increases air pollution by 25–40% at peak times, can be shortened [7].

Parking forecasts have been investigated for different purposes using a variety of methods. Machine learning approaches e.g. support vector machines or neural networks have frequently been used to predict the number of free parking lots at a given time [7, 8]. Within those studies often the influence of variables such as weather, day of the week, holidays or traffic flow was examined. Other research uses queuing models to simulate driver behaviour by accounting e.g. currently available parking lots, distance, traffic congestions and price [9]. The typical goal of such investigations are recommendations and parking guidance for drivers. Further work is aimed at supporting car park operators. For example, dynamic pricing and revenue management methods have been used to maximise the expected revenue for parking managers [10].

It was pointed out by Caicedo et al. [11], that the management of parking lots needs to accommodate the needs of different customer segments, e.g. monthly payers with reservations and short-term parkers without reservations. In a very specific context, different customer types were considered in the work of Cai et al. [3]. They have developed a method for allocating the parking spaces of five public buildings that are shared by users of these buildings and private individuals. The underlying demand for parking space for the two customer groups was randomly generated.

We are extending existing research by developing an approach to control access to parking spaces in car parks. As it is common in many parking garages, we consider two different types of customers: Firstly, there are registered customers (RCs) with reservations, who pay a monthly fee and can park at any time. The second type are public customers (PCs) without reservations. These can park depending on parking lot availability and pay according to parking time. While there has to be always enough space for RCs, PCs are more profitable. Our approach allows the parking manager to maximise the number of PCs. For this purpose, we estimate the future demand of RCs and derive the number of PCs that will be admitted. In this way, we try to guarantee a parking space for arriving RCs. Our solution is based on a time-dependent model for parking demand and uses real-world data to predict the number of inbound and outbound customers of both types as well as their parking time. Real-time deviations from the forecast parking occupancy are continuously adjusted. We test our solution in a case study using data from a car park in a German city. At peak times, when the demand for parking is high, our approach results in approximately 22% more parking space being available for PCs.

The paper is organised as follows: Related work is presented in Sect. 2. In Sect. 3 we derive our approach for parking demand. The case study follows in Sect. 4. Finally, we close with concluding remarks and an outlook.

2   Related Work

Predictions of car park occupancy were investigated for different objectives. A variety of scenarios were studied and different methods were applied. Several approaches investigate the dependence of parking forecasts for specific points in time on external variables, such as weather, holidays or traffic flow (see e.g. [7–9]). Typically, the impact of the considered variables on prediction accuracy is evaluated within different models. Off-street [7] and on-street [8] scenarios are addressed. Distinctions between different types of offers, e.g. for short- and long-term parking, or different pricing schemes were not in focus. For modelling, machine learning approaches with e.g. neural networks are commonly used in this domain.

Some studies focus on efficiently guiding drivers to free parking spaces. They often deal with predictions for parking availability and web applications for driver routing (see e.g. [12, 13]). Reducing traffic congestions, saving fuel, time and reduction of air pollution as well as stress are the main motivations for this type of research. Most data on historic parking space occupancy, locations of parking lots and cars as well as traffic congestion are used as input data. Also in these studies, only one type of parking offer is considered. Use is made of machine learning approaches [7, 12, 13] or queuing models with e.g. Markov chains [9, 14, 15]. Results are usually evaluated using data from real-world settings [15] or via simulations covering high and low traffic situations [9].

The approaches discussed above often focus on driver support. They are not necessarily suitable for parking garage management. Maximising revenue is the typical goal of car park operators. For this purpose, revenue management techniques are applied in e.g. [10, 16, 17]. They usually include dynamic pricing depending on demand, i.e. expected arrivals and the number of free parking spaces (see e.g. [17]) as key variables.

In real-world settings, it is often important to consider the link between parking availability and reservations, as pointed out by Caicedo et al. [11]. For example, car parks often block parking spots for regular customers paying monthly fees. In addition to corresponding offers for reservations, almost all car parks provide ad-hoc parking too. The challenge is to find a balance between the two types of offers to maximise the use of available space and increase profit.

A first study in this direction was conducted by Cai et al. [3]. They have considered the usage of parking lots in public buildings by people visiting and working in those buildings as well as by private individuals. While parking space should be reserved for the first type of user, this is not necessary for the second type. To efficiently allocate parking space between these two groups of customers, a parking allocation method has been developed. It uses a genetic algorithm to optimise parking fees and the share of private parking in specific time windows. Randomly generated demand for parking is used as the main input. The resulting algorithm is evaluated in a scenario with five parking garages for public buildings and compared to a traditional "all time all space" parking strategy, where everyone is allowed to park everywhere at any time.

A general concept that helps car park operators to efficiently manage the occupancy of parking spaces in a typical environment, where both customers with and without reservations are served, is still lacking. Our approach presented in this paper addresses this gap.

3 Approach for Data-Driven Control of Parking Lots

In our approach, we consider customers with reservations, RCs, and customers without reservations, referred to as PCs. Garages control the number of cars that are allowed to park by capacities Cap^{RC} and Cap^{PC}. Once a capacity is reached vehicles of that customer type are not allowed to enter the facility unless a vehicle of the same customer type leaves the garage. Our goal is, to find the maximum capacity Cap^{PC} that can be assigned to PCs in a time interval $t_k \leq t \leq t_{k+1}$ which we denote by $\Delta_{k,\,k+1}$. The constraint is that parking spaces must always be available for incoming RCs within the total capacity Cap^{tot} of the garage.

In a first step, we derive a probability-based description of upcoming departures. We then outline our approach for calculating the maximum capacity for PCs.

3.1   Estimate of Departures

The average number of cars entering the garage during the time interval $\Delta^E_{i,\,i+1}$ ranging from t_i until t_{i+1} with fixed external conditions $f_1, \ldots, f_n$ is denoted by:

$$E\left(\Delta^E_{i,\,i+1}|f_1 \ldots f_n\right) \tag{1}$$

Typical external conditions or features f_i are time, weekday, weather, public holiday, or events. In practice, E can be obtained in different ways, e.g., by an average of appropriate data from the past, or through machine learning approaches (see e.g. [7]). Similarly, the average number of cars leaving the parking facility during the time interval Δ^L after having entered during the time interval Δ^E is:

$$L\left(\Delta^L_{j,\,j+1}, \Delta^E_{i,\,i+1}|f_1 \ldots f_n\right) \tag{2}$$

with $j \geq i$. The ratio

$$P\left(\Delta^L_{j,\,j+1}, \Delta^E_{i,\,i+1}|f_1 \ldots f_n\right) = \frac{L\left(\Delta^L_{j,\,j+1}, \Delta^E_{i,\,i+1}|f_1 \ldots f_n\right)}{E\left(\Delta^E_{i,\,i+1}|f_1 \ldots f_n\right)} \tag{3}$$

can then be interpreted as the probability of cars leaving the garage during $\Delta^L_{j,\,j+1}$ after having entered during $\Delta^E_{i,\,i+1}$, assuming that E and L are normally distributed.

The observed number of cars leaving the garage at a certain time usually differs from the average number described by the function L. Consequently, one must constantly adjust the expected number of departures in response to the observed number of vehicles that have already left. For this purpose, we denote the observed number of cars leaving the garage during the time interval Δ^L after entering during the time interval Δ^E as:

$$O\left(\Delta^L_{j,\,j+1}, \Delta^E_{i,\,i+1}|f_1 \ldots f_n\right) \tag{4}$$

Then the total number of cars that have left the garage by time t_k with $k > i$ is:

$$\sum_{j=i}^{k-1} O(\Delta^L_{j,\,j+1}, \Delta^E_{i,\,i+1}|f_1 \ldots f_n) \tag{5}$$

This observation until $t = t_k$ determines the adjustment of the expected number of cars leaving the garage at a time interval $\Delta^L_{l,\,l+1}$, with $l > k$, after having entered at $\Delta^E_{i,\,i+1}$.

It is given by the number of cars remaining in the garage and the recalculated probability P_k for cars leaving during $\Delta^L_{l,\,l+1}$:

$$L_k\left(\Delta^L_{l,\,l+1},\ \Delta^E_{i,\,i+1}|f_1\ldots f_n\right) = \left[E\left(\Delta^E_{i,\,i+1}|f_1\ldots f_n\right) - \sum_{j=i}^{k-1} O\left(\Delta^L_{j,\,j+1},\ \Delta^E_{i,\,i+1}|f_1\ldots f_n\right)\right] \\ *P_k\left(\Delta^L_{l,\,l+1},\ \Delta^E_{i,\,i+1}|f_1\ldots f_n\right) \tag{6}$$

with

$$P_k\left(\Delta^L_{l,\,l+1},\ \Delta^E_{i,\,i+1}|f_1\ldots f_n\right) = \frac{P\left(\Delta^L_{l,\,l+1},\ \Delta^E_{i,\,i+1}|f_1\cdots f_n\right)}{\sum_{j=k} P\left(\Delta^L_{j,\,j+1},\ \Delta^E_{i,\,i+1}|f_1\ldots f_n\right)} \tag{7}$$

3.2 Capacity of Parking Lots for Public Customers

Our goal is, to maximise the parking space that can be opened for PCs while meeting RC's incoming demand. To do so, we start by predicting the demand of parking space for RCs. Consider the situation at $t = t_k$. At this point in time, the number of vehicles $C_{ob}^{RC/PC}\,(t_k\,|\,f_1\ldots f_n)$ of RC and PC in the car park is known by observation.

The predicted number $C_{pr}^{RC}(t_{k+1}\,|\,f_1\ldots f_n)$ of RC cars in the parking garage at the time t_{k+1} results from the number of observed cars at $t = t_k$, plus the predicted number E_{pr}^{RC} of cars entering the garage during the time span $\Delta^E_{k,\,k+1}$ that do not leave during the same time interval. In addition, one must correct for the vehicles L_k^{RC} that entered before t_k and are expected to depart during the time interval $\Delta^L_{k,\,k+1}$:

$$C_{pr}^{RC}\,(t_{k+1}|f_1\ldots f_n) = C_{ob}^{RC}(t_k|f_1\ldots f_n) + E_{pr}^{RC}\left(\Delta^E_{k,\,k+1}|f_1\ldots f_n\right) \\ *\left[1 - P^{RC}\left(\Delta^L_{k,\,k+1},\ \Delta^E_{k,\,k+1}|f_1\ldots f_n\right)\right] \\ -\sum_{i=0}^{k-1} L_k^{RC}\left(\Delta^L_{k,\,k+1},\ \Delta^E_{i,\,i+1}|f_1\ldots f_n\right) \tag{8}$$

Similarly, one can obtain the predicted number of cars at a later point in time, e.g. at $t = t_{k+2}$:

$$C_{pr}^{RC}\,(t_{k+2}|f_1\cdots f_n) = C_{ob}^{RC}(t_k|f_1\cdots f_n) + E_{pr}^{RC}\left(\Delta^E_{k,\,k+1}|f_1\cdots f_n\right) \\ *\left[1 - P^{RC}\left(\Delta^L_{k,\,k+1},\ \Delta^E_{k,\,k+1}|f_1\cdots f_n\right)\right. \\ \left. -P^{RC}\left(\Delta^L_{k+1,\,k+2},\ \Delta^E_{k,\,k+1}|f_1\cdots f_n\right)\right] \\ +E_{pr}^{RC}\left(\Delta^E_{k+1,\,k+2}|f_1\cdots f_n\right) \\ *\left[1 - P^{RC}\left(\Delta^L_{k+1,\,k+2},\ \Delta^E_{k+1,\,k+2}|f_1\cdots f_n\right)\right] \\ -\sum_{i=0}^{k-1} L_k^{RC}\left(\Delta^L_{k,\,k+1},\ \Delta^E_{i,\,i+1}|f_1\cdots f_n\right) \tag{9}$$

Focusing on the demand for RCs within the time interval $\Delta_{k,\,k+1}$, the total parking capacity available for PCs during this time span is:

$$Cap^{PC}_{k,\,k+1}\big(\Delta_{k,\,k+1}|f_1 \dots f_n\big) = Cap^{tot} - Max\big(C^{RC}_{pr}(t|f_1 \dots f_n),\ with\ t_k \le t \le t_{k+1}\big) \quad (10)$$

given by the difference of Cap^{tot}, the total capacity of the parking garage, and the maximum of the predicted parking demand for RCs in the considered time interval. Since at time t_k the number $C_{ob}{}^{PC}$ of PCs is observed and known, the additional space $E^{PC}{}_{k,\,k+1}$ that is available for PCs during $\Delta_{k,\,k+1}$ is:

$$Cap^{PC}_{k,\,k+1}\big(\Delta_{k,\,k+1}|f_1 \dots f_n\big) = C^{PC}_{ob}(t_k|f_1 \dots f_n) + E^{PC}_{k,\,k+1}\big(\Delta_{k,\,k+1}|f_1 \dots f_n\big) \quad (11)$$

However, PCs that are allowed to enter the parking garage during the time interval $\Delta_{k,\,k+1}$ have also to meet the demand of RCs at a later time. In this way, one obtains further conditions on the additional space E^{PC}. For example, considering the demand for RCs within the time interval $t_{k+1} \le t \le t_{k+2}$ one gets:

$$
\begin{aligned}
Cap^{PC}_{k+1,\,k+2}\big(\Delta_{k,\,k+1}|f_1 \dots f_n\big) = {}& Cap^{tot} - Max\big(C^{RC}(f_1 \dots f_n),\ with\ t_{k+1} \le t \le t_{k+2}\big)\\
= {}& C^{PC}_{ob}(t_k|f_1 \dots f_n) + E^{PC}_{k+1,\,k+2}\big(\Delta_{k,\,k+1}|f_1 \dots f_n\big)\\
& * \Big[1 - P^{PC}\Big(\Delta^{L}_{k+1,\,k+2},\ \Delta^{E}_{k,\,k+1}|f_1 \dots f_n\Big)\Big]\\
& - \textstyle\sum_{i=0}^{k} L^{PC}_{k}\Big(\Delta^{L}_{k+1,\,k+2},\ \Delta^{E}_{i,\,i+1}|f_1 \dots f_n\Big)
\end{aligned}
\quad (12)
$$

Here one has to take into account that PCs entering within the time interval $\Delta^{E}_{k,\,k+1}$ will leave the garage with probability P^{PC} during $\Delta^{L}_{k+1,\,k+2}$. Adjustments must also be made for PCs that depart in the same time interval while having entered before t_k, as described by the term $L_k{}^{PC}$.

Similarly, further constraints on the additional capacity E^{PC} for PCs are obtained from RC demands for later time intervals $t_{k+i} \le t \le t_{k+i+1}$. In the end, the total available capacity for PCs during the time interval $\Delta_{k,\,k+1}$ is obtained by the most restrictive constraint, which is equivalent to the minimum of the corresponding capacities:

$$
\begin{aligned}
Cap^{PC}\big(\Delta_{k,\,k+1}|f_1 \cdots f_n\big) = {}& Min\big(Cap^{PC}_{k+i,\,k+i+1}(\Delta_{k,\,k+1}|f_1 \cdots f_n)\big)\\
= {}& C^{PC}_{ob}(t_k|f_1 \cdots f_n)\\
& + Min\big(E^{PC}_{k+i,\,k+i+1}(\Delta_{k,\,k+1}|f_1 \cdots f_n)\big),\ with\ i \ge 0
\end{aligned}
\quad (13)
$$

In practice, the range for i should cover the typical parking time of PCs.

4   Case Study

Our approach is now applied to the management of parking space in a car park of a city in Germany. The car park offers the two services described in the previous section:

Parking for RCs and parking for PCs without reservations. A RC pays a monthly fee and should be able to park at any time while a PC may park if space is available and pay according to parking time. RCs provide a basic income and have to be supported due to municipal contracts. On the other hand, PCs are more profitable. Therefore, the goal of the car park operator is to provide as much space as possible for PCs while still meeting RC's demand.

For our case study, we use parking data covering three months from December 2019 to February 2020 with 39576 records. The data records for parked vehicles describe the time of entry, the time of departure, and the customer segment, i.e. PC or RC. In addition, we use data describing the maximum available capacity of PCs and RCs vehicles on the days of our study.

In total, the car park, which is located in an urban area, offers 245 parking spots. Peak times for occupancy are primarily on weekdays around midday, between 11 am and 2 pm.

4.1 Unused Parking Space

The number of vehicles of customer groups RC and PC that can enter the car park is controlled by capacities: At the beginning of each full hour an operator sets the capacity for RC and PC for vehicles in the garage, which are then valid for the next hour. Once a capacity limit is reached, no additional RC or PC vehicles are allowed to enter unless a vehicle from the same customer group exits. The capacities are manually selected by a staff member and are based on her or his experience. This brings many challenges, such as a late and unsystematic adjustment of capacity to actual demand. Inefficient use of the available parking space is the result.

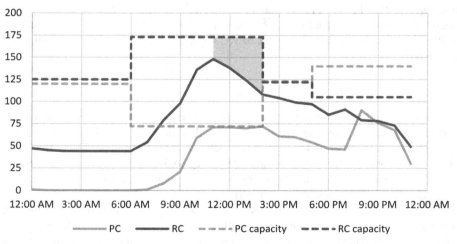

Fig. 1. Amount of cars and capacity for RCs and PCs for a typical case

Figure 1 illustrates a typical case from January 31st, 2020: Between 6 am and 2 pm the capacity for PCs has been set to 72. The number of vehicles of PCs in the garage reached this limit around 11 am. From now on until 2 pm PCs could only enter the garage if a PC's vehicle had left the garage beforehand. During the same period, i.e. from 11 am to 2 pm, the number of RC vehicles did not reach the capacity for RCs of 173. On average, 37 parking spaces that could be used for PCs remained unoccupied during this time, as indicated by the shaded area in Fig. 1. This example underlines the need for demand-driven and systematic capacity management for RCs and PCs.

4.2 Implementation

To implement the approach for data-driven control of parking lots from Sect. 3, we proceed as follows: At peak times, which we are investigating, the parking time of most vehicles is not less than one hour. Therefore, in a first simple approach, we consider the parking situation in time intervals of one hour. Starting at a particular hour, we always look at the parking situation for the next 24 h. As input, we calculate the average number of RC and PC cars entering and leaving, E and L from Eqs. (1, 2) respectively, during December 2019. As features f_i, we currently use weekday only. We obtain from Eq. (3) the probabilities P of cars leaving the garage. For this purpose, we assume normal distributions, which turn out to be well justified at times of high parking demand.

Taking the values for E, and L from the last four previous similar day and hour combinations as input for January and February 2020, we can determine Cap^{PC}, a car park operator should set for PC vehicles at a specific day and time t_k, for the next hour. For this purpose, we use the parking data from these two months to determine the number of cars leaving the garage on a specific day until the time t_k. This enables the calculation of L_k from Eq. (6). It describes the number of vehicles leaving the car park after t_k, taking into account earlier departures.

We then need to calculate the expected number of RC cars in the garage, i.e. C_{pr}^{RC} from Eqs. (8, 9). It has been found that it is sufficient to do this for 5 h, i.e. until $t = t_{k+5}$. Finally, we obtain the capacity Cap^{PC} from Eqs. (10–13). To this end, we use in Eqs. (8, 9) values for the predicted number of RC vehicles at the end of the time intervals considered.

4.3 Results

With our approach, we obtain at each hour the capacity Cap^{PC}, which is valid for the then following hour. If the parking operator sets this limit at the beginning of an hour, it determines the number of PC vehicles, which can enter the garage during this hour, taking into account PC cars being already in the garage or leaving the garage. We compare Cap^{PC} with the capacities manually set by the operator and the actual number of cars in the garage during January and February 2020.

Figure 2 illustrates our results for the example already discussed above (see Fig. 1): In the early hours of the day, demand for RCs increases steadily due to daily parking patterns. In comparison, the predicted capacity for PCs drops more sharply until 6 am. This is because the usual parking time of PCs arriving at this time is around 8 to 10 h. It is taken into account to avoid scenarios where space is used by PCs who leave the garage after the said space is needed for RC demand. Therefore, there is a decrease in the predicted capacity for PCs. The average parking time of PCs arriving at 6 am contrasts with around 4 to 5 h. Therefore, additional PCs may enter, resulting in a higher predicted capacity for PCs. A further increase in RC demand leads to a decreasing capacity for PCs in the following hours.

The operator has set the capacity for PCs manually to 72 from 6 am to 2 pm. During the period from 11 am until 2 pm the number of PCs hit the capacity limit – although space is still available as shown in Fig. 1. On the other hand, the suggested capacity from our approach, Cap^{PC}, is considerably higher than the manual one, set to 97 at 11 am. This opens up significantly more space for PCs as indicated by the shaded area in Fig. 2.

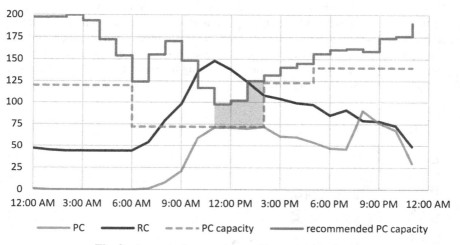

Fig. 2. Amount of cars and capacities on a typical case

To assess the potential of our approach, we look at the parking data from January and February 2020 for periods when manually set PC capacity was utilised by vehicles up to more than 95%. In these critical periods, our approach allowed to release 734 additional hours of parking for PCs. 9 h of parking time were lost when Cap^{PC} was lower than the limit set manually even though there was space. In these few cases, the predictions for the upcoming demand for RC vehicles were slightly higher than the actual demand and the expected parking time for PCs was marginally overestimated.

Table 1. Case study results

Comparison with manual capacity control	Parking hours
Additional parking lot hours for PCs with our approach	734
Parking lot hours for PCs where our approach provided less parking lots	9
Parking lot hours where capacity for PCs exceeds potential RC demand	49
Hours where RCs could not enter (manual vs. current approach)	12 vs. 8

If the calculated capacity Cap^{PC} overestimates the potentially available parking space for PCs, it can happen that RC vehicles do not find free parking lots. In our simulation, this risk existed for 49 parking lot hours within two months. This value is quite low. The reason for it is a deviation of the predicted demand of RCs from the observed demand, which occurred in a few hours. This risk however only materialises if all parking spaces that can be occupied by PCs have been used by them. In practice, one can minimise this risk further by introducing a small capacity buffer. On the other hand, during the two months of our study parking space was not available for RCs for 12 h. The approach presented in this paper would have reduced this to 8 h. In Table 1 these results are summarised.

Figure 3 shows the distribution of additional parking hours from our approach depending on the time of day. Only critical periods were considered in which the parking capacity was utilised up to 95%. It can be seen that our approach can provide additional parking space for PCs, especially during the midday hours. For example, the proposed approach could have provided 332 additional parking hours for PCs from 11–12 am on 11 days in January and February 2020.

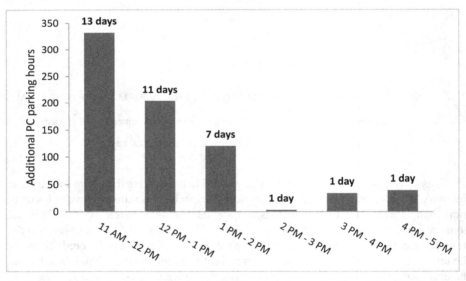

Fig. 3. Aggregated additional parking hours for PCs depending on the time of day. Also indicated is the number of single days where additional parking capacity for PCs could have been provided.

5   Summary and Outlook

We proposed an approach to control access to an off-street parking lot with two different customer offers. RCs who pay a monthly fee and always have to be provided with a free parking space, while PCs are more profitable and therefore should be maximised. Our approach achieves this, by reserving only as many parking spaces as necessary to meet RC demand of upcoming hours.

The proposed demand-driven approach is tested in a case study with a historical data set. Compared to the original control by the parking operator, our approach released significantly more parking spaces for PCs during the period of the case study.

While the results speak for themselves, there is still room for improvement. The input parameters of our approach are dependent on weekdays. In a future study, an extension to a wider range of features such as holidays or weather is planned. Then machine learning approaches will be used to train the corresponding probability distributions e.g. neural networks.

References

1. Manville, M., Shoup, D.: Parking, People, and Cities. J. Urban Plann. Dev. **131**(4), 233–245 (2005). https://doi.org/10.1061/(ASCE)0733-9488(2005)131:4(233)
2. van Ommeren, J., Wentink, D., Dekkers, J.: The real price of parking policy. J. Urban Econ. **70**, 25–31 (2011). https://doi.org/10.1016/j.jue.2011.02.001
3. Cai, Y., Chen, J., Zhang, C., Wang, B.: A parking space allocation method to make a shared parking strategy for appertaining parking lots of public buildings. Sustainability **11**, 120 (2019). https://doi.org/10.3390/su11010120
4. MOBIX Homepage. https://mobix.ai/2021/10/07/the-iaa-mobility-2021-mobix-deep-parking-showcase/. Accessed 23 Feb 2022
5. Buehler, R., Pucher, J., Gerike, R., Götschi, T.: Reducing car dependence in the heart of Europe: lessons from Germany, Austria, and Switzerland. Transp. Rev. **37**, 4–25 (2017). https://doi.org/10.1080/01441647.2016.1177799
6. The Buffalo News Homepage. Buffalo's zoning code steps into the 21st century. https://buffalonews.com/news/local/buffalos-zoning-code-steps-into-the-21st-century/article_a8b81e45-f6f3-526e-99fe-dde988ef9c78.html. Accessed 23 Feb 2022
7. Arjona, J., Linares, M.P., Casanovas, J.: A deep learning approach to real-time parking availability prediction for smart cities. In: Hoballah, I. (ed.) Proceedings of the Second International Conference on Data Science, E-Learning and Information Systems - DATA 2019, Dubai, United Arab Emirates, 02.12.2019–05.12.2019, pp. 1–7. ACM Press, New York, New York, USA (2019). https://doi.org/10.1145/3368691.3368707
8. Badii, C., Nesi, P., Paoli, I.: Predicting available parking slots on critical and regular services by exploiting a range of open data. IEEE Access **6**, 1–12 (2018). https://doi.org/10.1109/ACCESS.2018.2864157
9. Abdeen, M.A.R., Nemer, I.A., Sheltami, T.R.: A balanced algorithm for in-city parking allocation: a case study of Al Madinah City. Sensors. **21**, 3148 (2021). https://doi.org/10.3390/s21093148
10. Tian, Q., Yang, L., Wang, C., Huang, H.-J.: Dynamic pricing for reservation-based parking system: a revenue management method. Transp. Policy **71**, 36–44 (2018). https://doi.org/10.1016/j.tranpol.2018.07.007
11. Caicedo, F., Blazquez, C., Miranda, P.: Prediction of parking space availability in real time. Expert Syst. Appl. **39**, 1–9 (2012). https://doi.org/10.1016/j.eswa.2012.01.091
12. Stolfi, D.H., Alba, E., Yao, X.: Can I park in the city center? Predicting car park occupancy rates in smart cities. J. Urban Technol. **27**, 27–41 (2019). https://doi.org/10.1080/10630732.2019.1586223
13. Vlahogianni, E.I., Kepaptsoglou, K., Tsetsos, V., Karlaftis, M.G.: A real-time parking prediction system for smart cities. J. Intell. Transp. Syst. **30**, 192–204 (2016). https://doi.org/10.1080/15472450.2015.1037955

14. Geng, Y., Cassandras, C.G.: New "smart parking" system based on resource allocation and reservations. IEEE Trans. Intell. Transport. Syst. **30**, 192–204 (2013). https://doi.org/10.1109/TITS.2013.2252428

15. Wu, E.H.-K., Sahoo, J., Liu, C.-Y., Jin, M.-H., Lin, S.-H.: Agile urban parking recommendation service for intelligent vehicular guiding system. IEEE Intell. Transport. **6**, 35–49 (2014). https://doi.org/10.1109/MITS.2013.2268549

16. Saharan, S., Kumar, N., Bawa, S.: An efficient smart parking pricing system for smart city environment: A machine-learning based approach. Future Gener. Comput. Syst. **106**, 222–240 (2020). https://doi.org/10.1016/j.future.2020.01.031

17. Guadix, J., Onieva, L., Muñuzuri, J., Cortés, P.: An overview of revenue management in service industries: an application to car parks. Serv. Indust. J. **31**, 91–105 (2011). https://doi.org/10.1080/02642069.2010.491543

On Web Service Quality Using Multi-criteria Decision-Making and Fuzzy Inference Methods

Diana Kalibatienė[1]([⊠]) [iD] and Jolanta Miliauskaitė[2] [iD]

[1] Vilnius Gediminas Technical University, 10223 Vilnius, Lithuania
diana.kalibatiene@vilniustech.lt
[2] Institute of Data Science and Digital Technologies, Vilnius University, 08663 Vilnius, Lithuania
jolanta.miliauskaite@mif.vu.lt

Abstract. Quality of service (QoS) is a concept that has been widely explored over the last decade to characterize Web Services (WS) from a non-functional perspective. However, QoS of WS is dynamic, different for each user, and complex by its nature; therefore, it is challenging to determine. Nevertheless, various authors have proposed different approaches for QoS finding. However, there is a gap in knowing how different QoS determining approaches affect QoS value and what is the relationship between the obtained QoS values. This paper presents the QoS value finding and analysis approach, which allows us to investigate the relationship between the applied methods and evaluate the correlation of results. The experiments were conducted by applying a fuzzy control system (FCS) and multi-criteria decision-making methods TOPSIS and WASPAS to determine QoS values and find the relationship between the obtained QoS values. The obtained results show that there is a strong positive linear relationship between QoS values obtained by WASPAS and TOPSIS, WASPAS and FCS, a very strong positive linear relationship between TOPSIS and FCS, and a very strong monotonic relationship between WASPAS and TOPSIS, WASPAS and FCS, and TOPSIS and FCS. Consequently, the three analysed QoS determining approaches can be successfully applied as alternatives.

Keywords: Web service · Quality of service · Fuzzy control system · Multi criteria decision making · WASPAS · TOPSIS · Correlation

1 Introduction

Nowadays, Web Services (WS) with the same functionality are compared considering their non-functional attributes that may impact the quality of service offered by WS [1], collectively named as Quality of Service (QoS). Based on QoS, a number of authors have proposed WS selection and ranking [2, 3], service planning [4], service composition [5–7], service discovery [8], service recommendation [9–11], etc. However, QoS is dynamic, different for each user, and complex by its nature [1]. Therefore, it is challenging to determine QoS in WS domain.

© The Author(s), under exclusive license to Springer Nature Switzerland AG 2022
M. Ivanovic et al. (Eds.): Baltic DB&IS 2022, CCIS 1598, pp. 31–46, 2022.
https://doi.org/10.1007/978-3-031-09850-5_3

Ghafouri et al. [1] have reviewed memory-based, model-based and context-aware methods for QoS prediction. Memory-based methods apply statistical equations to calculate QoS values by the values of similar users or services. Model-based methods use a particular dataset to develop and train a model. The QoS value is then predicted based on the obtained model. Context-aware methods use context information of a user or a service, such as the user geographical data, service invocation time, etc., to improve QoS value prediction.

In the WS selection and ranking context, authors apply a particular multi-criteria decision making (MCDM) method to determine the QoS value [2, 3] according to the predefined attributes, such as response time, availability, throughput, etc. Based on these attributes, the QoS value for each alternative WS is calculated, and further, these values are compared.

In all the cases described above, the QoS determining approaches depending on the task to be solved are presented. They all use similar or the same attributes (i.e., non-functional attributes, context attributes, etc.) to obtain the QoS value, but those QoS determining approaches differ in the model for obtaining the QoS value.

Therefore, the questions arise as follows: 1) *how different approaches for determining QoS affect QoS value?* and 2) *what is the relationship between QoS values obtained using different approaches?*. We aim to investigate these two questions by presenting the QoS performance determining and analysis approach, which allows us to explore the relationship between applied methods and evaluate the correlation of results.

This study contributes to the body of knowledge on WS quality by investigating the impact of the used QoS determining approaches on the obtained QoS values that affect the WS selection during the business process implementation and the WS recommendation in practice. The main contributions of this paper can be summarized as follows:

1. We propose an approach for investigating the effect of the used QoS performance determining approaches on the obtained QoS performance values.
2. We have applied statistical analysis to investigate the relationship between the QoS performance determining approaches.
3. The results of our experiments with 2 506 WS confirm that the three analysed approaches for determining QoS values are correlating with each other.
4. The practical contribution is that the three analysed approaches for determining the QoS performance can be successfully applied as alternatives in the practice depending on the context of WS used.

The rest of this paper is structured as follows. Section 2 introduces related works on QoS determining methods and approaches. Section 3 presents the proposed approach of the research. Section 4 describes the case study and shows the obtained results. Section 5 discusses the results obtained in the paper. Finally, Sect. 6 concludes the paper.

2 Related Work

Based on [1], existing approaches on WS QoS prediction are classified as follows: memory-based, model-based, and context-aware.

Memory-based approaches or neighbourhood-based approaches apply statistical equations to calculate WS QoS values for a user using the values of similar users or similar web services known as neighbours. First, they calculate similarities and, second, predict unknown WS QoS value by the value of similar users or web services. Although memory-based approaches have a high perceptual capability, easy implementable, and have acceptable accuracy, they suffer from data sparsity (i.e., users have used a small amount of available WS), cold-start (i.e., when a new WS/user is introduced, there are no neighbours for them, since new WS have not been used by any user or new users have not used any WS), scalability (i.e., in case of high number of users/WS, the cost of computing neighbours is also high), trust (the prediction of WS QoS values strongly depend on the users' shared values).

Model-Based Approaches. Using a particular dataset, a model is designed and trained using training data. Then WS QoS value prediction is made based on the obtained model. Different learning techniques, like clustering (fuzzy C-means [12], etc.), matrix factorization (based on the user-service matrix) [13], time series (presenting time-dependent values of properties) [14] and machine learning [10, 11], are popular. The main limitation of model-based approaches is high computation time [1].

Context-aware approaches use context information of a user or WS to improve QoS value prediction. The important context information employed here is the user's geographical data, WS invocation time and trustworthiness of data. Since using context-based approaches additional parameters are set, additional calculation, which increases computation time, is necessary.

In this research, we are going to use classical fuzzy controller [15, 16] (i.e., model-based method) to predict WS QoS value based on the chosen WS QoS dataset.

In MCDM field, we can find plenty of works proposing WS selection based on their QoS attributes [2, 3, 17]. Regarding the multiple conflicting qualitative and quantitative criteria, which should be taken into consideration to predict WS QoS value, MCDM methods are suitable for solving this task [2, 18–20]. In MCDM, the WS QoS value is calculated by applying a particular utility function (Multiple Attribute Utility Theory (MAUT) method [21], Analytic Hierarchy Process (AHP) [22], Weighted Sum Method (WSM) [22], Weighted Product Method (WPM) [22, 23], VIKOR [24]), the distance measure (the Technique for Order Preference by Similarity to Ideal Solution (TOPSIS) [25–27], EDAS [28]), priority scores (COPRAS [29, 30], etc.).

In this research, we are going to use TOPSIS and WASPAS to obtain WS QoS values. TOPSIS solves multi-dimensional problems, where each attribute can be associated with different units of measure and each attribute have tendency of monotonically increasing or decreasing utility. The main advantage of TOPSIS is that it ranks different alternatives measuring their relative distances to ideal positive and negative solutions, providing a meaningful performance measurement for each candidate [31]. Its employment has been proven to be robust in dealing with MCDM problems in different application areas. Finally, a number of its extensions were developed, like fuzzy TOPSIS [31–33], grey TOPSIS [34], etc.

The weighted aggregated sum product assessment (WASPAS) [35] method is a combination of WSM and WPM. It has advantages of both WSM and WPM [36]. WASPAS validates a final performance scores of alternatives using a linear relation and power and multiplication aggregation [35].

3   Determining QoS Performance Values

In this section, we describe the approach (Fig. 1) used to investigate how different approaches for determining QoS affect QoS values and what is the relationship between obtained QoS values using different approaches.

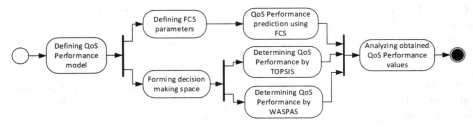

Fig. 1. The reference schema of the QoS performance determining approach.

This schema is universal and QoS determining methods can be changed if necessary.

3.1   QoS Performance Model

QoS values depend on different attributes [1, 37]. Based on [1, 38–40], QoS performance model is presented in Fig. 2.

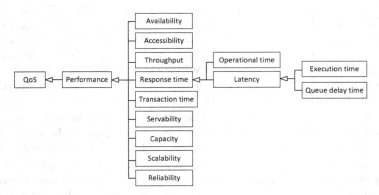

Fig. 2. The QoS performance tree

QoS attributes may vary depending on the application domain, user categories, and WS usage context. A more complete list of QoS attributes can be found in [1, 38], and the tree of QoS attributes considering various quality factors such as reputation, security, correctness, monetary, etc. is presented in [39]. In this research, we are concentrating on the QoS performance.

3.2 Fuzzy Control System for QoS Performance Value Prediction

According to [15, 41], a classical fuzzy control system (FCS) consists of the following components (Fig. 3):

- *Fuzzification* – converts crisp input values into fuzzy values using a particular fuzzification method. This method presents a way of determining the degree to which input variables belong to each of the appropriate fuzzy sets using membership functions (MFs).
- *Fuzzy Inference* – simulates human thinking applying fuzzy rules from the Knowledge Base. Based on the fuzzy inference model applied in FCS, they are Mamdani [41], Takagi-Sugeno [16], etc.
- *Defuzzification* – converts fuzzy values got from Fuzzy Inference to crisp values using a particular defuzzification method.
- *Knowledge Base* stores fuzzification methods and their parameters, fuzzy rules for inferencing, and defuzzification methods and their parameters.

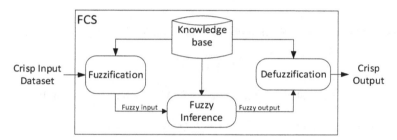

Fig. 3. The reference schema of FCS (used from [15])

In this research, we use FCS to predict QoS values.

3.3 Forming Decision-Making Space

A decision-making space consists of assessed alternatives, attributes and their weights as follows:

- a set of alternatives $A = \{A_i | i = 1, \ldots, n\}$, where n is a number of alternatives;
- a set of attributes $X = \{x_j | j = 1, \ldots, m\}$, where m is a number of attributes;
- a set of weights $W = \{w_j | j = 1, \ldots, m\}$, where each w_j denotes the weight of importance of the j-th criterion. The sum of the weights values should be equal to 1.

Consequently, the decision making matrix (DMM) is as follows: $\overline{X} = \{w_j \bar{x}_{ij}\}$, where $\bar{x}_{ij}$ is a normalized attribute value. The normalization techniques are described below with the applied MCDM methods WASPAS and TOPSIS.

3.4 WASPAS for Determining QoS Performance

The Weighted Aggregated Sum Product Assessment (WASPAS) method is proposed in [42] and is based on three criteria of optimality.

The first criterion of optimality is based on WSM (Eq. (1)):

$$Q_i^{(1)} = \sum_{j=1}^{n} \bar{x}_{ij} w_j,$$ (1)

where normalization of initial criteria values is performed as follows in Eq. (2), if $\max_i x_{ij}$ is preferable:

$$\bar{x}_{ij} = \frac{x_{ij}}{\max_i x_{ij}},$$ (2)

or Eq. (3), if $\min_i x_{ij}$ is preferable:

$$\bar{x}_{ij} = \frac{\min_i x_{ij}}{x_{ij}}.$$ (3)

The second criterion of optimality is based on WPM (Eq. (4)):

$$Q_i^{(2)} = \prod_{j=1}^{n} \left(\bar{x}_{ij} \right)^{w_j}.$$ (4)

The third joint generalized criterion of WASPAS is determined using Eq. (5):

$$Q_i = \lambda Q_i^{(1)} + (1 - \lambda) Q_i^{(2)}, \lambda \in [0, 1].$$ (5)

When $\lambda = 0$, WASPAS becomes WPM; when $\lambda = 1$, WASPAS becomes WSM. In our case, we use $\lambda = 0, 5$ to find QoS Performance values by WASPAS. Therefore, the final equation of the third joint generalized criterion of WASPAS looks as in Eq. (6):

$$Q_i = 0, 5 Q_i^{(1)} + 0, 5 Q_i^{(2)}.$$ (6)

The best alternative will have the highest Q_i value [35].

3.5 TOPSIS for Determining QoS Performance

The main idea of the TOPSIS method, proposed in [43], is that the selected alternative should be the most similar to the best alternative and the least similar to the worst alternative [22]. The normalized DMM is developed using explanations in Sect. 3.3 and Eq. (7) for normalization of attributes:

$$\bar{x}_{ij} = \frac{x_{ij}}{\sqrt{\sum_{i=0}^{n} x_{ij}^2}}.$$ (7)

The best alternative, denoted as A^+, and the worst alternative, denoted as A^-, are calculated as presented in Eq. (8) and (9):

$$A^+ = \{a_i^+, i = \overline{0, n}\} = \left\{ \left[\left(\max_i \overline{\overline{x}}_{ij} | j \in J \right), \left(\min_i \overline{\overline{x}}_{ij} | j \in J' \right) \right], i = \overline{0, n} \right\}, \quad (8)$$

$$A^- = \{a_i^-, i = \overline{0, n}\} = \left\{ \left[\left(\min_i \overline{\overline{x}}_{ij} | j \in J \right), \left(\max_i \overline{\overline{x}}_{ij} | j \in J' \right) \right], i = \overline{0, n} \right\}, \quad (9)$$

where $J = \{j = 1, \ldots, m$ and j is associated with benefit criteria$\}$; $J' = \{j = 1, \ldots, m$ and j is associated with loss criteria$\}$.

Next, the n-dimensional Euclidian distance method is applied to measure the separation distances of each alternative from the positive-ideal solution (Eq. (10)) and negative-ideal solution (Eq. (11)) [22].

$$S_i^+ = \sqrt{\sum_{j=1}^{m} \left(\overline{\overline{x}}_{ij} - a_j^+ \right)^2}, \quad (10)$$

$$S_i^- = \sqrt{\sum_{j=1}^{m} \left(\overline{\overline{x}}_{ij} - a_j^- \right)^2}. \quad (11)$$

The *relative closeness to the optimal solution* is calculated as in Eq. (12):

$$K_i^* = \frac{S_i^-}{S_i^+ + S_i^-}, \quad i = \overline{0, m} K_i^* \in [0, 1]. \quad (12)$$

The option with K_i^* closest to one is closest to the optimal solution. Obviously, $K_i^* = 1$, if $A_i = A^+$, and $K_i^* = 0$, if $A_i = A^-$. Consequently, the higher K_i^* is closest to the optimal solution.

3.6 Determining Correlation

Finally, the QoS Performance values obtained by applying FCS, TOPSIS and WASPAS are analysed using the Pearson's (Eq. (13)) [44] and the Spearman's [44] correlation coefficients, which are the most popular to measure linear and non-linear relationships respectively.

$$r_{xy}^{Pears} = \frac{\sum_{i=1}^{n} (x_i - \overline{x})(y_i - \overline{y})}{\sqrt{\sum_{i=1}^{n} (x_i - \overline{x})^2} \sqrt{\sum_{i=1}^{n} (y_i - \overline{y})^2}}, \quad (13)$$

where n is a sample size, x_i and y_i are the compared *i-th* variables; $\overline{x}$ and $\overline{y}$ are the sample means of two samples respectively.

The Spearman's rank correlation coefficient [44] is calculated using the same equation (Eq. (13)), but instead of variables x_i and y_i, we use the ranks R_{xi} and R_{yi} of those variables, and the mean ranks $\overline{R_X}$ and $\overline{R_Y}$ instead of $\overline{x}$ and $\overline{y}$ respectively.

4   Case Study and Results

For the case study, we used a real-world QWS dataset [45, 46] consisting of 13 attributes values for 2 506 WS. For our research, we have chosen only benefit or cost attributes, which are not correlating (i.e., the Pearson's correlation coefficient is less than 0,5), since inclusion of correlating attributes may lead to skewed or misleading results and the standard error of the coefficients will increase [47].

Table 1. Attributes to find the QoS Performance values.

Attributes	Description	Units	Weights (w_j)
Response Time (x_1)	Time taken to send a request and receive a response	ms	0,35
Availability (x_2)	Number of successful invocations/total invocations	%	0,22
Throughput (x_3)	Total Number of invocations for a given period of time	invokes/second	0,14
Reliability (x_4)	Ratio of the number of error messages to total messages	%	0,085
Compliance (x_5)	The extent to which a WSDL document follows WSDL specification	%	0,155
Documentation (x_6)	Measure of documentation (i.e. description tags) in WSDL	%	0,05

The attribute weights, which influence the preferences on WS and have an impact on the whole QoS performance of WS, are determined using [48, 49].

For determining QoS performance values, we used the whole dataset. Only the main results, which sufficiently reflect the entire sample, are presented below.

4.1   QoS Performance Value Prediction Using FCS

A FCS for QoS performance value prediction was implemented into the prototype for evaluation using the MATLAB/Simulink 2021 software.

The input parameters of the FCS correspond to attributes from Table 1. Each of them was partitioned into five linguistic terms (i.e., very high, high, moderate, low, and very low), using the grid partition method in the Fuzzification component (see Fig. 3). An example of partitioning the most significant input attributes Response Time (x_1) and Availability (x_2) are presented in Fig. 4 and Fig. 5.

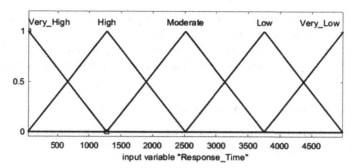

Fig. 4. The MFs of response time.

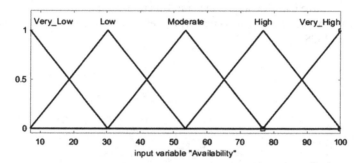

Fig. 5. The MFs of availability.

The predefined output of QoS performance is also partitioned into five MFs (Fig. 6). Note that Availability and Response Time are benefit and cost attributes respectively.

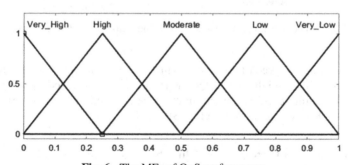

Fig. 6. The MFs of QoS performance.

Using combinatorial and rule consolidation approaches, a set of 235 fuzzy rules was generated and used in the Fuzzy Inference component (see Fig. 3), which uses the Takagi-Sugeno fuzzy model. The general structure is presented in Eq. (14), and an example of one fuzzy rule from our used Fuzzy Inference component is presented in Eq. (15).

$$\textbf{IF } input\_term \text{ is } A \textbf{ AND } input\_term \text{ is } B \textbf{ THEN} Z = f(x, y) \quad (14)$$

IF is *VeryHigh* **AND** is *VeryHigh* **AND** is *VeryHigh* **AND** is *VeryHigh* **AND** is *Moderate*
AND is *Moderate* **THEN** Z is *VeryHigh*

$$(15)$$

where $Z = f(x, y)$ presents the output obtained after applying a particular fuzzy rule. In this research, we have used the aggregate sum function for $f(x, y)$.

The snapshot of the obtained QoS performance values using the FCS is presented in Table 2 (column FCS).

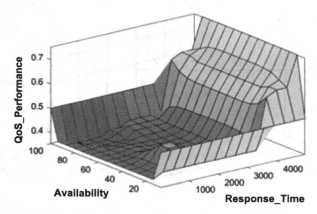

Fig. 7. The dependency between inputs and output QoS Performance.

The relationships between two inputs, which have the highest weights (Response Time and Availability) and the output QoS Performance is presented by the 3-D plot in Fig. 7. How the output depends on the inputs is determined by the fuzzy rules, which are stored in the Knowledge Base (see Fig. 3).

4.2 Determining QoS Performance Values by FCS, WASPAS and TOPSIS

Below in Table 2, we have presented the initial DMM and QoS performance values obtained using FCS, WASPAS and TOPSIS.

Figure 8 presents distribution of 101 QoS performance values obtained by FCS, WASPAS (Q_i) and TOPSIS (K_i^*). We can see from the figure that there is a certain dependence between the obtained QoS Performance values. The correlation analysis is provided below.

Table 2. Initial DMM and QoS performance values by FCS, WASPAS and TOPSIS.

	Attributes						QoS performance values		
	x_1	x_2	x_3	x_4	x_5	x_6	WASPAS (Q_i)	TOPSIS (K_i^*)	FCS
w_j	0,35	0,22	0,14	0,085	0,155	0,05			
a_1	41	97	43,1	73	100	5	0,819	0,958	0,909
a_2	48,35	10	14,9	67	78	4	0,434	0,857	0,675
a_3	62,75	56	7,8	83	89	10	0,499	0,850	0,529
a_4	71,54	18	4,3	60	78	9	0,364	0,830	0,664
a_5	105,92	9	9,3	67	89	11	0,315	0,840	0,706
a_6	255,08	12	8,1	53	78	62	0,269	0,832	0,711
a_7	524	94	22,5	67	89	65	0,420	0,868	0,852
a_8	541	91	20,3	73	100	35	0,404	0,858	0,863
a_9	573,81	11	3,5	67	78	11	0,181	0,790	0,647
a_{10}	1387,5	78	3,5	73	78	4	0,249	0,687	0,551
a_{11}	1471,92	61	2,1	73	67	96	0,242	0,671	0,334
a_{12}	2150	83	7,4	73	89	1	0,261	0,560	0,512
a_{13}	3157,61	23	1,3	78	89	5	0,155	0,359	0,451
a_{14}	3768,33	63	1,4	83	50	56	0,188	0,246	0,246
a_{15}	4989,67	93	1,6	73	100	5	0,249	0,090	0,517

Note that for experimentation we have used values of all 2 506 WS. Table 2 presents results of 15 WS, which sufficiently reflect the entire sample.

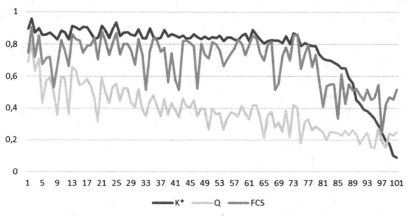

Fig. 8. The distribution of QoS Performance values by FCS, WASPAS and TOPSIS.

Table 3. The Pearson's/Spearman's correlation of QoS performance values.

	WASPAS (Q_i)	TOPSIS (K_i^*)	FCS
WASPAS (Q_i)	1/1	0,643/0,926	0,696/0,746
TOPSIS (K_i^*)	0,643/0,926	1/1	0,733/0,713
FCS	0,696/0,746	0,733/0,713	1/1

Table 3 presents the Pearson's/Spearman's correlation coefficient of QoS performance values obtained by FCS, WASPAS and TOPSIS.

The Pearson's correlation coefficients showed a strong positive linear relationship between QoS performance values obtained by WASPAS and TOPSIS, WASPAS and FCS, a very strong positive linear relationship between TOPSIS and FCS.

The obtained Spearman's correlation coefficients showed a very strong monotonic relationship between QoS performance values obtained by WASPAS and TOPSIS, WASPAS and FCS, and TOPSIS and FCS.

Comparing the obtained Pearson's and Spearman's correlation coefficients, the Spearman's correlation coefficients have higher values that means a stronger monotonic relationship than the linear relationship.

5 Discussion

In the beginning of the research, we have defined two questions – *how different approaches for determining QoS affect QoS value?* and *what is the relationship between QoS values obtained using different approaches?*. After performing the research, we can answer these questions.

First, we have presented an approach for analysing the effect of QoS determining approaches on the obtained QoS values, which is based on the statistical comparison of the found QoS performance values. For the experiment, we have chosen WASPAS, TOPSIS and FCS. While WASPAS and TOPSIS belong to the same class of tasks to be solved, i.e., MCDM, and use a strictly defined mathematical formalism to calculate QoS values, FCS is based on the fuzzy set theory and developed to predict unknown values applying fuzzy inferencing model.

Second, the real-world QWS dataset was used to conduct the experiment and to obtain QoS performance values applying WASPAS, TOPSIS and FCS. The correlation analysis of the obtained results showed a strong positive linear relationship between QoS performance values obtained by WASPAS and TOPSIS ($r_{xy}^{Pears} = 0,643$), WASPAS and FCS ($r_{xy}^{Pears} = 0,696$), and a very strong positive linear relationship between TOPSIS and FCS ($r_{xy}^{Pears} = 0,733$). A very strong monotonic relationship exists between QoS performance values obtained by WASPAS and TOPSIS ($r_{xy}^{Spear} = 0,926$), WASPAS and FCS ($r_{xy}^{Spear} = 0,746$), and TOPSIS and FCS ($r_{xy}^{Spear} = 0,713$).

Those results can be understand as follows. The relationship between WASPAS and TOPSIS should exist, since they solve the same task. However, the strength of that relationship may vary because it depends on the difference of the mathematical formalisms used in the MCDM methods. The main question was raised about a relationship between the QoS performance values obtained by FCS and MCDM methods, since they differ by their nature and are addressed to solve different tasks. This research proves the existence of a strong positive linear relationship and a very strong monotonic relationship between those methods. Consequently, we have learned that the analysed three approaches for determining QoS performance can be successfully applied as alternatives in the practice depending on the context of WS used.

The main limitation of the current research is the limited number of methods analysed. In future works, we are going to extend the set of analysed methods and conduct new and more complex experiments. Those researches provide a better understanding of the relationship between QoS performance values obtained applying different approaches. Moreover, based on those results, recommendations can be developed for the use of different QoS performance determining approaches.

In addition, we plan to perform an analysis of the efficiency of methods used for determining QoS performance values. This research allows us to determine which approach for determining QoS performance is the most appropriate under certain conditions. For example, which approach for determining WS QoS performance values is more appropriate for devices with limited resources? or which approach has less computational complexity?

Finally, we found that additional tuning of fuzzy rules is necessary to improve the performance of FCS. This research allows us to develop a more accurate FCS, and, consequently, investigate more closely the relationship between QoS values obtained using different approaches.

6 Conclusions

The analysis of the related works revealed that there is a plenty of approaches for determining QoS based on similar or the same attributes (i.e., non-functional attributes, context attributes, etc.), but they differ in how the QoS value is obtained. However, there is a knowledge gap how different approaches for determining QoS affect QoS value, and what is the relationship between QoS values obtained using different approaches.

The approach for the determining of the QoS performance value that is proposed in this paper allows us to investigate the relationship between the applied approaches and evaluate the correlation of results. The main advantage of the proposed approach is that it allows us to perform statistical analysis of the QoS performance values obtained applying different QoS determining approaches.

The found relationships between the analysed QoS performance determining approaches allow us to state that they can be successfully applied as alternatives in the practice depending on the context of WS used.

In summary, the benefit of this study is that researchers and practitioners become familiar to the relationships that exist between different QoS performance determining approaches, regardless of their purpose in addressing different tasks.

References

1. Ghafouri, H., Hashemi, M., Hung, P.C.K.: A survey on web service QoS prediction methods. IEEE Trans. Serv. Comput. (2020). https://doi.org/10.1109/TSC.2020.2980793n
2. Masdari, M., Khezri, H.: Service selection using fuzzy multi-criteria decision making: a comprehensive review. J. Ambient. Intell. Humaniz. Comput. 12(2), 2803–2834 (2020). https://doi.org/10.1007/s12652-020-02441-w
3. Hosseinzadeh, M., Hama, H.K., Ghafour, M.Y., Masdari, M., Ahmed, O.H., Khezri, H.: Service selection using multi-criteria decision making: a comprehensive overview. J. Netw. Syst. Manage. 28(4), 1639–1693 (2020). https://doi.org/10.1007/s10922-020-09553-w
4. Miliauskaitė, J.: Some methodological issues related to preliminary QoS planning in enterprise systems. Balt. J. Mod. Comput. 3, 149–163 (2015)
5. Yaghoubi, M., Maroosi, A.: Simulation and modeling of an improved multi-verse optimization algorithm for QoS-aware web service composition with service level agreements in the cloud environments. Simul. Model. Pract. Theory. 103, 102090 (2020). https://doi.org/10.1016/j.simpat.2020.102090
6. Chen, L., Ha, W.: Reliability prediction and QoS selection for web service composition. Int. J. Comput. Sci. Eng. 16, 202–211 (2018). https://doi.org/10.1504/IJCSE.2018.090442
7. Chattopadhyay, S., Banerjee, A.: QoS-aware automatic web service composition with multiple objectives. ACM Trans. Web. 14, 1–38 (2020). https://doi.org/10.1145/3389147
8. Adarme, M., Jimeno, M.: Qos-based pattern recognition approach for web service discovery: Ar_wsds. Appl. Sci. 11, 8092 (2021). https://doi.org/10.3390/app11178092
9. Chang, Z., Ding, D., Xia, Y.: A graph-based QoS prediction approach for web service recommendation. Appl. Intell. 51(10), 6728–6742 (2021). https://doi.org/10.1007/s10489-020-02120-5
10. Dang, D., Chen, C., Li, H., Yan, R., Guo, Z., Wang, X.: Deep knowledge-aware framework for web service recommendation. J. Supercomput. 77(12), 14280–14304 (2021). https://doi.org/10.1007/s11227-021-03832-2
11. Xiong, R., Wang, J., Zhang, N., Ma, Y.: Deep hybrid collaborative filtering for Web service recommendation. Expert Syst. Appl. 110, 191–205 (2018). https://doi.org/10.1016/j.eswa.2018.05.039
12. Hasan, M.H., Jaafar, J., Watada, J., Hassan, M.F., Aziz, I.A.: An interval type-2 fuzzy model of compliance monitoring for quality of web service. Ann. Oper. Res. 300(2), 415–441 (2019). https://doi.org/10.1007/s10479-019-03328-6
13. Ghafouri, S.H., Hashemi, S.M., Razzazi, M.R., Movaghar, A.: Web service quality of service prediction via regional reputation-based matrix factorization. Concurr. Comput. Pract. Exp. 33 (2021). https://doi.org/10.1002/cpe.6318
14. Wang, M., Liu, B., Li, J., Li, Y., Chen, H., Zhou, Z., Zhang, W.: A location-based approach for web service QoS prediction via multivariate time series forecast. In: Proceedings of the IEEE International Conference on Software Engineering and Service Sciences, ICSESS, pp. 36–39 (2020). https://doi.org/10.1109/ICSESS49938.2020.9237713
15. Kalibatiene, D., Miliauskaitė, J.: A hybrid systematic review approach on complexity issues in data-driven fuzzy inference systems development. Informatics 32, 85–118 (2021). https://doi.org/10.15388/21-INFOR444
16. Takagi, T., Sugeno, M.: Fuzzy Identification of systems and its applications to modeling and control. IEEE Trans. Syst. Man Cybern. SMC-15, 116–132 (1985). https://doi.org/10.1109/TSMC.1985.6313399
17. Jatoth, C., Gangadharan, G.R., Fiore, U., Buyya, R.: SELCLOUD: a hybrid multi-criteria decision-making model for selection of cloud services. Soft. Comput. 23(13), 4701–4715 (2018). https://doi.org/10.1007/s00500-018-3120-2

18. Wang, S., Sun, Q., Zou, H., Yang, F.: Particle swarm optimization with Skyline operator for fast cloud-based web service composition. Mob. Netw. Appl. **18**, 116–121 (2013). https://doi.org/10.1007/s11036-012-0373-3
19. Xu, J., et al.: Towards fuzzy QoS driven service selection with user requirements. In: Proceedings of 2017 International Conference on Progress in Informatics and Computing, PIC 2017. pp. 230–234 (2017). https://doi.org/10.1109/PIC.2017.8359548
20. Ghobaei-Arani, M., Souri, A.: LP-WSC: a linear programming approach for web service composition in geographically distributed cloud environments. J. Supercomput. **75**(5), 2603–2628 (2018). https://doi.org/10.1007/s11227-018-2656-3
21. Keeney, R.L., Raiffa, H.: Decisions with Multiple Objectives. John Wiley & Sons, New York (1976)
22. Triantaphyllou, E.: Multi-criteria Decision Making Methods. Springer, Boston (2000). https://doi.org/10.1007/978-1-4757-3157-6_2
23. Kumar, A., et al.: A review of multi criteria decision making (MCDM) towards sustainable renewable energy development. Renew. Sustain. Energy Rev. **69**, 596-609 (2017). https://doi.org/10.1016/j.rser.2016.11.191
24. Yazdani, M., Graeml, F.R.: VIKOR and its applications. Int. J. Strateg. Decis. Sci. **5**, 56–83 (2014). https://doi.org/10.4018/ijsds.2014040105
25. Hwang, C.-L., Yoon, K.: Methods for Multiple Attribute Decision Making. Springer, Berlin (1981). https://doi.org/10.1007/978-3-642-48318-9_3
26. Triantaphyllou, E.: Multi-criteria Decision Making Methods: A Comparative Study. Springer, Boston (2000). https://doi.org/10.1007/978-1-4757-3157-6
27. Vafaei, N., Ribeiro, R.A., Camarinha-Matos, L.M.: Data normalisation techniques in decision making: case study with TOPSIS method. Int. J. Inf. Decis. Sci. **10**(1), 19 (2018). https://doi.org/10.1504/IJIDS.2018.090667
28. Ghorabaee, M.K., Zavadskas, E.K., Olfat, L., Turskis, Z.: Multi-criteria inventory classification using a new method of evaluation based on distance from average solution (EDAS). Informatics **26**, 435–451 (2015). https://doi.org/10.15388/Informatica.2015.57
29. Roy, J., Sharma, H.K., Kar, S., Zavadskas, E.K., Saparauskas, J.: An extended COPRAS model for multi-criteria decision-making problems and its application in web-based hotel evaluation and selection. Econ. Res. Istraz. **32**, 219–253 (2019). https://doi.org/10.1080/1331677X.2018.1543054
30. Alinezhad, A., Khalili, J.: COPRAS method. In: New Methods and Applications in Multiple Attribute Decision Making (MADM). ISORMS, vol. 277, pp. 87–91. Springer, Cham (2019). https://doi.org/10.1007/978-3-030-15009-9_12
31. Bottani, E., Rizzi, A.: A fuzzy TOPSIS methodology to support outsourcing of logistics services. Supply Chain Manag. **11**, 294–308 (2006). https://doi.org/10.1108/13598540610671743
32. Nădăban, S., Dzitac, S., Dzitac, I.: Fuzzy TOPSIS: a general view. Procedia Comput. Sci. **91**, 823–831 (2016)
33. Junior, F.R.L., Hsiao, M.: A hesitant fuzzy topsis model to supplier performance evaluation. DYNA **88**, 126–135 (2021). https://doi.org/10.15446/DYNA.V88N216.88320
34. Feng, Y., et al.: A novel hybrid fuzzy grey TOPSIS method: supplier evaluation of a collaborative manufacturing enterprise. Appl. Sci. **9** (2019). https://doi.org/10.3390/app9183770
35. Chakraborty, S., Zavadskas, E.K., Antucheviciene, J.: Applications of WASPAS method as a multi-criteria decision-making tool. Econ. Comput. Econ. Cybern. Stud. Res. **49**, 5–22 (2015)
36. Yazdani, M., Zarate, P., Kazimieras Zavadskas, E., Turskis, Z.: A combined compromise solution (CoCoSo) method for multi-criteria decision-making problems. Manag. Decis. **57**, 2501–2519 (2019). https://doi.org/10.1108/MD-05-2017-0458

37. Pandharbale, P.B., Mohanty, S.N., Jagadev, A.K.: Recent web service recommendation methods: a review. Mater. Today Proc. (2021). https://doi.org/10.1016/j.matpr.2021.01.783
38. Polska, O., Kudermetov, R., Shkarupylo, V.: The approach for QoS based web service selection with user's preferences. Probl. Model. Des. Autom. 19–27 (2020). https://doi.org/10.31474/2074-7888-2020-2-19-27
39. Polska, O., Kudermetov, R., Shkarupylo, V.: Model of web services quality criteria hierarchy. Visnyk Zaporizhzhya Natl. Univ. Phys. Math. Sci. 2, 43–51 (2021). https://doi.org/10.26661/2413-6549-2020-2-06
40. Miliauskaitė, J.: The membership function construction in view-based framework. In: Haav, H.-M., Kalja, A., Robal, T. (eds.) 11th International Baltic Conference on Database and Information Systems (Baltic DB&IS 2014), pp. 125–132. Tallinn University of Technology Press, Tallinn (2014)
41. Mamdani, E.H.: Application of fuzzy algorithms for control of simple dynamic plant. Proc. Inst. Electr. Eng. 121, 1585–1588 (1974). https://doi.org/10.1049/piee.1974.0328
42. Zavadskas, E.K., Turskis, Z., Antucheviciene, J., Zakarevicius, A.: Optimization of weighted aggregated sum product assessment. Elektron. ir Elektrotechnika. 122, 3–6 (2012). https://doi.org/10.5755/j01.eee.122.6.1810
43. Hwang, C.-L., Yoon, K.: Methods for multiple attribute decision making. In: Multiple Attribute Decision Making. LNEMS, vol. 186. pp. 58–191. Springer, Heidelberg (1981). https://doi.org/10.1007/978-3-642-48318-9_3
44. Cleff, T.: Exploratory Data Analysis in Business and Economics. Springer, Cham (2014). https://doi.org/10.1007/978-3-319-01517-0
45. Al-Masri, E.: QWS Dataset. https://qwsdata.github.io/. Accessed 24 Feb 2022
46. Al-Masri, E., Mahmoud, Q.H.: Investigating web services on the world wide web. In: Proceeding of the 17th International Conference on World Wide Web 2008, WWW 2008, pp. 795–804 (2008). https://doi.org/10.1145/1367497.1367605
47. Daoud, J.I.: Multicollinearity and regression analysis. IOP Conf. Ser. J. Phys. 949(1), 1–6. (2017). https://doi.org/10.1088/1742-6596/949/1/012009
48. Ouadah, A., Benouaret, K., Hadjali, A., Nader, F.: SkyAP-S3: a hybrid approach for efficient skyline services selection. In: Proceedings - 2015 IEEE 8th International Conference on Service-Oriented Computing and Applications, SOCA 2015, pp. 18–25. IEEE (2016). https://doi.org/10.1109/SOCA.2015.22
49. Sun, L., Ma, J., Zhang, Y., Dong, H., Hussain, F.K.: Cloud-FuSeR: fuzzy ontology and MCDM based cloud service selection. Futur. Gener. Comput. Syst. 57, 42–55 (2016). https://doi.org/10.1016/j.future.2015.11.025

Universal Methodology for Objective Determination of Key Performance Indicators of Socioeconomic Processes

Girts Karnitis[1]([✉]) [iD], Janis Bicevskis[1] [iD], Andris Virtmanis[2] [iD], and Edvins Karnitis[1] [iD]

[1] University of Latvia, Raina Blvd. 19, Riga 1586, Latvia
{Girts.Karnitis,Janis.Bicevskis,Edvins.Karnitis}@lu.lv
[2] Riga Technical University, Meza Street 1 k1, Riga 1048, Latvia
Andris.Virtmanis@rtu.lv

Abstract. The progress in the majority of socioeconomic processes (Processes) can usually be characterized by some headline indicator/index that is compliant with the essence of the Process. The Process develops by performing various process-driving actions; thereby a large amount of data is generated, which forms specific indicators that are more or less distinctive for the Process and its headline indicator. No Process management can really perform all the relevant actions to achieve progress of the whole set of indicators. Hence, prioritization of the action lines and determination of the key performance indicators (KPIs) has become an essential factor. Unfortunately, KPIs and their weighting are still largely subjectively defined and there is a lack of qualitative and quantitative justifications for choices. The article describes the universal methodology developed for objective mathematical computation of KPIs of the Processes and determining their weighting. By means of the regression analysis algorithms for statistically significant KPIs are computed and mathematical expression has been obtained showing the impact of each selected KPI on the headline indicator. The methodology has been tested in several Processes, achieving convincing results; applying it to variety of Processes requires mediocre programming skills only. Process management can put the methodology into practice to monitor the achieved development level of the Process in statics and dynamics, to observe progress and deficiencies in separate aspects, to take these into account when making the sustainable planning and strategic decisions.

Keywords: Socioeconomic process · Key performance indicators · Mathematical modelling

1 Introduction. More Data is Better, But is It All Significant?

The ongoing digital transformation of a wide range of socioeconomic processes (Processes), together with the direct benefits, also provides an increase in the availability of various generated data which is collected in public and private data bases. There are two kinds of new data. Part of them only increases the amount of data in the existing data series, which are the basis for indicators that describe various aspects of the respective Process. However, this quantitative change sometimes can generate a qualitative effect; the data of time series is a convincing example (e.g., [1]).

Another part of new data creates new data series (indicators) that can qualitatively improve the description of the Process and its progress; they emerge or lose their relevance as the Process evolves. Comparing the sets of indicators forming Digital Economy and Society Index (DESI) [2, 3] and European Innovation Scoreboard (EIS) [4] in 2016 and 2021, it can be seen that the indicators, which have lost their significance as a result of sociotechnical development, have been replaced by more advanced ones. Thus, the indicators reflecting the effect of digital transformation and green course on innovation are added to the set of EIS indicators; the innovation performance currently is assessed against 32 indicators, while in 2016 – only against 25 indicators (for more details on the evolution of DESI see Sects. 3.3 and 3.5).

Academic discussions demonstrate benefits generated by the use of large amounts of data (e.g., [5, 6]). Developing new indicators is proposed with a view to improve the assessment of Processes in different sectors: economy [7–9], ecology [10], social sectors [11], etc. Radically increasing number of indicators is also used to create various national and municipal scale indicator sets and composite indices. Hence, the Global Competitiveness Index (GCI) is composed of 103 different national-size indicators [12]; 141 indicators are approved by *Saeima* (the parliament of Latvia) to evaluate implementation of the National Development Plan of Latvia for 2021–2027 [13].

Clearly, in many cases national, sectoral or local management cannot perform all the activities to achieve progress in all the indicators, due to the insufficient capacity and inability to invest simultaneously in all action lines. The same relates to businesses, which apparently are carefully considering the pay-back of the required investment. Many of the indicators could be insignificant, but which ones? The prioritization of the indicators (and hence, the related action lines) has become an essential, sometimes – even critical factor.

This encourages analysts to create methods that determine which indicators from the large data set are decisive Process drivers, the key performance indicators (KPIs). Discussion papers are published [14, 15] to reflect this issue, presenting the advantages, as well as the disadvantages of large data sets [16]. Various procedures for selection of KPIs are proposed in a variety of sectors, including economy [17–19], social services, [20, 21], environment [22], etc.

It is still popular to rely on the experts' subjective choices in the KPI selection procedure [22–25]. In a number of cases, experts directly subjectively carry out the weighting of the selected KPIs too [11, 13]. In other cases, various mathematical methods are additionally used for processing expert assessments, for example, fuzzy analytical hierarchical process [19], decision making method DEMATEL [20], qualitative scoring method and analytical hierarchical process [17]. The results of these calculations, of course, maintain the subjectivity of the experts' assessments.

However, some methodologies, which aim at obtaining as objective as possible selection of KPIs, have also been proposed, involving mathematical tools. Weighting calculations can also be performed at the same time. There are applied data envelop and correlative analyses [18], ontologies [26], machine learning algorithms [27], regression analysis [21, 28]. Unfortunately, the methodologies proposing the application of mathematical tools for selection of KPIs are not opened in referred publications, which make their re-apply for similar tasks practically impossible.

The aim of this study is development of universal transparent methodology for mathematical computation of KPIs of the socioeconomic processes and determining their weighting. Objective computation of KPIs from the set of Process indicators is important for the creation of high-quality Process models, enabling the correct reflection of the impact of key drivers in the model. The actual KPIs are the basis for a model that is accurate as possible and at the same time simple and understandable to its users – non-IT professionals. Furthermore, a transparent KPI computing methodology is one of the key aspects for trust in the model. Therefore, only the application of mathematical tools for determination of KPIs has been considered acceptable.

Selection of the appropriate mathematical tool is described in Sect. 2, while the Sect. 3 is devoted to the methodology itself. Section 4 discusses the results obtained and provides conclusions.

2 Regression Analysis: A Suitable Mathematical Tool

To achieve the stated aim, a working hypothesis was put forward: let us consider that any Process contains k static units of observation, at which the achieved level of the Process development is indicated by the characteristic headline indicator (Y_k), the value of which depends on values of n KPIs $(p_{1k}, p_{2k},....p_{nk})$. Then the Process as a whole can be described by the mathematical model of the Process, where the achieved level of the Process development is described by target/dependent variable (Y) that is a multiparameter function (f) from the set of KPIs $(p_1, p_2,....p_n)$:

$$Y = f\left(p_1, p_2, ...p_n\right) \qquad (1)$$

Changes in the value of (Y) reflect the progress achieved. Each KPI p_n shows progress in some aspect of the Process that has been achieved due to the performance of relevant action lines. Thus, the identification of KPIs will also mean the identification of related action lines, which performance is a priority for the Process development, whereas determination of KPIs weighting will show the impact of a specific KPI on the Process.

Today, no direct theoretical calculation is possible for the function (f) and the subsequent measurement of progress in the Process. However, there are several data mining technologies that are suitable for studying cause and effect relationships between x input/independent variables $(i_1, i_2, ..., i_x)$ and target variable (Y) without exploring the internal aspects of the Process (black box principle).

Various data mining procedures could be used to simulate socioeconomic processes. The adaptation of the data processing methods for the selection of KPIs is an innovative approach that provides significant benefits, which are shown in the following sections. The regression analysis was chosen as the most preferable mathematical tool. It is directly focused on the revealing causalities between several independent variables and the dependent variable. Most of regression analysis algorithms do not require normalization of indicators' data; although normalization is widespread and is performed by maintaining the ratio of data point values for a particular indicator, the choice of min/max values affects the inter-indicator comparison. The obtained modelling result is a decoded mathematical expression (1); it is understandable and convincing for non-IT professionals too. The procedures of analysis are relatively easy to apply.

The authors have modeled several Processes over the years: regularities of EU economies [29], the impact of digitalization on economic growth [30], priority actions for urban sustainable development [31], and the efficiency of district heating networks [32]. For the control of stability and sustainability, a computation of KPIs for the digitalization process was also performed, using highly modified in 2021 set of indicators for recalculated DESI 2019–2020 (for greater detail see Sects. 3.3 and 3.5). By means of regression analysis algorithms we have disclosed and extracted the most significant indicators, i.e., the KPIs, reducing a large number of potential Process drivers ($n \ll x$). The practice of applying regression analysis shows its suitability for the analysis of the *status quo* and for revealing causal relationships between the independent and dependent variables, as well as for forecasting.

Specific assumptions to be considered when using regression analysis:

- The model cannot be an abstract representation of the data scope. Respectively, the analyst, using observational data, must carefully justify if and why a relationship between two variables has a causal interpretation, or why the existing relationships have a predictive power for a new content.
- A full data set (values of independent variables and target variable in observation points) is necessary to determinate causalities.
- An impact of external factors on all observation points should be similar.

Applying mutually absolutely independent modelling tools very different mathematical expressions of the Process model can be obtained, but they usually give very comparable qualitative results, as shown by the usage of different modelling procedures for the same task [33, 34]. Thus, Fig. 1 shows an excellent coincidence of both the nonlinear regression and neural network models of heat transmission costs.

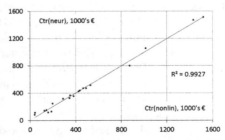

Fig. 1. The mutual coincidence of the neuron network model Ctr(neur) and the nonlinear regression model Ctr(nonlin) of heat transmission costs.

3   Methodology: Sequential Steps

The methodology consists of 5 sequential steps (Fig. 2). The single target (dependent) variable (Y) should be determined in the first step of the modelling procedure. Indicators (independent variables) that describe the target variable as comprehensively as possible from different aspects are selected in the step 2. Computing of KPIs is taking place in the third step by the multistage linear regression procedures. In the step 4, the KPIs weights are specified by adding nonlinearity at the level of KPIs and/or the level of the mathematical expression of the model. Varied application-related tests can be applied in the step 5 to check stability and sustainability of the models.

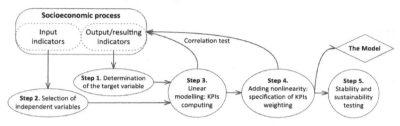

Fig. 2. Design of the methodology.

3.1   Determination of the Target Variable

The most complete and comprehensive headline indicator of the Process is usually used as the target variable to reflect a progress toward the set strategic goal. Result-oriented indicators are preferable, in addition to describing the development process, they characterize the achieved result. Determining the target variable is a critical step toward obtaining a reliable result. If the target variable is determined incorrectly (inaccurately), KPIs will also be selected incorrectly.

So, if the Process relates to the national economy, Gross Domestic Product (GDP) or its derivatives can be used. Similarly, the level of the socioeconomic development is generally described by the Human Development Index (HDI) [35]. Both indicators are accepted by experts and politicians. Success of the business activities could be characterized by the profit obtained, performance of the health care system – by treatable mortality, level of education – by years of schooling, efficiency of services at a defined quality/performance – by price (tariff), etc.

If there is no corresponding comprehensive indicator, in individual cases it is necessary and possible to create one. For instance, there was no indicator to show the sustainable development (SD) level achieved by countries according to the UN globally accepted SD paradigm – integrity and balance of the economic, social and environmental dimensions. Therefore the appropriate indicator – an Advanced Human Development Index (AHDI) was created to use it as a target variable in modelling the SD process [31] (Fig. 3).

A targeted analysis to this end opened several aspects that were considerably taken into account: heredity and simplicity of the target variable, authority of the HDI calculation methodology, the need to use an already accepted comprehensive headline environment indicator. AHDI was created by supplementing HDI with the comprehensive Environmental Performance Index (EPI), which provides an incomparably wider coverage of the environmental aspects in comparison with that of the other options. HDI calculation methodology was precisely adapted to obtain the mathematical expression of the AHDI and to use it as target variable for modelling.

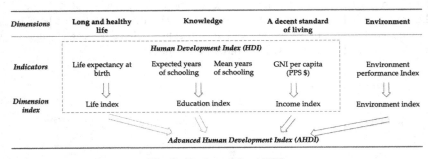

Fig. 3. Design of the AHDI.

3.2 Selection of Independent Variables

Sometimes the set of independent variables (indicators) that characterize the Process is already defined (e.g., [30]), at other times one's own has to be created. So, for many-sided reflection of the growth of EU economies, and their gradual transformation on innovation-driven growth path, the indicator set of the EIS was supplemented by DESI and energy productivity indices [29]. The set of the sustainable development goals (SDGs) have detailed the UN's understanding on the urban SD format, therefore, selected independent indicators ($i_1, i_2, ..., i_x$) should associate with one of the 13 SDGs related to city-level performance [31]; 49 selected indicators were grouped in 13 separate groups related to one of the SDGs. The existence and availability of data sometimes is a constraint on the set formation (this was the case when modelling heat transmission [32]).

The need to compile the most comprehensive set of independent variables sometimes may lead to contradiction. To obtain reliable modelling results based on the causal relationships between the x independent variables and the dependent variable (Y) and to exclude individual deviations, a number of observation points $k >> x$ is required. The stronger this inequality, the more accurate causal relationship (from the point of view of general causality) can be created. If $k \leq x$, we could certainly find several relationships that perfectly reflect all the points of observation, but without the possibility of further generalization (which is needed for prediction and forecasting).

In cases with an insufficient number of observation points, an individual innovative approach is needed to overcome this shortage. So, using the fact that the DESI methodology had not been changed for several years, the data on EU countries for four years (2014–2017) were combined, thus virtually quadrupling the number of observation points [30]. For modelling SD [31], a combined multi-stage modelling process was developed, dividing the indicators into separate modelling procedures under specific conditions (more than 1.7 million procedures were performed in total), and combining a common computation of KPIs. The general algorithms and standard software package had to be adapted and supplemented to perform these specific tasks.

3.3 Linear Modelling: KPI Computing

The choice of the optimal modelling method can be determined by the requirements set by the task to be solved: (1) the mode and tool of modelling should allow easy repeatability of the modelling if data and/or indicators change, and (2) the model should be implementable, recomputable and adaptable to a specific task by a person with mediocre programming skills. The multiple linear regression algorithm was chosen as the first option, because (1) it is mathematically the simplest method, (2) the obtained model is a linear expression, there is a simple and clear interpretation of the model, (3) basic knowledge in mathematics and programming is sufficient for model computation, and (4) using the mathematical expression of the model it can be easily calculated by spreadsheet or even by calculator. The linear regression presents the model in the form of a simple linear equation that shows well the effect of each KPI on the dependent variable, which characterizes the overall process.

Several general and specialized programming languages are suitable for our task. We used the well-developed and user-friendly **R** statistics environment, and a connected development environment **R**Studio. A modelling result includes the estimated weighting and p-value for each indicator. The coefficient of determination R^2 is serving as a quality criterion during the modelling.

The first modelling procedure is performed including all indicators i_x. Using a linear algorithm, the general mathematical function (f) is expanded in linear expression:

$$Y_{m1} = \alpha + \beta_1 \times i_1 + \beta_2 \times i_2 + \cdots + \beta_x \times i_x \tag{2}$$

where α is the intercept and β_x is the modelled weight of the indicator i_x in the linear model.

The post-modelling selection of statistically significant indicators (KPIs) can be done either manually or by supplementing the standard modelling procedure; it is based on two features:

- The KPI is by definition the driver of the function Y_{m1}; so, the indicators i_x should be selected, for which the coefficient β_x has a sign that drives the progress of Y_{m1}: a (+) sign if the increase of i_x promotes an increase of Y_{m1}, but a (−) sign if the increase of Y_{m1} is promoted by a decrease of i_x.
- Indicators i_x should be selected, for which the p-value is less than a certain cut-off value; usually 0.05 or 0.1 is used as a threshold. It should be noted that other values also may be used.

Modelling procedure is repeated with only those indicators that have both features; the others relate to factors that are insignificant and even burdensome for the progress of Process. It is possible that in this narrower set of indicators some of them have lost statistical significance. They can be discarded and the next modelling procedure performed.

After repeating the modelling procedure several times, we obtain an expression of resulting Ymlin, in which p-values of all indicators are small, while correlation between the (Ymlin) and (Y) remains strong (e.g., outputs of three-stage linear modelling of DESI 2019–2020 are shown in the Table 1; indicators' symbols comply with [3]). High statistical significance of these indicators shows their decisive role in the model's regularity; it clearly means that they are the sought-for KPIs (p_1, p_2,....p_n). Action lines, which lead to progress in these KPIs, can be recommended to provide the overall progress of Process. Impact of other indicators on target variable (resp., progress of Process) is insignificant, even random.

Table 1. Output data in DESI 2019–2020 multistage linear modelling. Significance codes: 0 '***' 0.001 '**' 0.01 '*' 0.05 '.' 0.1 ' '1

1st modelling procedure			2nd modelling procedure			3rd modelling procedure		
Indic.	Estimate	p-value	Indic.	Estimate	p-value	Indic.	Estimate	p-value
1a1	2.254e−03	0.350947***	1b1	0.0074910	0.02474*	1b1	0.0094988	0.00276**
1a2	−3.105e−04	0.732016	2b1	0.0006251	0.03654*	2b1	0.0007550	0.00530**
1a3	−7.071e−04	0.758560	3b2	0.0006766	0.10212	3b3	0.0016639	0.00647**
1b1	1.809e−02	0.008904**	3b3	0.0012171	0.05697.	4a1	0.0005243	0.00772**
1b2	7.449e−04	0.371116	3b7	0.0001773	0.34889	4a5	0.0968844	2.19e−05***
1b3	−1.958e−04	0.666097	4a1	0.0004773	0.01450*			
1b4	−6.329e−03	0.008443**	4a5	0.0770913	0.00122**			
2a1	−3.410e−04	0.457984						
2a2	3.999e−04	0.147012						
2a3	8.261e−04	0.440479						
2b1	8.462e−04	0.010701*						
2b2	−2.153e−04	0.048438*						
2c1	−4.064e−03	0.090427.						
2c2	6.483e−05	0.631385						
2c3	NA	NA						
2c4	−2.749e−04	0.586070						
2d1	−6.899e−05	0.848519						
3a1	−5.490e−05	0.941947						
3b1	−7.426e−04	0.071429.						
3b2	1.311e−03	0.001997**						
3b3	2.456e−03	0.000141***						
3b4	−3.193e−03	0.000178***						
3b5	−4.795e−04	0.216064						
3b6	−3.079e−04	0.411530						
3b7	7.587e−04	0.004916**						
3c1	1.574e−03	0.118141						

(continued)

Table 1. (*continued*)

1st modelling procedure			2nd modelling procedure			3rd modelling procedure		
Indic.	Estimate	p-value	Indic.	Estimate	p-value	Indic.	Estimate	p-value
3c2	5.645e−04	0.642668						
3c3	2.141e−04	0.854528						
4a1	4.479e−04	0.054915.						
4a2	−1.628e−04	0.487793						
4a3	4.841e−04	0.142318						
4a4	−5.864e−04	0.105467						
4a5	8.120e−02	0.001513**						

3.4   Adding Nonlinearity: Specification of KPIs Weighting

High numerical characteristics have been achieved creating linear models. Nevertheless sometimes a detailed post-modelling analysis of residuals points toward an incomplete compliance of the actual data with the linear model. **R** diagnostic plots (frequency of residuals, residuals vs fitted, Q-Q, etc.) can show that the linear model does not fully capture the existing nonlinear relationship between the target variable and KPIs. E.g., the **R** diagnostic plot of the linear urban SD model [31] (Fig. 4a) shows that residuals are not relatively evenly spread around a horizontal zero line.

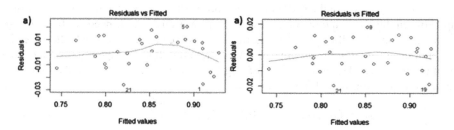

Fig. 4. Residual characteristic of the urban SD (a) linear model, (b) final non-linear model.

It is possible to improve the model by adding nonlinearity to obtain the stronger causality and to specify the impact of KPIs on the target variable, i.e., KPIs weighting. This can be done both at the level of KPIs and the level of the mathematical expression of the model. We used the **R**Studio NLS function, which determines the nonlinear (weighted) least-squares estimates of the parameters of the nonlinear model.

The individual causal relationships between each KPI (p_n) and the target variable (Y) were checked to process the level of KPIs. The real impact of specific KPI on (Y) is, of course, different from the individual regularity (e.g., due to some mutual impact of KPIs). Nevertheless, the strong qualitative difference of some individual (e.g., p_2) causal relationship from the optimum linear one indicates a reduced quality of the linear model.

E.g., the strongly nonlinear data set p_2 was tested by several relative nonlinear relationships, finding the $f_N(p_2)$, which provides the strongest possible correlation between the modified $Np_2 = f_N(p_2)$ and Y. By repeating the linear modelling, a corrected version of the expression (2) was obtained:

$$Y_{ml} = \alpha + \beta_1 \times p_1 + \beta_2 \times f_N(p_2) + \cdots + \beta_n \times p_n \qquad (3)$$

In this way in the case of urban SD the G6.2 data set (Fig. 5a) was transformed into a new data set $G_N6.2$, achieving a stronger linear relationship between $G_N6.2$ and AHDI. The strongest correlation (Fig. 5b) was achieved by modelling the inverse proportionality expression.

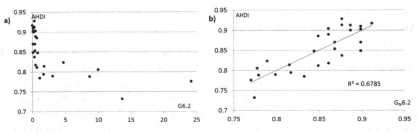

Fig. 5. (a) Regularity G6.2. vs AHDI and (b) regularity $G_N6.2$ vs AHDI.

To process the level of the mathematical expression of the model the causal relationship between the Y_{mlin} and the target variable (Y) was checked. It needs to be clarified whether the linear trendline provides the highest possible correlation, or whether there is some nonlinear function f_P that improves the correlation. If so, the quantitative parameters of the model can be refined by modifying expression (3) accordingly, obtaining the final nonlinear expression of the model (Y_m):

$$Y_m = f_P(\alpha + \beta_1 \times p_1 + \beta_2 \times f_N(p_2) + \cdots + \beta_n \times p_n) \qquad (4)$$

Thus, a corresponding scatterplot in [31] shows that the linear trendline of the data points is slightly skewed with respect to the axis of symmetry in case of urban SD. As a result, smaller fitted values of $AHDI_{lin}$ are generally slightly above the corresponding AHDI values, while large fitted values are below them. Such shifts indicate that the sigmoidal function is best-suited for improving the model. Several S-shaped functions were checked to decrease the aforementioned offset.

The **R** plot of the final nonlinear model (Fig. 4b) shows an improvement of the model quality in comparison with the one depicted in Fig. 3a due to adding nonlinearity. Thereby, a more exact weighting of KPIs has been achieved.

3.5 Stability and Sustainability Testing

As each Process evolves, the numerical values of KPIs are changing in observation points. In addition to these justified changes, data holders are typically revising and updating the raw data repeatedly in order to reflect reality more accurately. We checked if and how these data changes affect the Process model, with respect to whether the model is stable against such data variability.

The model of EU economies was created for 2008–2015, that was a period of hard economic crisis, post-crisis recovery and return to sustainable growth [29]; there were very different preconditions for the progress in particular years of the period. Calculations, which were made for each year using the created joint regularity, show a gradual increasing of correlation (Fig. 6a); it reflects the sustainability of both EU innovation-driven economic policy and the model, as well as an increasing convergence of the EU economics on the innovation-driven growth strategy. The fact that a single functional regularity could be used for years of such diversity, even that the regularity of deep crisis year 2008 could be used for growth year 2014 (Fig. 6b), attests to the universality and sustainability of the model.

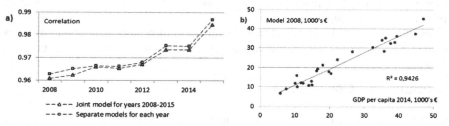

Fig. 6. (a) Correlations of fitted GDP pc models 2008–2015 and (b) coincidence of GDP pc 2014 vs model 2008.

To quantify the stability of the urban SD model [31] several AHDIm5% control models were computed using the modified data, with 5% chosen as the maximum level of random variability of the input data; 5% is close to the median change in EU27 data over the previous 3 years. Of course, these changes have a corresponding effect on the modelled assessment of each individual country; however, the shift using models AHDIm and AHDIm5% does not exceed 0.2% across the EU27 countries.

Both cases clearly show that for practical applications annual calibration of models is not necessary.

European Commission in 2021 strongly adjusted the approach to DESI to reflect technological developments and the major political initiatives that impact sustainable digital transformation of EU countries, namely, Green Deal, Recovery and Resilience Facility and the 2030 Digital Decade Compass. The target function is extended from economic to socioeconomic development. An increased number of indicators is concentrated around four principal and interconnected policy areas: human capital, connectivity, integration of digital technology and digital public services. It was worth to repeat DESI modelling according to the updated indicator set and to compare the KPI selection with 2014–2017 for aforementioned policy areas; the data of 2019–2020 was used to avoid a possible Covid-19 impact in 2021.

Inclusion of the indicator "ICT specialists" in both KPI scopes clearly indicates that a lot of skilled ICT workers are necessary for socioeconomic development. As in 2017, the deficiency of ICT workforce remains a pan-European long-term problem. On the other hand, Internet use in 2020 in the EU27 countries has already become a common practice in society and therefore it has lost its statistical significance.

The connectivity to broadband networks (BB) should be evaluated as very valuable driver of digital development. Both our models recognized fixed BB as a key technology, but technological development is reflected: overall fixed BB coverage was important in 2014–2017, while fast BB (NGA and VHCN) coverage in particular became essential in 2021. Despite the good availability of spectrum and stable y-o-y growth of the mobile data traffic, mobile BB still has a small weight in total broadband. 5G is still a technology of the future that has no significant impact on socioeconomic development today.

Both the big data (large data massifs) and open data (general availability of data) reflect the principles that have become strong enablers of any application and service in both private and public sectors. They are a basis for business transactions, they determine the current rapid spread of e-governance. Their selection justifies the exclusion of the narrower parameter "Electronic information sharing" from the set of indicators at the current level of development.

In general, despite the drastic changes in the set of indicators, the heritability of the choice of KPIs is visible; they represent all four policy areas in DESI 2021 approach.

4   Results and Conclusions

The achieved accuracy of the Processes' linear models, excellent correlations with the real Processes and microscopic p-values of the models (Table 2) clearly demonstrate the correctness of the trend of the current study and practical perspective of obtained results and conclusions. Statistical significance of mathematically selected KPIs confirms that these KPIs are the real drivers of the Processes.

Table 2. Parameters of the processes' models.

Model type	Parameter	GDP pc 2008–2015	DESI 2014–2017	Heat transmission costs 2017	CSDI 2019	DESI 2019–2020
	Indicators (x)	25	31	5	49	33
	KPIs (n)	3	7	2	6	5
Linear	Coefficient of determination R^2	0.9305	0.766	0.9636	0.9421	0.7506
	p-value	<2.2E−16	<2.2E−16	5.9E−13	2.5E−11	2.1E−13
Non-linear	Coefficient of determination R^2			0.9747	0.9638	
	p-value			7.9E−16	<2.2E−16	

Table 3. Numerical characteristics of linear and non-linear urban SD models.

Model	R^2	p-value	Residual standard error	Number of residuals, whose value		
				>2.5%	1.5–2.5%	<1.5%
Linear	0.9421	2.5×10^{-11}	0.01472	2	8	17
Non-linear	0.9638	$<2.2 \times 10^{-16}$	0.01042	0	3	24

Of course, an always linear causal relationship between the KPI and the process variable cannot be expected; the location of the residuals in the **R** diagnostic plots is a reliable indicator that model can be further refined, reducing the effect of existing nonlinear causalities. One can see that by adding nonlinearity in the model numerical characteristics are further improved (Table 3); the nonlinear model coincides better with the actual values of target indicator in comparison with the linear one. Thus, a more exact weighting of KPIs has been achieved.

Varied tests show stability and sustainability of the models. For practical applications annual update of the KPI set due to technological and/or economic development is not necessary; this needs to be done with significant changes of the set of indicators i_x (e.g., due to differences in DESI 2015 and DESI 2020 methodologies).

The developed universal methodology is a reasonable compromise between accuracy, stability, and simplicity, which is a strong advantage for the practical applications. KPIs and their weighting, found in this way, are mathematically computed, and modelling quality (accuracy) is quantifiable. Likewise modelling takes into account the complicated crosslinks between KPIs, as well as the integrity and interplay of separate action lines. Despite of the small number of selected KPIs that are the key drivers of the corresponding Process, the correlations between the modelled and the actual values of the target indicator are very, even extremely strong. The convincing results have obtained applying the mathematical calculation of KPIs; it shows a huge advantage over the methodologies using the voluntarily selected set of indicators and their weighting.

The popular Pareto principle, which over time has even been called "universal truth", states that typically 20% of inputs determine 80% of outputs. The computed pilot projects show that the described universal KPI computation methodology provides an even better outcome. While the average number of KPIs is around 20% of number of independent indicators (Table 2), the average degree of variability in the target variables that is explained by the KPIs (i.e., R^2) is close to 0.9.

The methodology is applicable for variety of Processes; currently we are working on creation of models of the urban heating system for its management and renovation programs to reduce CO2 emissions and to achieve the climate goals, set by EU package "Fit for 55".

Only mediocre programming skills are needed for the application of the methodology. Its transparency, detailed description and open access to mathematical expressions computed for reported cases provide an opportunity for Process management to put the methodology into practice in order to monitor the achieved development level of the Process in statics and dynamics, to see progress and backwardness in particular aspects. It should be mentioned that KPIs reflect relevant action lines. This can be taken into account in strategic planning and decision-making; it will undoubtedly constitute a significant contribution to the Process development and management.

Based on the results of the study, the answer to the introductory question can be formulated, as follows: yes, it is always desirable to obtain more data that provide new data series for a comprehensive description of a particular Process from different aspects and for increasing the number of observation points. For the practical use of large amounts of data, it is recommended to find the KPIs driving the Process, using a mathematical algorithm that provides an objective choice of KPIs. The larger the amount of input data, the more accurate is the computation of KPIs and their weighting.

Acknowledgment. The study has been supported by the Latvian Council of Science project lzp-2021/1-0108 "Sustainable management of the urban heating system under EU Fit for 55 package: research and development of the methodology and tool".

References

1. Wauchope, H.S., et al.: Evaluating impact using time-series data. Trends Ecol. Evol. **36**(3), 196–205 (2021). https://doi.org/10.1016/j.tree.2020.11.001
2. CDN Homepage. https://cdn.prohardver.hu/dl/cnt/2015-02/116080/desimodszertan.pdf. Accessed 28 Feb 2022
3. EC Homepage. https://digital-strategy.ec.europa.eu/en/policies/desi. Accessed 28 Feb 2022
4. EC Homepage. https://ec.europa.eu/info/research-and-innovation/statistics/performance-indicators/european-innovation-scoreboard_en#european-innovation-scoreboard-2021. Accessed 28 Feb 2022
5. Philips-Wren, G., Daly, M., Burstein, F.: Reconciling business intelligence, analytics and decision support systems: more data, deeper insight. Decis. Supp. Syst. **146**, 113560 (2021). https://doi.org/10.1016/j.dss.2021.113560
6. Randsborg, P.H.: Unstable Osteochondritis Dissecans in the Mature Knee: internal fixation works, but we need more data. Aarthrosc. J. Arthrosc. Relat. Surg. **35**(8), 2523–2524, 2019. https://doi.org/10.1016/j.arthro.2019.05.040
7. Li, J., et al.: A new indicator for a fair comparison on the energy performance of data centers. Appl. Energy **276**, 115497 (2020). https://doi.org/10.1016/j.apenergy.2020.115497
8. Gabbi, G., et al.: The biocapacity adjusted economic growth developing a new indicator. Ecol. Indicat. **122**, 107318 (2021). https://doi.org/10.1016/j.ecolind.2020.107318
9. Eggenberger, C., Rinawi, M., Backes-Gellner, U.: Occupational specificity: a new measurement based on training curricula and its effect on labor market outcomes. Labour Econ. **51**, 97–107 (2018). https://doi.org/10.1016/j.labeco.2017.11.010
10. Zhang, Y., et al. Antibiotic resistance genes might serve as new indicators for wastewater contamination of coastal waters: spatial distribution and source apportionment of antibiotic resistance genes in a coastal bay. Ecol. Indicat. **114**, 106299 (2020). https://doi.org/10.1016/j.ecolind.2020.106299
11. Onel, T., et al.: Leptin in sperm analysis can be a new indicator. Acta Histochem. **121**, 43–49 (2019). https://doi.org/10.1016/j.acthis.2018.10.006
12. World Economic Forum Homepage. https://www3.weforum.org/docs/WEF_TheGlobalCompetitivenessReport2019.pdf. Accessed 13 Feb 2022
13. Cross-Sectoral Coordination Center Homepage. https://www.pkc.gov.lv/sites/default/files/inline-files/NAP2027__ENG_3.pdf. Accessed 28 Feb 2022

14. Goldstein, E.J.: More data, more problems? Incompatible uncertainty in Indonesia's climate change mitigation projects. Geoforum **132** (2022). https://doi.org/10.1016/j.geoforum.2021. 11.007
15. Trerotola, S.O., Roy-Chaudhury, P., Saad, T.F.: Drug-coated balloon angioplasty in failing arteriovenous fistulas: more data, less clarity. Am. J. Kidney Dis. **78**(1), 13–15 (2021). https:// doi.org/10.1053/j.ajkd.2021.02.331
16. Analytics India Magazine Homepage. https://analyticsindiamag.com/is-more-data-always-better-for-building-analytics-models/. Accessed 28 Feb 2022
17. Li, Y., Gu, Y., Liu, C.: Prioritising performance indicators for sustainable construction and development of university campuses using an integrated assessment approach. J. Clean. Prod. **202**, 959–968 (2018). https://doi.org/10.1016/j.jclepro.2018.08.217
18. Tesic, M., et al.: Identifying the most significant indicators of the total road safety performance index. Acct. Anal. Prevent. **113**, 263–278 (2018). https://doi.org/10.1016/j.aap.2018.02.003
19. Kaur, M., Hewage, K., Sadiq, R.: Integrated level of service index for buried water infrastructure: selection and development of performance indicators. Sustain. Cities Soc. **68**, 102799 (2021). https://doi.org/10.1016/j.scs.2021.102799
20. Jiang, S., et al.: A large group linguistic Z-DEMATEL approach for identifying key performance indicators in hospital performance management. Appl. Soft Comput. J. **86**, 105900 (2020). https://doi.org/10.1016/j.asoc.2019.105900
21. You, J.W.: Identifying significant indicators using LMS data to predict course achievement in online learning. Internet Higher Educ. **29**, 23–30 (2016). https://doi.org/10.1016/J.IHEDUC. 2015.11.003
22. Pakzad, P., Osmond, P., Corkery, L.: Developing key sustainability indicators for assessing green infrastructure performance. Procedia Eng. **180**, 146–156 (2017). https://doi.org/10. 1016/j.proeng.2017.04.174
23. Zacepins, A., et al.: Model for economic comparison of different transportation means in the smart city. Balt. J. Mod. Comput. **7**(3), 354–363 (2019). https://doi.org/10.22364/bjmc.2019. 7.3.03
24. Kibira, D., et al.: Procedure for selecting key performance indicators for sustainable manufacturing. J. Manuf. Sci. Eng. **140**(1), 011005 (2018). https://doi.org/10.1115/1.403 7439
25. Krumins, K., Cakula, S.: Input determination for models used in predicting student performance. Balt. J. Mod. Comput. **8**(1), 154–163 (2020). https://doi.org/10.22364/bjmc.2020.8. 1.08
26. Roldan-Garcia, M.M., et al.: Ontology-driven approach for KPI meta-modelling, selection and reasoning. Management **58**, 102018 (2021). https://doi.org/10.1016/j.ijinfomgt.2019.10.003
27. Chalmers University of Technology Homepage. Thorstrom, M. Applying machine learning to key performance indicators. https://publications.lib.chal-mers.se/records/fulltext/250254/ 250254.pdf. Accessed 28 Feb 2022
28. Kubiszewski, I., et al.: Toward better measurement of sustainable development and wellbeing: a small number of SDG indicators reliably predict life satisfaction. Sustain. Dev. **30**, 139–146 (2021). https://doi.org/10.1002/sd2234
29. Karnitis, G., Karnitis, E.: Sustainable growth of EU economies and baltic context: characteristics and modelling. J. Int. Stud. **10**(1), 209–224 (2017). https://doi.org/10.14254/2071-8330.2017/10-1/15
30. Karnitis, G., Virtmanis, A., Karnitis, E.: Key drivers of digitalization; EU context and Baltic case. Balt. J. Mod. Comput. **7**(1), 70–85 (2018). https://doi.org/10.22364/bjmc.2018.7.1.06
31. Karnitis, E., et al.: Sustainable development model of EU cities compliant with UN settings. Mathematics **9**(22), 2888 (2021). https://doi.org/10.3390/math9222888

32. Sarma, U., et. al.: Toward solutions for energy efficiency: modeling of district heating costs. In: Tvaronaviciene, M., Slusarczyk, B. (eds.) Energy Transformation towards Sustainability, vol. 1, pp. 219–237. Elsevier, Amsterdam (2019). https://doi.org/10.1016/B978-0-12-817688-7.00011-2

33. Zuters, J., Valeinis, J., Karnitis, G., Karnitis, E.: Modelling of adequate costs of utilities services. In: Dregvaite, G., Damasevicius, R. (eds.) ICIST 2016. CCIS, vol. 639, pp. 3–17. Springer, Cham (2016). https://doi.org/10.1007/978-3-319-46254-7_1

34. Sarma, U., et al.: District heating networks: enhancement of the efficiency. Insights Regional Dev. **1**(3), 200–213 (2019). https://doi.org/10.9770/ird.2019.1.3(2)

35. UNDP Homepage. http://hdr.undp.org/sites/default/files/hdr2020_technical_notes.pdf. Accessed 28 Feb 2022

Knowledge and Knowledge Technologies for Digital Business and Intelligent Systems

Automatic Speech Recognition Model Adaptation to Medical Domain Using Untranscribed Audio

Askars Salimbajevs[1,2]([✉]) [ID] and Jurgita Kapočiūtė-Dzikienė[3,4] [ID]

[1] Tilde SIA, Vienibas Street 75a, Riga 1004, Latvia
[2] University of Latvia, Raina blvd. 19, Riga 1050, Latvia
askars.salimbajevs@tilde.lv
[3] Tilde IT, Naugarduko Street 100, 03160 Vilnius, Lithuania
[4] Faculty of Informatics, Vytautas Magnus University,
Vileikos Street 8, 44404 Kaunas, Lithuania
jurgita.dzikiene@tilde.lt

Abstract. Automatic speech recognition (ASR) technologies can provide significant efficiency gains in the health sector, by saving time and financial resources, allowing specialists to shift more time to high-value activities.

Creating customized ASR models requires domain- and task-related transcribed speech data. Unfortunately, producing such data usually is too expensive for medical institutions: it requires a lot of financial, human resources, and expertise. Consequently, his paper explores a semi-supervised medical domain adaptation method for the Latvian language that benefits from the untranscribed speech recordings. For the initial model, we use the currently available general-purpose hybrid ASR system with the core of a lattice-free maximum mutual information method used to train its acoustic model. The initial system is applied to the domain-related untranscribed data to extract sequences of pseudo-labels. Such automatic transcriptions are later added to the supervised and used together to update the acoustic model. To improve our ASR system further, we have also updated its language model with additional in-domain texts.

We have achieved significant improvements in the quality of speech recognition on all evaluation datasets. On the epicrises, psychiatry, and radiology datasets word error rate (WER) decreased by 39%, 27%–29%, and 21%, respectively.

Keywords: Hybrid ASR · Semi-supervised · Medical domain · Health sector · Latvian language

1 Introduction

Specialists working in the health sector face the daily need to have lots of written information (patient surveys, history of illnesses, descriptions of examinations and analyzes, descriptions of medical and rehabilitative processes, referrals, reports,

M. Ivanovic et al. (Eds.): Baltic DB&IS 2022, CCIS 1598, pp. 65–79, 2022.
https://doi.org/10.1007/978-3-031-09850-5_5

etc.). In most cases, the material is recorded on audio first and only then manually transcribed to have all it in the textual format. Even a relatively small medical institution produces thousands of hours of recordings a year, therefore the level of demand for such an automatic transcription system is unquestionable.

State-of-the-art automatic speech recognition (ASR) technologies that automatically convert spoken content into written form can provide significant efficiency gains: it would save time, financial resources, and would allow medics to dedicate time to their main high-value activities.

Despite there being a general-purpose hybrid ASR created for the Latvian language, high-quality speech recognition requires customization and adaptation to this specific medical domain. The improvement of such a system can be performed in two directions: by improving its acoustic and language models. The acoustic model (AM) adaptation involves the learning of the acoustic environment and user speaking manners related to the targeted domain. While the language model (LM) adaptation learns the language and terms of the target domain from the medical textual data.

Creating customized supervised machine learning models requires precise speech transcriptions (not only some of recording parts or summaries made by medics), therefore this vital training data almost does not exist. Despite there being plenty of audio recordings, their manual transcription is a slow, expensive and complicated process, which medical institutions usually do not have the resources and expertise to perform. As the solution to it, we use the semi-supervised ASR training approach to benefit from the very small transcribed and large untranscribed speech data. Besides, we interpolate the existing general domain LM with domain-specific LMs trained on the automatic ASR transcripts (obtained from medical domain-related recordings) and the additionally collected domain-related texts.

2   Related Work

The most crucial thing when creating a modern ASR system is the training data: the supervised system's accuracy mostly depends on its amount, diversity, and orientation towards the targeted domain. Unfortunately, transcribed data is rare and its preparation process is expensive and time-consuming. Not surprisingly so many researchers put their efforts into collecting necessary data in different ways.

The most advanced approach to this problem is semi-supervised training, especially knowing its superiority over the strongest data-augmentation or weakly-supervised techniques [17]. During the semi-supervised training, the additional training data are obtained by decoding the typically much larger untranscribed dataset with initial ASR trained on the smaller transcribed dataset.

It is important to notice, that end-to-end (E2E) ASR systems are much more sensitive to the quality of the "seed" ASR systems. The experimental investigation proves that improvements can be achieved only if starting from relatively good initial models (i.e., models trained on the large amounts of transcriptions) [1,6]. Whereas semi-supervised training of the hybrid ASR systems can boost its performance even starting with relatively small supervised training resources. Besides, almost all forces for the creation of the semi-supervised hybrid ASR system are directed towards the improvement of the AM, because the domain-related training data for the LM is much easier to get.

The lattice-free maximum mutual information (LF-MMI) objective used to train AMs in hybrid supervised ASR systems was transferred to a semi-supervised scenario [9]. The offered LF-MMI ASR system has effective solutions to deal with the unsupervised data: lattices obtained during decoding are rescored with the strong LM. Unfortunately, the traditional LF-MMI approach has its weak spot: its performance degrades if applied on small or limited in-domain datasets. To address this issue, the authors in [16] offer two error detection-driven semi-supervised AM training approaches. Error detectors (used to modify the supervision lattice/best-path hypothesis) effectively control the supervision provided for learning from unlabeled datasets.

Not all semi-supervised ASR training approaches limit to one iteration. There are different so-called scheduling strategies how to assure even larger improvements. The authors in [7] offer an LM-MMI-based AM training approach in which the unlabeled dataset is split into multiple subsets that are processed incrementally. With each subset, the previous AM becomes the "seed" for the next one. The authors report significant improvements on English, Lithuanian and Bulgarian datasets. Despite semi-supervised training being focused on obtaining the transcribed data, the importance of LM (in hybrid ASR systems) cannot be underestimated. The comprehensive investigation (including variations of initial systems, quantities of transcribed data, etc.) [22] of various semi-supervised approaches for the AM in hybrid ASR systems proves that having a good (e.g., domain-related, task-related) LM, the initial AM quality becomes far less important and can be effectively boosted via semi-supervised training.

Overall, semi-supervised approaches that use pseudo labels created by the existing ASR system have been shown to be very effective in general domain speech recognition settings and achieve state-of-the-art performance [18]. While untranscribed datasets are typically much larger than the available transcribed dataset, some research [16] shows that such an approach also works in the opposite case: performance of a model trained of a large amount of transcribed out-of-domain data can be improved by adding a smaller amount of untranscribed in-domain data.

The aim of this research is the ASR system accurately performing on the medical domain in the Latvian language. It is important to notice, that we do not have to start from scratch: there is a rather accurate hybrid general purpose ASR for the Latvian language. However, the availability of in-domain data is the big problem, we have only a moderate amount of raw in-domain audio recordings and in-domain texts.

The topic of automatic speech recognition for radiology examination reports in Latvian only recently has gained some attention [4]. Researchers focused more on the adaptation of language and pronunciation models using supervised datasets of much larger size (30h of speech, 135M tokens of text data), while this work takes advantage of untranscribed data and a much smaller amount of text data is available. Moreover, radiology is only one of 3 domains that we worked on.

The contribution of our research is two-fold: 1) we are creating multiple ASR systems adapted to the medical subdomains for the Latvian language; 2) we show that significant improvements in ASR quality are possible by using semi-supervised method (as presented in [16]) even on moderate amounts (hundreds of hours) of available in-domain data.

3 Method

This section describes the automatic speech recognition system used in this paper, collected data from medical domain and methods used for adaptation of ASR models to medical target using collected untranscribed speech data.

3.1 Semi-supervised Training of ASR with Error Detection

Most of the approaches to semi-supervised AM training generate an automatic transcription of speech data using a seed ASR model trained from supervised (transcribed) speech data. Typical approaches processes select new speech-transcription pairs based on different filtering schemes (see [9] for relevant references).

This work adopts semi-supervised speech recognition training with the error detection module [16] to train domain-adapted acoustic and language models. The idea of this method is to use a small amount of manually transcribed data to train the error detection model which can later mark errors in automatically transcribed data.

This method has been chosen for the following reasons:

- Modern ASR error detectors [2,8,19] are more powerful than the lattice posterior-based confidence scores used to weight per-frame gradients [9] or to discard erroneous words [20,21] or utterances [3,23] in most semi-supervised neural AM training studies;
- Transcripts obtained by this method can also be used for LM training and adaptation;
- We have already had a positive experience with this method in other domains.

Our idea is that this method can be used to improve speech recognition quality of medical speech by adapting both AM and LM. In this case, untranscribed speech data from medical domain is transcribed by baseline unadapted ASR and processed by error detector. Words marked as incorrect are replaced with the special token "<unk>". Next, both baseline and automatically transcribed datasets are concatenated and used to re-train the AM. This means that only words marked as incorrect are discarded and all remaining further used in training. The same transcripts with "<unk>" token are also used for LM training and adaptation. In both cases, after training "<unk>" token is removed from the ASR vocabulary preventing the system to output this token instead of real hypotheses.

3.2 Speech Recognition

The Kaldi toolkit was used to train both general-purpose initial (baseline) and customized (medical domain-adapted) speech recognition AMs [12], which deal with the raw audio waveforms of human speech, predicting what phoneme each waveform corresponds to, at the character or subword level. The architecture of AM used in this paper is the TDNN deep neural network trained with the LF-MMI loss function [13]. In this work, the only difference between the baseline and adapted models is the training data. Adapted models take advantage of automatically transcribed in-domain medical data obtained using method described in previous section.

N-gram LMs were trained with the KenLM tool [5] and RNN neural network LMs trained with the Kaldi RNNLM tool. All models are trained on a 40M sentence general domain text corpus collected from web news portals. Word n-gram models are used for semi-supervised adaptation because the method used in this study does not support the subword LMs. Generation of automatic transcripts was done in two steps:

– a pruned 2-gram model was used during decoding to create lattices that contain multiple hypotheses;
– lattices were rescored, LM weights were refined with larger and more accurate 3-gram models.

In turn, after training the AMs, BPE [15] subword LMs were used to evaluate them. Such an approach allows to use the RNNLM LM and achieve much better WER (word error rate) and CER (character error rate). Recognition was performed in three steps:

– a pruned 4-gram model is used during decoding to create lattices that contain multiple hypotheses;
– lattices were rescored, LM weights were refined with larger and more accurate 6-gram models;
– rescored lattices were rescored again, hypotheses were evaluated with RNNLM models, new costs were combined with costs from the 6-gram model.

The speech recognition quality was assessed by calculating WER and CER using the following formula:

$$WER/CER = \frac{S + D + I}{N}$$

where S is the number of substitutions, D is the number of deletions, I is the number of insertions, N is the number of words or characters in the reference.

3.3   Language Model Adaptation

As mentioned in Sect. 3.1, pseudo-labels obtained by the initial ASR can also be used for adapting the LM to the target domain. The following steps were performed to train domain-adapted LMs:

- Transcripts of untranscribed adaptation data were obtained using the initial ASR system;
- Transcripts were split into BPE subwords and the 6-gram LM was trained;
- ASR error token "<unk>" was filtered out from the vocabulary of the trained LM;
- The similar 6-gram subword LM was trained on real in-domain texts;
- A small held-out set was created from real transcripts of in-domain data;
- Both LMs were interpolated with a general domain 6-gram LM using a held-out set to optimize interpolation weights.

3.4   Data

The following datasets were used for training of the general domain ASR AMs:

- 100 h Latvian Speech Recognition Corpus [10];
- 8 h Latvian Dictation Speech corpus [11];
- 180 h the Saeima speech corpus which was created automatically [14];

For the AM adaptation, audio recordings were collected from 4 medical sub-domains (see Table 1). Some of these recordings have been collected from hospital dictaphone centers (8 kHz sample rate, telephone call quality), while some have been re-recorded from real transcripts using mobile devices (16 kHz sample and high quality). Such diversity is valuable because allows assessing the effect of adaptations on the recognition quality with both high-quality and low-quality audios.

Table 1. Collected untranscribed data

Domain	Source	Size
Epicrises	Dictaphone center	1964 recordings, 140 h
Pediatrics	Dictaphone center	3024 recordings, 188 h
Psychiatry	Mobile devices	56 recordings, 14 h
	Dictaphone center	1162 recordings, 90 h
Radiology	Mobile devices	244 recordings, 19 h
	Dictaphone center	841 recordings, 49 h

To ensure the anonymity of the collected data by the dictaphone centers, the beginning of each audio recording was cut off because it contains a personal code and other information that could allow identifying the patient. Re-recording was performed by the authorized medical personnel who were additionally instructed to omit sensitive information.

Audio recordings were collected separately for each subdomain (epicrises, pediatrics, psychiatry, radiology) and automatically divided into segments (utterances) by pauses. Subsets of randomly chosen utterances from each subdomain were manually transcribed. As a result of it, several evaluation datasets were created (see Table 2). Unfortunately, due to time constraints, the transcription of the pediatrics evaluation set was not completed.

Table 2. Evaluation data

Domain	Source	Size
Epicrises	Dictaphone center	2293 utterances, 2.5 h
Psychiatry	Mobile devices	2000 utterances, 3 h
	Dictaphone center	1626 utterances, 1.6 h
Radiology	Mobile devices	3423 utterances, 3 h

In addition, a development dataset was created, consisting of 2,314 utterances ($\approx$2 h) from recordings of the epicrises subdomain. This set was used for the training of the error detection model.

For training the adapted LMs, related medical texts were collected from psychiatry, radiology, and epicrises subdomains (see Table 3). Collected texts were also split into sentences and shuffled. Unfortunately, we were not able to collect a sufficient amount of texts from the pediatrics subdomain. Only narrative or descriptive parts were copied from medical information systems, omitting the information that could identify patients.

Table 3. Text data

Domain	Sentences	Words
Epicrises	14M	118M
Psychiatry	0.2M	2.8M
Radiology	0.2M	2.4M

4 Results

Using above described methods separate domain-adapted ASR systems were developed for each subdomain. Detailed adaptations and evaluation results for each subdomain are described in the following subsections.

4.1 Adaptation to the Epicrises Domain

A significant amount of audio recordings performed in the health sector belong to the epicrises domain. For the adaptation of the AM, 140 h of audio recordings of epicrises were processed using the semi-supervised method mentioned in

Sect. 3.1. The resulting audio transcripts were added to the generic training data and a new adapted AM was trained.

The evaluation was performed on two evaluation sets for:

- Psychiatry (dictaphone center), to check if adaptations improve the quality of speech recognition for audio in other domains.
- Epicrises, to test the effectiveness of adaptation on target domain data.

The results are summarized in Table 4. After adaptation to the epicrises domain, WER decreased from 41.1% to 37.8% (8% relative improvement) and CER from 18.2% to 15.7% (14% relative improvement). The quality of ASR hasn't changed on audio recordings from the psychiatry domain.

Table 4. AM adaptation to the epicrises domain

	Psychiatry (dictaphones)		Epicrises	
	WER, %	CER, %	WER, %	CER, %
Baseline	28.5	11.9	41.1	18.2
Adapted AM	28.5	11.9	**37.8**	**15.7**

The results suggest that a semi-supervised adaptation method can improve the quality of ASR in the target domain, but although both evaluation sets are from the medical field, there is no improvement on the records in the other psychiatry subdomain. This could mean that the method is sensitive to a particular subdomain of the adaptation data.

Finally, a LM adaptation was performed. Separate subword n-gram LMs were trained on collected texts and automatically generated transcripts of adaptation data. These models were interpolated with the general domain subword n-gram LM.

Table 5. LM adaptation to the epicrises domain

AM	LM adaptation texts	WER, %	CER, %
Baseline	No adaptation	41.1	18.2
Adapted	No adaptation	37.8	15.7
Adapted	Automatic transcripts	33.8	14.1
Adapted	Collected texts and automatic transcripts	25.7	**10.1**
Adapted	Collected texts only	**25.2**	10.3

As expected (see Table 5) LM adaptation significantly improves both WER and CER. Results show that, if no in-domain texts are available, automatic transcripts can be used instead. However, using real in-domain texts will yield a significantly better result. It is not clear if interpolation of LMs trained on real and automatic texts improves ASR quality, results show simultaneous WER degradation and CER improvement (both - statistically significant).

4.2 Adaptation to Psychiatry Domain

In psychiatry (more than in other specialties), medical records are based on long narratives, entering such long texts is time-consuming. Also, an important part of the treatment process in psychiatry is the establishment of therapeutic contact with the patient/family. The entry of electronic documentation during the visit significantly interferes with the establishment of therapeutic contact (in fact, makes it impossible).

As before, the first experiments were performed on the following two evaluation sets:

- Psychiatry (dictaphone center), to test the effectiveness of adaptation on target domain data.
- Epicrises, to check if adaptations improve the quality of speech recognition for audio in other domains.

Table 6 summarizes the results of the first experiments. It can be seen that it is important that the audio quality of the adaptation data coincides with the data quality of the target subdomain evaluation. Using high-quality psychiatry domain audio for semi-supervised adaptation, no improvement in WER and CER was observed.

Table 6. AM adaptation to the psychiatry domain. Evaluation on low-quality data

Adaptation data	Psychiatry (dictaphones)		Epicrises	
	WER, %	CER, %	WER, %	CER, %
No adaptation	28.5	11.9	42.6	18.8
Psychiatry data (mobile)	28.5	11.9	42.6	18.8
Psychiatry and radiology (mobile)	28.4	11.7	42.0	18.0
Downsampled psychiatry data (mobile)	28.1	11.5	42.9	18.3
Psychiatry data (dictaphone)	25.3	10.6	42.7	18.6
Combining all above	**23.6**	**10.0**	**40.2**	**17.9**

Attempts were made to use data from another subdomain, radiology, in addition to psychiatric data. Although the data come from a different subdomain, minimal improvement in WER and CER was found. Downsampling high-quality adaptation data to an 8 kHz sampling rate (which matches the recording quality of the dictaphone center) shows a greater improvement (WER from 28.5% to 28.1%, CER from 11.9% to 11.5%). On the other hand, performing ASR adaptation on psychiatry data from dictaphone center, an improvement in WER to 25.3% (11% relative improvement) and an improvement in CER to 10.6% (11% relative improvement) can be seen.

Finally, combining all the above achieved the best results and a significant improvement in the quality of speech recognition. WER improved to 23.6% (17% relative improvement) and CER to 10.0% (16% relative improvement).

The improvement is also visible on the evaluation data from another subdomain (epicrises). This could suggest that extending the scope of the adaptation data could lead to an improvement in the quality of ASR on multiple domains. However, the WER and CER are still higher than using adaptation data from the corresponding domain (40.2% vs. 37.8% and 17.9% vs. 15.7%; see Table 4).

The effectiveness of the adaptation was also tested on psychiatry domain evaluation data of high audio quality. Two adapted ASR models were evaluated:

- The best model adapted using only high-quality audio data;
- The model that achieved the best result on the evaluation data from the dictaphone center.

The results in Table 7 semi-supervised adaptation on high-quality data provides a significant improvement compared to the previous experiment (where the evaluation was performed on dictaphone center data). This again shows the importance of the adaptation data to match the target domain. WER improved from 17.5% to 16.1% (8% relative improvement) and CER from 6.6% to 6.0% (9% relative improvement).

However, the best result was achieved with the model adapted on combined data, which also achieved the best result on the data of the dictaphone center. WER improved to 14.0% (20% relative improvement) and CER to 5.5% (17% relative improvement).

Table 7. AM adaptation to the psychiatry domain. Evaluation on high-quality data

Adaptation data	WER, %	CER, %
No adaptation	17.5	6.6
Psychiatry and radiology (mobile)	16.1	6.0
Combined (see Table 6)	**14.0**	**5.5**

Finally, a LM adaptation was performed. As before separate subword n-gram, LMs were trained on collected texts and automatically generated transcripts of adaptation data. These models were interpolated with general domain n-gram LM.

Table 8. LM adaptation to the psychiatry domain

	Psychiatry (dictaphones)		Psychiatry (mobile)	
	WER, %	CER, %	WER, %	CER, %
Baseline AM and LM	28.5	11.9	17.5	6.6
Best adapted AM + baseline LM	23.6	10.0	14.0	5.5
Best adapted AM + adapted LM	**20.7**	**8.5**	**12.4**	**5.0**

Results in Table 8 show improvements in WER and CER on both evaluation sets. Compared with the baseline unadapted system, WER improved by 27%

relative on the dictaphone quality data and by 29% on mobile devices, while CER improved by 29% and 24%.

4.3   Adaptation to the Radiology Domain

Radiology uses the services of the dictaphone center quite intensively, the descriptions are long and often non-standard. Therefore, radiology was chosen as the next domain for adaptations.

Collected audio recordings from radiology (both dictaphone center and mobile recordings), psychiatry, and pediatrics were used for the semi-supervised adaptation of the AM. The results are summarized in Table 9.

Despite the radiology evaluation set consisting of high-quality audio, both the WER and CER of the systems tested are very high. This result shows that radiology is much more complex for the ASR. We believe it can be explained with a complex specific language with many terms, foreign words, numbers, and abbreviations.

The largest improvement in WER was achieved through semi-supervised adaptation with audio data from radiology (mobile devices only). WER was reduced from 46.6% to 44.2% (5% relative improvement). CER, on the other hand, rose from 18.1% to 21.1%. By supplementing training data with psychiatric audio (high quality), the WER remains the same, but the CER increases to 21.5%. Adaptation with radiological audio recordings from the dictaphone center increases both WER and CER.

Table 9. AM adaptation to the radiology domain

Adaptation data	WER, %	CER, %
No adaptation	46.6	**18.1**
Radiology (mobile)	**44.2**	21.1
Radiology and psychiatry (mobile)	**44.2**	21.5
Radiology (dictaphone)	47.0	18.3
Radiology (all)	44.4	21.7
Radiology, psychiatry, epicrises, pediatrics (all)	44.8	23.0

Data Vocabulary. While analyzing previous results, we hypothesized that a small improvement in WER could be due to a mismatch between evaluation and adaptation data (obtained by the semi-supervised method). To test this, a comparison of vocabularies between general domain data, adaptation data, and evaluation data was made:

– vocabularies of all unique words were retrieved from each data set;
– vocabularies were transformed into vectors;
– by calculating the cosine similarity between these vectors, the correspondence of the vocabularies was measured.

The results (see Table 10) show that the adaptation data are textually consistent with the evaluation data (cosine similarity - 0.7526), while general domain data is quite different. Adding adaptation data to the general domain data brings it closer to the target domain and significantly reduces OOV from 25% to 11%. Therefore, it can be concluded that the hypothesis was not confirmed.

Table 10. Correspondence of vocabularies between adaptation and evaluation data

Transcript	Cosine similarity	OOV, %
General domain	0.4291	25%
Radiology	0.7526	17%
Combined	0.4346	11%

Improving Seed LM. A small improvement in WER could also be due to the high WER of the seed ASR system, which limits the quality of automatic transcription and degrades the performance of the semi-supervision transcription. To test this hypothesis, seed LM in semi-supervised training was replaced with an adapted radiology LM (as literature [22] seem to indicate that having better seed LM is more important than AM). This model is a 3-gram model that was trained on collected radiology texts. The results of the experiment (see Table 11) do not allow to draw of unambiguous conclusions. Although the WER improved to 40.7% (13% relative to baseline and 8% relative to the previous best), the CER increased to 25% (38% relative). Such a result could indicate overfitting of the ASR to specific words (word forms), ignoring what was actually said.

Table 11. Adaptation to the radiology domain using improved seed LM

Adaptation data	WER, %	CER, %
No adaptation	46.6	**18.1**
Radiology (mobile)	44.2	21.1
Radiology (all) + improved seed LM	**40.7**	25.0

Radiology LM. Finally, a LM adaptation was performed using both automatically generated transcripts and real in-domain texts.

The results (see Table 12) adaptation of the LM is an effective way to improve WER on the radiology recordings. With baseline AM adapted LM adaptation improves WER from 46.6% to 37.0% (22% relative), and CER from 18.1% to 14.3% (21% relative). However, combining with AM adaptations does not provide an unambiguous improvement. While WER slightly improved to 36.6%, the CER significantly degraded to 17.5%.

Table 12. LM adaptation to the radiology domain

AM	LM	WER, %	CER, %
No adaptation	No adaptation	46.6	18.1
Best adapted	No adaptation	40.7	25.0
No adaptation	Adapted	37.0	**14.3**
Best adapted	Adapted	**36.6**	17.5

5 Conclusion and Future Work

In this paper, we investigated the adaptation of speech recognition models to the medical sector for the Latvian language by using untranscribed audio recordings and in-domain texts. To tackle this problem we 1) have applied a semi-supervised training method with the error detector [16] to adapt the AM and 2) performed LM adaptation using in-domain texts.

The semi-supervised method was applied to the transcribed audio recordings covering multiple subdomains (epicrises, psychiatry, pediatrics, and radiology). A small part of the collected data was transcribed for evaluation and training of the error detection model.

The obtained evaluation results are promising: significant speech recognition quality improvements were achieved on each evaluation dataset. The largest WER improvement by 39% was observed on the epicrises domain (which had the largest text and audio data available for adaptation, so there could be a correlation). WER improved by 27% and 29% on evaluation sets from the psychiatry domain. The smallest 21% WER improvement was obtained in the radiology domain.

From our experience WER has to be lower than 25% for ASR system to be usable. Therefore, the achieved promising results allow us to assume that ASR system for psychiatry domain can already be applied in practice (especially with high-quality audio inputs). However, the radiology and epicrises ASR systems still need improvements and therefore becomes our important future direction.

Our experimental investigation also reveals the necessity of targeted domain data. Unfortunately, the data from another medical subdomain demonstrates very little or even no improvement.

However, the demand for ASR systems coming from the medical sector is huge. It encourages us not only to adapt and improve the ASR systems for the subdomains targeted in this paper but also to expand to other subdomains. We also believe that these findings can be generalized to any other language.

Acknowledgements. This research has been supported by the ICT Competence Centre (www.itkc.lv) within the project "2.8. Automated voice communication solutions for the healthcare industry" of EU Structural funds, ID no 1.2.1.1/18/A/003.

References

1. Chen, Y., Wang, W., Wang, C.: Semi-supervised ASR by end-to-end self-training. arXiv abs/2001.09128 (2020)
2. Errattahi, R., El Hannani, A., Salmam, F.Z., Ouahmane, H.: Incorporating label dependency for ASR error detection via RNN. Procedia Comput. Sci. **148**, 266–272 (2019)
3. Grezl, F., Karafiát, M.: Semi-supervised bootstrapping approach for neural network feature extractor training. In: 2013 IEEE Workshop on Automatic Speech Recognition and Understanding, pp. 470–475. IEEE (2013)
4. Gruzitis, N., Dargis, R., Lasmanis, V.J., Garkaje, G., Gosko, D.: Adapting automatic speech recognition to the radiology domain for a less-resourced language: the case of Latvian. In: Nagar, A.K., Jat, D.S., Marín-Raventós, G., Mishra, D.K. (eds.) Intelligent Sustainable Systems. LNNS, vol. 333, pp. 267–276. Springer, Singapore (2022). https://doi.org/10.1007/978-981-16-6309-3_27
5. Heafield, K.: Kenlm: faster and smaller language model queries. In: Proceedings of the Sixth Workshop on Statistical Machine Translation, pp. 187–197 (2011)
6. Kahn, J., Lee, A., Hannun, A.: Self-training for end-to-end speech recognition. In: ICASSP 2020–2020 IEEE International Conference on Acoustics, Speech and Signal Processing (ICASSP), pp. 7084–7088. IEEE (2020)
7. Khonglah, B.K., Madikeri, S.R., Dey, S., Bourlard, H., Motlícek, P., Billa, J.: Incremental semi-supervised learning for multi-genre speech recognition. In: ICASSP, pp. 7419–7423. IEEE (2020)
8. Lybarger, K., Ostendorf, M., Yetisgen, M.: Automatically detecting likely edits in clinical notes created using automatic speech recognition. In: AMIA Annual Symposium Proceedings, vol. 2017, p. 1186. American Medical Informatics Association (2017)
9. Manohar, V., Hadian, H., Povey, D., Khudanpur, S.: Semi-supervised training of acoustic models using lattice-free mmi. In: 2018 IEEE International Conference on Acoustics, Speech and Signal Processing (ICASSP), pp. 4844–4848. IEEE (2018)
10. Pinnis, M., Auziņa, I., Goba, K.: Designing the Latvian speech recognition corpus. In: Proceedings of the 9th Edition of the Language Resources and Evaluation Conference (LREC 2014), pp. 1547–1553 (2014)
11. Pinnis, M., Salimbajevs, A., Auzina, I.: Designing a speech corpus for the development and evaluation of dictation systems in Latvian. In: Chair, N.C.C., et al. (eds.) Proceedings of the Tenth International Conference on Language Resources and Evaluation (LREC 2016). European Language Resources Association (ELRA), Paris, France (2016)
12. Povey, D., et al.: The kaldi speech recognition toolkit. In: IEEE 2011 Workshop on Automatic Speech Recognition and Understanding. IEEE Signal Processing Society, December 2011. iEEE Catalog No.: CFP11SRW-USB
13. Povey, D., et al.: Purely sequence-trained neural networks for ASR based on lattice-free MMI. In: Proceedings of the Annual Conference of the International Speech Communication Association, INTERSPEECH, vol. 08-12-Sept, pp. 2751–2755 (2016). https://doi.org/10.21437/Interspeech.2016-595
14. Salimbajevs, A.: Creating lithuanian and Latvian speech corpora from inaccurately annotated web data. In: Calzolari, N., et al. (eds.) Proceedings of the Eleventh International Conference on Language Resources and Evaluation, LREC 2018, Miyazaki, Japan, 7–12 May 2018. European Language Resources Association (ELRA) (2018). http://www.lrec-conf.org/proceedings/lrec2018/summaries/258.html

15. Sennrich, R., Haddow, B., Birch, A.: Neural machine translation of rare words with subword units. In: Proceedings of the 54th Annual Meeting of the Association for Computational Linguistics (vol. 1: Long Papers), pp. 1715–1725 (2016)
16. Sheikh, I., Vincent, E., Illina, I.: On semi-supervised LF-MMI training of acoustic models with limited data. In: INTERSPEECH 2020, Shanghai, China (2020). https://hal.inria.fr/hal-02907924
17. Singh, K., et al.: Large scale weakly and semi-supervised learning for low-resource video ASR. In: INTERSPEECH, pp. 3770–3774. ISCA (2020)
18. Synnaeve, G., et al.: End-to-end ASR: from supervised to semi-supervised learning with modern architectures. CoRR abs/1911.08460 (2019). http://arxiv.org/abs/1911.08460
19. Tam, Y.C., Lei, Y., Zheng, J., Wang, W.: ASR error detection using recurrent neural network language model and complementary ASR. In: 2014 IEEE International Conference on Acoustics, Speech and Signal Processing (ICASSP), pp. 2312–2316. IEEE (2014)
20. Thomas, S., Seltzer, M.L., Church, K., Hermansky, H.: Deep neural network features and semi-supervised training for low resource speech recognition. In: 2013 IEEE International Conference on Acoustics, Speech and Signal Processing, pp. 6704–6708. IEEE (2013)
21. Veselý, K., Burget, L., Cernocký, J.: Semi-supervised DNN training with word selection for ASR. In: Interspeech, pp. 3687–3691 (2017)
22. Wallington, E., Kershenbaum, B., Klejch, O., Bell, P.: On the learning dynamics of semi-supervised training for ASR. In: Proceedings of Interspeech 2021, pp. 716–720 (2021). https://doi.org/10.21437/Interspeech.2021-1777
23. Zhang, P., Liu, Y., Hain, T.: Semi-supervised DNN training in meeting recognition. In: 2014 IEEE Spoken Language Technology Workshop (SLT), pp. 141–146. IEEE (2014)

On the Automatisation of the Realisation of a *Banduke* Table

Antoine Bossard[✉][ID]

Graduate School of Science, Kanagawa University, 2946 Tsuchiya,
Hiratsuka, Kanagawa 259-1293, Japan
abossard@kanagawa-u.ac.jp

Abstract. *Banduke* tables are a traditional Japanese mean of communicating rankings and other organisation charts. They are well-known in Japan especially thanks to their continued usage to announce details of sumo wrestling competitions. Such tables were also used in earlier centuries for instance to publish the names of the wealthiest individuals in the country. Traditional *banduke* tables feature a characteristic, visually impacting design which is difficult to reproduce on computer systems. And, the automatisation of the generation of such a chart is even more challenging. In this paper, in order to keep this cultural heritage alive, we investigate this automatisation issue and propose a system which generates *banduke* tables. The obtained results are very promising in that the charts that can be produced by our proposal look very realistic. Besides, we have also quantitatively evaluated the generated tables by comparing them to original documents, some of which were obtained with the help of museums of Japanese history.

Keywords: Digitalisation · Cultural heritage · Japan · Character · Language

1 Introduction

Traditionally, Japan has relied on organisation charts, called *banduke* (IPA: [banzɯike]), to make public, written announcements with respect to various purposes. For instance, and it is now one of the most well-known usage example of *banduke* tables, all the parties involved in sumo wrestling competitions, starting with wrestlers themselves, are detailed on such an organisation chart. Names and ranks are central to such documents.

Banduke tables are however not restricted to this characteristic sportive usage: such charts can be found in archives of libraries and museums, listing for example the wealthiest individuals in the country – such tables are typically called 長者 *chōja* "wealthy person" either 集 *shū* "list" [8], 鑑 *kagami* "example" [5] or 番付 *banduke* "organisation chart", literally "order assignment" [3,6]. This second sample usage seems also to be characteristic of *banduke* tables. A part of such an organisation chart is illustrated in Fig. 1.

© The Author(s), under exclusive license to Springer Nature Switzerland AG 2022
M. Ivanovic et al. (Eds.): Baltic DB&IS 2022, CCIS 1598, pp. 80–92, 2022.
https://doi.org/10.1007/978-3-031-09850-5_6

Fig. 1. A part of a *banduke* table (cropped from a photograph of [8]). The "crowded" aspect is characteristic of such organisation charts.

Although characteristic of the Japanese society of the previous centuries, such listings remain part of the Japanese culture and some are thus still edited in our modern society. For example, H. Kikuchi authored a few years ago a book on post-war Japanese billionaires which is in the form of a *banduke* chart, albeit modern [6]. That is, its content conforms to that of a traditional *banduke*, but not its format: in order to benefit from facilitated editing as provided by mainstream word processing software and facilitated printing and commercial distribution, such modern editions are edited as regular books and have thus lost the typical design of *banduke* tables, and thus part of their appeal. An exception is made for sumo wrestling organisation charts [3], which retain the traditional, visually impacting design of ancient tables (e.g. [5,8]).

The objective of this research is thus to enable automatic generation of a *banduke* table that retains their traditional, characteristic style in order to keep this cultural heritage alive for the current and next generations. In other words, we investigate and measure whether it is feasible and practical to supersede the arguably bland typesetting of modern *banduke* table editions without having to resort to manual typesetting.

The rest of this paper is organised as follows: the basic structure and core properties of a *banduke* table are reviewed in Sect. 2. The proposed automatic generation system is described in Sect. 3 and experimentally evaluated in Sect. 4. Finally, Sect. 5 concludes this paper.

2 Preliminary Analysis of *Banduke* Tables

In this section, we briefly recall essential properties of the considered writing system, Japanese, before describing in detail the structure of a typical *banduke* table.

2.1 Writing System

First and foremost, we make a recall about the elements of the Japanese writing system. It is based on three main categories of characters: Chinese characters, called *kanji*, which represent the vast majority of the characters of the Japanese writing system, and the *kana* characters of the two syllabaries *hiragana* and *katakana*. Chinese characters are logograms, each having at least one reading and one meaning (yet often several) whereas the *kana* characters are used only for their readings and thus convey no semantic information [1].

In most cases, these characters are stacked vertically: in the Japanese writing system, characters traditionally flow from top to bottom and such character columns are positioned on the page from right to left [7]. And in some particular situations, such as titles or shop signs, characters can also be found stacked horizontally from right to left. This latter scenario is almost exclusively restricted to single line phrases though. (This is to be compared with the writing systems of Latin cultures: characters are stacked horizontally from left to right, with such character rows positioned on the page from top to bottom.) So, in the case of *banduke* tables, most text is typeset vertically and from right to left, with some exceptions, usually single lines, such as for titles which are typeset horizontally and from right to left.

2.2   Table Content and Structure

We next make several observations regarding the structure of a typical *banduke* table. These are obviously general guidelines which are more or less followed by *banduke* authors. We mostly relied on the three tables [4,5,8] which are of different origins and periods.

Such a chart can be typeset in both portrait or landscape mode, and it usually consists in five or six layers of persons' names. Layers are stacked vertically. They include lists of names written vertically from right to left, thus in accordance with traditional Japanese writings. The table is horizontally split at the centre to separate two sets of such layers: the left layers, called the "west", and the right layers, called the "east". East and west layers are separated by a vertical column at the centre which spans the entire table height and which includes additional information such as table details and sponsor information. A *banduke* table can have a title which spans its width or height, although some have no such title: they only rely on the middle column text to provide such information.

The typical ranks found in a *banduke* table are as follows (in descending order of importance): 横綱 *yokoduna*, 大関 *ōzeki*, 関脇 *sekiwake*, 小結 *komusubi* and 前頭 *maegashira*. It can be noticed that other, lower ranks do exist, for example 十両 *jūryō* and 幕下 *makushita* for sumo wrestling, but the corresponding titles are usually not explicitly displayed in the main, printed organisation charts (refer to Fig. 6a).

We now detail the structure of these five to six table layers. As explained, a layer is a list of entries, such as persons' names. Each entry of a layer usually consists of three parts: the rank, at the top, the location (e.g. prefecture, district), at the middle, and the name, at the bottom. So, each layer usually consists of three rows: the rank row, the location row and the name row. There may be of course slight variations; for instance, the rank row is abbreviated for the lower layers of [8].

Regarding the topmost layer, say layer 1, each entry is fully detailed: ranks are written without any abbreviation, locations are repeated even if appearing for two consecutive entries. See Fig. 1.

Regarding the next layer (i.e. the layer below layer 1), say layer 2, typically the rank of the first entry (i.e. the rightmost one) is fully written but that of the subsequent entries is abbreviated to only the character 同 "same". Similarly, when the location of several consecutive entries is identical, the first location is fully written and the succeeding ones are abbreviated to only that same *kanji* character 同.

The next layer, say layer 3, typically either completely omits ranks and abbreviates repeated consecutive locations with an even simpler glyph such as 〃 or 〆 (which corresponds to 同), or slightly abbreviates the rank of the first entry, for example 前頭 becomes simply 前, and succeeding ranks are denoted by 〆, just as repeated consecutive locations.

Layer 4 can be similar to the previous layer or can be even more abbreviated: for instance, repeated consecutive locations become the simple glyph 丶. The remaining layers are typeset on a par with the fourth layer.

A typical *banduke* table structure is illustrated in Fig. 2. This figure shows two such organisation charts side by side (*banduke* tables taken from [12]) so as to clearly designate the various table elements, without overlapping. The reader can also refer to the generated table given in appendix for an illustration (Fig. 7).

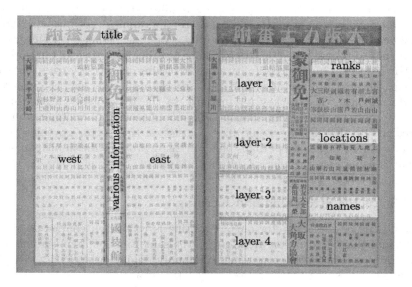

Fig. 2. Structure of a typical *banduke* table: the major elements are labelled. Two such organisation charts are here shown side by side (*banduke* tables from [12]) so as to clearly designate the various table elements.

Finally, it is important to mention that some glyphs used inside *banduke* tables are characteristic of such organisation charts and thus not present in conventional character encodings, such as Unicode [11], even with support for the ideographic variation database (IVD).

3   Methodology

Our implementation has been realised with the Scheme-based Racket programming language and framework [2].

3.1   Character Rendering

Two aspects are essential in our approach: a traditional *banduke* table is visually appealing first and foremost because of the font it uses and tightly spaced characters (sometimes even overlapping). So, no satisfactory result could be obtained without an appropriate font. To this end, we have selected a font that is similar to the one used to typeset *banduke* tables for sumo wrestling competitions [3]. It should be noted that the proposed system enables to seamlessly change fonts, which is obviously a significant improvement over manual production. Font selection is easily done in Racket with, for instance, the `make-font` procedure, which we use.

Second, for the realised digitalisation method to achieve optimal graphical rendering quality, notably when printing is required, the produced output needs to be based on vector graphics, and not raster graphics (i.e. bitmap). Vector graphics can be easily obtained in Racket by using, for instance, a PDF drawing context (`pdf-dc%`); we relied on this solution. Another advantage of our approach is that it induces a high accessibility since it retains character (string) information (e.g. the text is selectable, and thus searchable inside, say, the generated PDF document), which is key for instance to the text-to-speech accessibility feature [9]. Furthermore, accessibility is increased thanks to vector graphics as detailed in [10]. Finally, we would like to insist on this vector graphics feature since a *banduke* table could perhaps be more easily produced with bitmap graphics, that is using raster renderers, filters and so on.

3.2   Character Stretching and Kerning

The key issue of the character output routine is to stretch characters so that they fit into their destination area, but at the same time enforcing a maximum stretch ratio so that characters remain humanly readable, obviously. So, while kerning (i.e. the space between two consecutive characters) is set to the value provided as parameter, this value is in fact treated as the minimum kerning: when a stretching factor that is larger than the maximum tolerated stretch ratio would be required to make the character string fit its destination area, characters are stretched according to the maximum tolerated stretch ratio and kerning is automatically adjusted between characters so that they perfectly fit into their destination area.

The first task is to calculate the bounding box of each character, that is, to retrieve the precise width and height of each glyph. The `get-text-extent` method of the drawing context of the window canvas did not return satisfactory results. The best solution was to first retrieve the outline of the character as a path with the `text-outline` method of the `dc-path%` class and then retrieve the corresponding bounding box. The `get-path-bounding-box` method did not produce satisfactory results, although they were significantly better than those obtained with the above first method. Satisfactory results were eventually obtained by relying instead on the `get-bounding-box` method, which was applied to the result of `text-outline`.

The successive results are illustrated in Fig. 3, the red frame showing the calculated bounding box for the sample character 日 "day" (typeset with the system default Japanese font), and the acceptable method is detailed in Listing 1.1 (the source code has been simplified for the sake of clarity); the `dc` variable represents therein the drawing context that is used for graphical rendering.

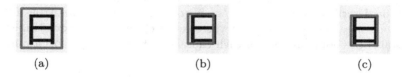

(a)   (b)   (c)

Fig. 3. The result of each of the three bounding box (red frame) calculation solutions for the sample character 日 "day": (a) with the `get-text-extent` method; then with the `text-outline` method combined with (b) the `get-path-bounding-box` method and with (c) the `get-bounding-box` method. (Color figure online)

Listing 1.1. Calculation of the bounding box of each character with the `get-bounding-box` method.

```
1  (let ([path-dc (new dc-path%)])
2    (send path-dc text-outline (send dc get-font) "日" 0 0)
3    (let-values ([(left top width height)
4                  (send path-dc get-bounding-box)])
5    (list left top width height))) ; return the bounding box
```

Then, this bounding box calculation method is applied to each character of the string to print out in order to calculate the dimensions (i.e. width and height) of the entire string. To this end, kerning that we call "manual" since manually specified (constant) in the program is added between every two consecutive characters of the string. There is no need to adjust such parameter: the default value is satisfactory.

Then, we deduce the tentative scaling factors (i.e. horizontal and vertical) from the specified destination area and the calculated string dimensions. These obtained scaling factors remain tentative: it is indeed possible to setup a maximum stretch ratio m, which acts as a threshold to determine whether kerning should be automatic or manual. If the tentative scaling factors do not induce a stretch ratio which goes beyond this threshold, then the scaling factors are fixed. Otherwise, that is the tentative scaling factors would overly stretch characters, the constant kerning value is discarded in favour of an automatic one which satisfies the threshold; in practice, the scaling factors are calculated so that character stretching equals the maximum stretch ratio, and space is evenly distributed between consecutive characters.

Let us consider vertical typesetting, which is the vast majority of the character strings of a *banduke* table. The horizontal scaling factor is directly fixed to $s_h = w_r/w_s$, with w_r the width of the destination rectangle and w_s the aggregated width of the character string (i.e. the width of the largest character since a vertical character string). The vertical scaling factor is tentatively set to $s_v = h_r/h_s$, with h_r the height of the destination rectangle and h_s the aggregated height of the character string. If $s_v/s_h > m$ holds, the vertical scaling factor s'_v is fixed to $m \times s_h$, and otherwise to s_v. Then, the "smart" kerning value calculation described above when $s_v/s_h > m$ holds is detailed in Listing 1.2 (the source code has been simplified for the sake of clarity). The `bounding-boxes` list contains the bounding box of each character of the string to print out.

Listing 1.2. Calculation of the automatic kerning value between consecutive characters. The value s'_v is the calculated vertical scaling factor.

```
1  (let ([remaining-space ; remaining space inside destination rectangle
2          (- rect-height ; height of the destination rectangle
3             (foldl (lambda (box current-height)
4                      (let ([height (* (fourth box) s'_v)])
5                        (+ height current-height)))
6                    0 bounding-boxes))])
7    (/ remaining-space (sub1 (length characters)) s'_v))
```

A sample vertical typesetting output in the case of manual kerning only and in the case of automatic kerning are given in Figs. 4a and 4b, respectively. In this example, the manual kerning method overly stretches characters, and this is corrected with the automatic kerning method: space is evenly distributed between consecutive characters so as to satisfy here a maximum stretch ratio vertical:horizontal of 2:1. (This ratio is of course a sample value: any maximum ratio can be specified.)

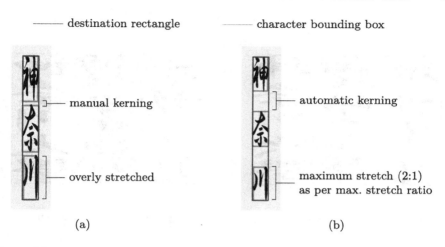

Fig. 4. (a) Manual kerning induces overly stretched characters. (b) Automatic kerning evenly distributes space between consecutive characters so as to satisfy here a maximum stretch ratio of 2:1.

3.3   Character String Filling and Margins

Then, such character string fitting is automatically repeated in order to fill in large zones of the *banduke* table. This step is thus about the automatic calculation of the position and dimensions of numerous destination areas, one for each entry of the chart. It also requires to take into account the margin value to be inserted between two consecutive character strings; such margin can be set to a negative value to reproduce the "crowded" aspect of *banduke* tables. Although rather tedious, such calculations are omitted here for the sake of conciseness. The adjustment of this margin setting is illustrated in Figs. 5a and 5b: a positive and a negative margin, respectively.

4   Experimental Evaluation

We have quantitatively evaluated the results obtained from the proposed generation system. This is detailed next.

4.1   Experimental Conditions and Results

An illustration of a generated sample *banduke* table is given in appendix (Fig. 7); the results are very promising in that the produced chart looks very realistic. Now, in an attempt to quantitatively evaluate the proposal, we have generated a *banduke* table with the proposed automatised generation system (Fig. 6b) and we have compared the obtained chart with two existing ones: an organisation

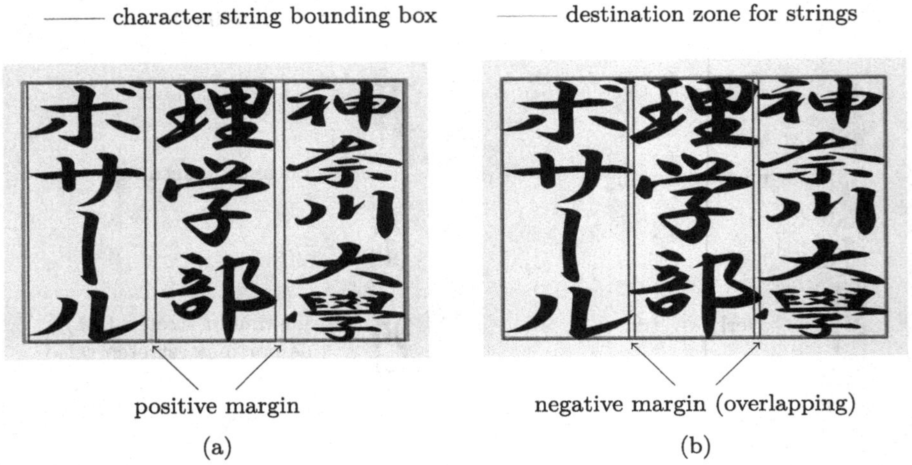

——— character string bounding box   ——— destination zone for strings

positive margin
(a)

negative margin (overlapping)
(b)

Fig. 5. An illustration of the margin setting between consecutive character strings: (a) a positive margin, (b) a negative margin, with thus character string bounding boxes overlapping.

chart for a sumo wrestling competition (Fig. 6a) and that of [8] (Fig. 6c). Then, after shearing and resizing these two original tables so that their dimensions very roughly match those of the generated table, we have applied several filters to the obtained images in order to more easily visualise the difference between the generated table and original ones.

Precisely, we have calculated the difference between images, then converted the result to a monochrome image and, finally, we have pixelized the result (8×8 pixels) to better identify similarities and differences with the original *banduke* tables of Figs. 6a and 6c. The obtained results are shown in Figs. 6d and 6e, respectively.

4.2   Discussion of the Results

The result of the calculated image difference should be understood as follows: black pixels (black areas) designate similarity between the original and generated charts. And white areas accordingly emphasise dissimilarities between the two images.

The first result (Fig. 6d), that is the difference between a *banduke* table for sumo wrestling competition and the generated one, reveals larger similarities in the bottom half of the chart. It should be noted that the table generated with the proposed system has been filled with generic, mostly Japanese names, that is, not the same names that appear on the sumo wrestling table so as to avoid any possible copyright infringement.

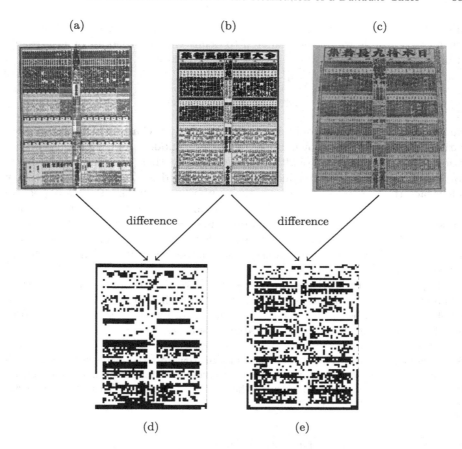

Fig. 6. The difference between original *banduke* tables and the generated one has been calculated and emphasised with pixelization. (a) is a photograph of [4], (b) is the generated table and (c) is a photograph of [8].

This first result induces a similarity rate of approximately 37%. One should note that this value is only given for reference: it could be easily increased by adjusting the table content so as to match the original. Rather than focusing on the exact similarity value, the purpose of this experiment is to identify areas inside the generated chart where improvements could be made in an attempt to reproduce such a *banduke* table with a higher fidelity.

On the other hand, the second result (Fig. 6e), that is the difference between a *banduke* table which lists wealthy individuals and the generated one, reveals larger similarities in the top and bottom third of the chart. This second result induces a similarity rate of approximately 40%. These results also show how much of each table we have considered to define the proposed automatic generation system.

5   Conclusions

Banduke tables are traditional Japanese organisation charts which are used for various purposes. Well-known usage examples include sumo wrestling competition tables and national wealth rankings. Due to their complex layout, so as to benefit from computer technologies the produced modern charts are mostly uncharacteristic, mere lists such as those published in books. In this paper, we have investigated the feasibility of automatising the creation of *banduke* tables while, importantly, retaining their characteristic design. The obtained results are very promising: the generated organisation chart looks very realistic. In addition, we have quantitatively measured the results in an attempt to identify high and low similarity areas in the output.

Regarding future works, some properties of vertical typography, which is an inherent part of the Japanese writing system, such as the rotation of several glyphs, remain to be implemented. In addition, an interface could be realised to facilitate the usage of this *banduke* table generator.

Acknowledgements. The author is grateful towards the Miyazaki Prefectural Museum of Nature and History (Japan) for providing and granting permission to use the *banduke* table of [8] for this study. The *banduke* tables included in this paper are copyright of their respective authors and owners.

A   Complete Sample Output

We reproduce the generated sample *banduke* table of Fig. 6b in a full-page sized version in Fig. 7 to allow for a more precise inspection. It be noted that this table has been realised for research purposes only: names are entirely fictitious; any similarity to actual persons, organisations or other entities is purely coincidental.

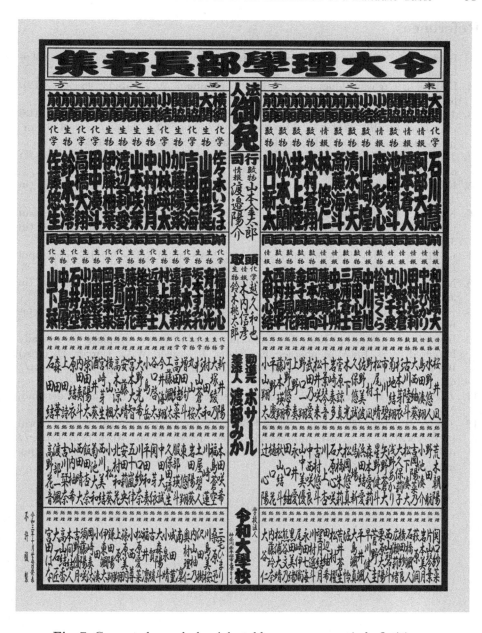

Fig. 7. Generated sample *banduke* table; names are entirely fictitious.

References

1. Bossard, A.: Chinese characters, deciphered. Kanagawa University Press, Yokohama, Kanagawa, Japan, March 2018
2. Flatt, M.: Creating languages in Racket. Commun. ACM **55**(1), 48–56 (2012). https://doi.org/10.1145/2063176.2063195
3. Japan Broadcasting Corporation (Nippon Hoso Kyokai): Ōzumō banduke tte, ittai nannano? (大相撲 番付って、いったい何なの？) May 2021. https://www3.nhk.or.jp/sports/story/13400/index.html. (in Japanese). Accessed Apr 2022
4. Japanese Sumo Association (Nihon Sumo Kyokai): (2021), Banduke table (番付表) of 1st March 2021. (in Japanese)
5. Katō, T.: Dainippon marumochi chōja kagami (大日本持丸長者鑑) (1879). (in Japanese)
6. Kikuchi, H.: Nihon no chōja banduke: sengo okuman chōja no seisui (日本の長者番付 ： 戦後億万長者の盛衰). Heibonsha, Tokyo, Japan (2015). (in Japanese)
7. Lunde, K.: CJKV Information Processing, 2nd edn. O'Reilly Media, Sebastopol (2009)
8. Nihon marumochi chōja shū (日本持丸長者集) (Tenpō period (1830–1844)). (in Japanese)
9. PDFlib GmbH: A technical introduction to PDF/UA. pDFlib Whitepaper, December 2015
10. Rotard, M., Otte, K., Ertl, T.: Exploring scalable vector graphics for visually impaired users. In: Miesenberger, K., Klaus, J., Zagler, W.L., Burger, D. (eds.) ICCHP 2004. LNCS, vol. 3118, pp. 725–730. Springer, Heidelberg (2004). https://doi.org/10.1007/978-3-540-27817-7_108
11. The Unicode Consortium: The Unicode Standard, Version 14.0. Print on demand, November 2021
12. Tōkyō Banduke Chōsakai (東京番附調査会): Kinko ō-banduke: nanajū yorui (今古大番附 ： 七十余類). Bunsankan Shoten, Tokyo, Japan, April 1923. https://doi.org/10.11501/1185061. National Diet Library of Japan (identifier no. info:ndljp/pid/1185061)

Improved Content Model in Personalized Adaptive E-Learning System

Vija Vagale[1]([✉]) [iD], Laila Niedrite[2] [iD], Andris Vagalis[1] [iD], and Svetlana Ignatjeva[1] [iD]

[1] Daugavpils University, Vienibas 13 Street, Daugavpils, Latvia
vija.vagale@gmail.com, {andris.vagalis,svetlana.ignatjeva}@du.lv
[2] Faculty of Computing, University of Latvia, Raina boulv.19, Riga, Latvia
laila.niedrite@lu.lv

Abstract. The article proposes an analysis of a personalized adaptive e-learning system LMPAELS, and an adaptation of a content model of this system to the trends of digital transformation in education and new pedagogical innovations. This research includes a survey on (i) students' attitude towards the need for independent work and its novelty, (ii) types and resources of independent work used in a learning process, and (iii) risks/factors that are most often encountered during the independent work. Trends in educational transformation and results of the survey demonstrated a need to improve the existing LMPAELS content model. Subjects of the survey were students from three Latvian universities. As a result, following attributes were added to the course described in the content model: competence, preconditions, and outcomes. Attributes included in a description of a learning object were – skills, knowledge, deadline, and learning time. The improved content model gives an opportunity to create different types of learning objects depending on the deadline, including organizing independent study hours. Introduction of a deadline and learning time for learning objects allows a learner to plan and control their own learning process. The use of different learning object types allows a more detailed description of the learning process components, and improves the adaptation offered by the system.

Keywords: Digital transformation · Moodle · Independent study · Personalized adaptive system · E-learning

1 Introduction

Society is constantly shaken by various adversities that affect both the economy and education. On the one hand, education is the main driver of the country's economic and social development [15]. On the other hand, education is still one of the most vulnerable areas [14]. Recently, the digitalization of education or the creation of a digital learning space has become very important [4, 9, 11, 16].

The development of computers and the Internet has driven a trend towards digital transformation in education and digitalization of educational processes relatively early. Although, until recently, it had a relatively low pace, as there were no external factors accelerating these processes. However, with the onset of the COVID-19 pandemic in

M. Ivanovic et al. (Eds.): Baltic DB&IS 2022, CCIS 1598, pp. 93–107, 2022.
https://doi.org/10.1007/978-3-031-09850-5_7

March 2020, a forced lockdown was introduced in many countries. That lead to people searching for new forms of work in all areas, including education [3, 4]. In 2020, a global pandemic led to a rapid shift of learning process from a physical classroom to a virtual classroom (digital space) [21]. Researchers in many countries have conducted studies analyzing the progress of this transition, and its successes and failures, such as Indonesia [3], Norway [4], and Saudi Arabia [1].

Higher education was one of the first to adapt quickly and transform the learning process by moving it to the digital environment. In many parts of the world, universities resumed a full-fledged study process in the digital environment within 1–2 weeks. This was possible because of the existing developments in the digitalization of education [4]. Additionally, teaching in a virtual classroom anticipates new teaching and learning activities and interaction models [21]. During this pandemic, also the amount of independent work in the learning process increased significantly [3].

However, despite the success stories, there have also been some failures when incorporating digital transformation in education. Some factors slowing down this process are insufficient technological and pedagogical support, lack of competence and experience in digital use, new requirements for the digital competencies of both teachers and students, and the difference between the levels of digital competencies of teachers and students [16, 21]. This gave rise to a need to improve and complement existing digital tools, such as learning management systems (LMS) to make them more efficient in the digital and online environment.

In the organization of the learning process, there is a constant search for ways to ensure and improve the quality of the education, considering the needs and requirements of modern society. Some recent tendencies in educational transformation are distance learning, lifelong learning, inclusive education, competence-based learning of the content [24], student-centered approach to organizing the learning and teaching process [18, 24], embracing flexible learning paths [24], learning "based on the desired learning outcomes for students and the workload required to achieve them" and considering students as active participants in their learning process [22].

To adapt the LMS to the specific needs of each individual as much as possible, the personalization and adaptation aspects of e-learning systems are important. For experimental purposes, a learner model based personalized adaptive e-learning system (LMPAELS) is used at Daugavpils University [18].

The above-mentioned technological and pedagogical innovations promoted the need to assess the pertinence of the LMPAELS e-learning system for current educational trends. An emphasis here is put on the competences, knowledge, skills, outcomes, and independent work of the learner, which is an integral part of any course learning process.

The research object here is a learner model based personalized adaptive e-learning system LMPAELS. The aim is to analyze the personalized adaptive e-learning system LMPAELS and to adapt the system content model to the trends of modern information technology and digital transformation in education.

First, the use of digitalization and the latest pedagogical tendencies in education were analyzed, with an emphasis on the use of an independent work in the learning process. Then, a detailed literature review on the importance of independent work in the learning process was performed in [7, 12, 17]. Next, a questionnaire for students was developed based on the aforementioned review articles. In the survey, students indicated their attitude toward the need for independent work and its novelty; the types and resources of independent work used in the learning process; and risks and factors that are most often encountered during a self-study. Students from three Latvian universities took part in the survey. The survey results were analyzed using descriptive and inferential statistics [8]. The results showed students are aware that they must actively take part in the learning process. Students also understand the role and importance of independent work in the learning process. The performance of the independent work is often influenced by factors and risks associated with a lack of time and resources.

Based on pedagogical tendencies and the results of the survey analysis, new attributes were added in the content model of LMPAELS: (i) to the course (competence, preconditions, and outcomes), and (ii) to the learning object (LO) (skills, knowledge, deadline, and learning time). LOs were divided into two groups – (i) in-class and (ii) outside the class LO. In addition, the latter was divided into two other groups – (i) graded and (ii) not graded LO. Introducing deadline and learning time for LO enables the learner to plan and control their learning process better. Using the LO type allows to describe the components of the learning process in more detail and improve the adaptation offered by the system.

The paper is organized as follows. Section 2 presents an explanation of the concepts related to the digitalization of education. Section 3 describes the personalized adaptive e-learning system LMPAELS used in the study. Section 4 describes the evaluation of the LMPAELS. The experiment is described in Sect. 5. Section 6 covers the improvement of LMPAELS content model. Section 7 lays out related works. Finally, conclusions and future work are discussed in Sect. 8.

2   Definitions and Assumptions

In this research, one of the tasks was to elucidate the concepts "digitalization" and "digital transformation" to understand the essence of these concepts and identify their impact on the object of research - LMPAELS.

2.1   Digitalization

The analysis of the use of the term "digitalization" in scientific publications has identified three interpretations of this term.

In the first, simplest case, the term "digitalization" means the same that the terms "digitalize". It refers to converting paper materials into a format used on a computer. For example, in education, the digitalization of learning materials [1, 11] and curriculum [6] as well as the storage of digital materials are mentioned.

Second, the broader term "digitalization" refers to transferring infrastructure and various processes to digital platforms [16]. For example, in [4], an attempt to digitalize followed two parallel tracks (dual digitalization): (i) digitalization of educational solutions such as LMS, MOOCs, library systems, and websites that are implemented and supported by IT specialists, and (ii) digitalization of learning subjects by academic staff.

Thirdly, "digitalization" can be interpreted as high digital technology and equipment accessibility for everyone involved in the learning process. This approach is typical for the Nordic educational system. For example, the Swedish education system is one of the most digitized in the European Union [21]. Most schools have at least one computer or tablet per student.

Digitalization promotes a paradigm shift and improves productivity in all areas where it is used [16]. This can also apply to education.

The combination of these three interpretations makes it possible to create a united digital learning space. It is a space in which learning activities take place physically, socially and epistemically (relating to knowledge and cognition), i.e. by students and teachers [9]. In the digital learning space, the learner's learning process (activities) is influenced by (i) set tasks, (ii) available tools and resources, and (iii) actions of people around.

2.2 Digital Transformation

The scientific literature review elucidates two interpretations of the "digital transformation" term.

Firstly, the development of an integrated learning space is called education digital transformation (DT) [4]. In such case, digital transformation means the change and transfer of educational processes to digital platforms and learning environments, also changing the approach to the organization of the learning process.

Secondly, DT is defined as the coordinated movement of culture, employees and technology towards a new model of education and operation that changes business processes, development directions and values [10]. In this interpretation, digital transformation means that digital use, besides improving and supporting traditional methods, fosters new forms of innovation and creativity in both business and society. DT is applicable in various, such as government, education, global communications, health, art, and science.

In this paper, the term "digitalization of education" refers to the use of various technological tools and IT solutions at different levels and fields of education to ensure the learning process [11]. The "digital transformation" of education refers to a transfer of traditional educational processes to digital educational spaces and a paradigm shift in the organization of the learning process, adapting to modern requirements.

3 Background

A learner model-based personalized adaptive e-learning system (LMPAELS) is used at Daugavpils University for experimental purposes. LMPAELS is based on the learning management system Moodle. Additional functionality has been added to Moodle for personalization and customization of the learning process [18]. This section considers the LMPAELS from the perspective of models. The system comprises three models: a learner model, a content model, and an adaptation model.

3.1 Learner Model

LMPAELS adapts the learning process based on the learner's characteristics and needs. Data characterizing the learner are described in the learner model (LM). Based on the data lifetime in the model, all learner-characterizing data are divided into three groups: basic data, additional data, and learning process data (see Fig. 1).

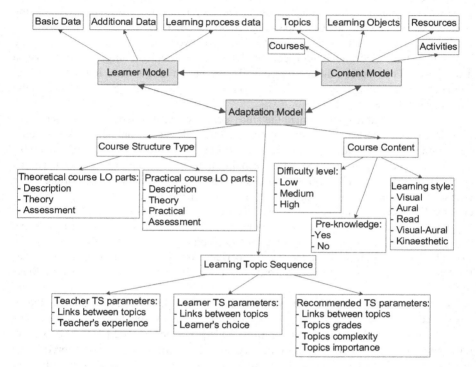

Fig. 1. Description of the LMPAELS system models.

Figure 1 shows the structure of LMPAELS models based on the data types used. In the figure, models are highlighted in grey. Arrows indicate the data types used.

Basic data have the longest lifespan, as they do not change at all or change rarely. This group includes data that describe the learner's personal data. Examples of included personal information about the learner are name, surname, email, gender, age, etc.

The personality of the learner is characterized by the additional data. They describe the learner's individual features (e.g. learning style), pedagogical data (e.g. courses, topics, topics sequences), preference data (e.g. language, presentation format), device data (e.g. hardware, screen resolution), and training system's usage experience. Values of these data change over time.

Learning process data describe the learning process of the learner. These data include learning history data and knowledge data at the current moment.

The developed LM contains data based on the data lifecycle, and can also be used in the lifelong learning learner profile. Data lifecycle indicates how long this data is valid in the system. The above-mentioned data types, their acquisition, and data lifecycle are described in more detail in the paper [19].

3.2 Adaptation Model

Types of adaptation in the LMPAELS are described by the adaptation model. There are three ways a system performs adaptation, based on: (i) the course structure type, (ii) the course content, and (iii) the topic learning sequence (see Fig. 1).

Based on the structure, it is possible to create two types of study courses in the learning system: theoretical and practical. The practical course comprises four parts: a description of the topic, a theory, a practical part, and an assessment. In the theoretical course, the practical part is omitted. More on this is explained in the description of the content model in Sect. 3.3.

The system is able to customize the study course content based on learner's (i) pre-knowledge (yes, no) in the study course, (ii) learning style (visual, aural, read, kinesthetic, the combination of visual and aural), and (iii) chosen difficulty level (low, medium, high).

Three topic sequences (TS) have been implemented in the course: teacher's TS (TTS), learner's TS (LTS), and recommended TS (RTS). At the beginning of the study course, the learner must choose the order in which the system offers topics for the course. TTS is set by default. All three TSs are based on links between topics. At the beginning of the course, the teacher defines links between the topics according to the skills required to acquire each subsequent topic. When choosing the TTS, in addition to the links between topics, the teacher's experience is also considered. As for the LTS, the learner can assemble the sequence of the topics, based on the links between these topics.

When developing the RTS, it was initially named the optimal topic sequence. It was based on the links between the topics and the grades obtained in these topics. This topic sequence was later refined and improved [18]. The newest addition to the existing parameters in the RTS are topic complexity and importance that are considered when creating an RTS. Topic complexity characterizes the topic's level of learning difficulty compared to the rest of the topics in the course. Topic importance shows the topic's position on the list of all course topics.

It is possible to change the topic learning sequence anytime during the learning process. A transfer to another TS is described with more details in [20]. A full description of the personalized adaptive system architecture used in the experiment can be found in [18].

3.3 Content Model

The learning content in the LMPAELS is described using the content model (CM). CM is based on the concept of learning object (LO). In LMPAELS, the definition of LO is based on the one used in [2]. A LO represents a unit of learning content with a theoretical part, a practical part, and an assessment, which are all used to achieve one goal. In the system, additionally to the aforementioned LO parts, a description part has been added (see Fig. 1). A LMPAELS study course comprises one or several topics. Each topic consists of one or more LO. Each part of the LO contains resources or activities depending on the learner's pre-knowledge, learning style, and chosen difficulty level [19].

4 Evaluation of the E-Learning System LMPAELS

In this section, an evaluation of the LMPAELS was performed to find out its compliance with the modern and educational digital transformation (paradigm shift following modern requirements) trends. The transfer of traditional educational processes to the digital education space determines the paradigm shift in the organization of the learning process following modern requirements. The main factors influencing the quality of education are student-centered learning, competence-based approach, lifelong learning, and inclusive learning.

Student-centered learning means that learners can plan their learning paths based on clear information to acquire knowledge, skills, and competences that meet both their personal goals and the needs of society [18, 22]. The LMPAELS adaptation model (AM) provides a student-centered approach where the learner can be active in the learning process. The AM takes into consideration several factors about the learner. It permits adapting the course content according to the learner's pre-knowledge level, the level of learning complexity, and the learning style. Besides the teacher's and recommended topic sequences, the system offers the learner to choose topics sequence on his/her own.

A competence-based approach in education means that the learner's achievements are described through competences. Competence is a set of knowledge, skills, and attitudes [23]. Moodle has also realized competencies but with a broader meaning. This term refers to both competence, knowledge, and skills. In a Moodle course, a teacher is not allowed to manage the list of Moodle competencies. It is allowed to use only the Moodle competencies pre-defined by the administrator. This approach does not allow the teacher to define knowledge, skills, competences, and learning outcomes within one course.

Learning outcomes are described by competence, knowledge and skills that are not included in specific competence [23]. Outcomes describe exactly what the learner will accomplish measurably. Over one measurable outcome, knowledge, and skill can be defined for each competence. Course prerequisites describe the knowledge and skills required to complete a course. In the course description, course prerequisites are used to indicate the location of the course throughout the curriculum. In LMPAELS, learning outcomes and course prerequisites are not implemented.

Competence-based education includes practical activities that help to strengthen the acquired knowledge and improve its understanding. The amount of practical work in class within the study course is limited. Therefore, in order to develop competences, it is necessary to determine the amount of independent work. Universities in their study course descriptions include a recommended amount of independent study hours (ISH). In the Latvian educational system, the amount of ISH is not defined. However, such requirements exist in other countries, under other names such as a self-managed directed study, and self-managed independent study [25]. Self-managed directed study (SMDS) refers to activities that take place outside the class as a continuation or preparation for the learning process. In the SMDS, resources or activities that need to be evaluated, such as homework, are used. Self-managed independent study (SMIS) includes activities defined by the students themselves without direct instructions from the teacher. These are called "topic activities". These activities are based on the learner's initiative and improve his/her knowledge of the topic. For example, reading specialized literature or developing practical skills. These activities are not being evaluated. Independent study hours in the LMPAELS content model are not implemented.

The first column of Table 1 summarizes the main issues that are important in the training process nowadays. The second column describes how each specific issue refers to LMPAELS.

Table 1. Analysis of the possibility of using pedagogical trends in the LMPAELS.

Issues	Implementation in LMPAELS
Student-centered approach	In LMPAELS, the learner manages his/her own learning process; the system offers content adaptation according to the learner's characteristics (provided by AM)
Lifelong learning	LM contains data that can be used for the user profile in lifelong learning
Learning path	Three TS for course acquisition (TTS, LTS, RTS) are implemented in AM
Competences	Implemented partially
Knowledge	Implemented partially
Skills	Implemented partially
Learning outcomes	Not implemented
Course preconditions	Not implemented
Independent work	Not implemented

5   Experiment and Data Analysis

To find out how students evaluate the independent work and study materials included in the teaching process, a questionnaire was developed, and an anonymous survey was organized. The survey took place in the spring semester of the academic year 2021/2022.

5.1   Survey Description

A questionnaire consists of seven parts: (i) "Characteristics of respondents" (9 questions), (ii) "Evaluation of the attitude towards independent work" (18 questions), (iii) "Assessment of the independent work novelty" (18 questions), (iv) "Assessment of the available resource quality " (9 questions), (v) "Assessment of the independent work types" (5 questions), (vi) "Assessment of the negative factor impact on the independent work performance" (9 questions), and (vii) "Assessment of the risks connected with the performance of independent work" (11 questions).

Likert scale, ranging from 1 to 5, was used to assess the questionnaires from parts 2–7. In the last part, respondents had to assess the probability (percentage) of the risk factor related to performing independent work. Therefore, in part 7, Likert scale values correspond to the following percentage: value 1 corresponds to 0–20%, 2 to 21–40%, 3 to 41–60%, 4 to 61–80%, and 5 to 81–100%.

5.2 Respondents Description

To get a more accurate picture of the situation regarding the importance of independent work and teaching materials used, the survey was conducted for respondents with the widest possible range of characteristics.

119 respondents from 3 Latvian universities took part in the survey. 95 respondents (79.8% of the total number of respondents) were from Daugavpils University, 15 (12.6%) from the University of Latvia, and 9 (7.6%) from the Ventspils University of Applied Sciences.

98 (82.4%) respondents are aged 18 to 25, 14 (11.8%) aged 26 to 35, 6 (5%) aged 36 to 45 and the rest over 46 years old. 39 (58%) respondents are men and 50 (42%) are women.

Analyzing the enrolled level of education, 107 (89.9%) respondents are currently students of academic or professional bachelor's study programs, 7 (5.9%) are students of the first level professional higher education program, and 5 (4.2%) are currently in a master's study program.

The questionnaire attempted to cover different study programs. The most respondents – 57 (47.9%) study the "Information technology" program, followed by 20 (16.8%) in the "Design" program, 19 (16%) – "Computer science", 8 (6.7%) – "Education science and teacher", 5 (4.2%) – "Art management", 5 (4.2%) – "Psychology", 3 (2.5%) – "Economics", and 1 (0.8%) in "Math" and "Electronics Engineer" each (see Fig. 2a).

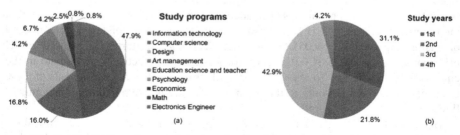

Fig. 2. Distribution of respondents based on study program (a) and study years (b).

Analyzing the study year of the respondents, 37 (31.1%) are in the 1st year, 26 (21.8%) – 2nd year, 51 (42.9%) - 3rd year, and 5 (4.2%) – 4th year (see Fig. 1b). 63 (52.9%) students of the total number also work in parallel to their studies. The analysis of the students' skills to study independently shows that 87 (73.1%) respondents have a previous experience in studying online courses (see Fig. 2b).

5.3 Results

The analysis of the survey data was performed with the help of the SPSS software. In this chapter, "independent study hours" (ISH) correspond to the description introduced in Sect. 4. According to the structure of the questionnaire, six indicators were identified: (i) attitudes towards ISH, (ii) ISH novelty, (iii) quality of ISH resources, (iv) types of ISH work, (v) ISH factors, and (vi) ISH risks. Due to the limitation of the article, only the most relevant results of this study are described below.

Attitudes towards ISH. Respondents rated 18 statements where they expressed their views on ISH. When analyzing the ratings, the mean scores ($\bar{x}$) for each statement were calculated. The following five statements received the highest rating: (i) "the student must actively take part in the acquisition of knowledge" ($\bar{x} = 4.26$), (ii) "high-quality independent work allows to receive a higher grade in the respective study course" ($\bar{x} = 4.21$), (iii) "ISH strengthens the knowledge and skills gained in the lessons "($\bar{x} = 4.21$), (iv) "ISH promotes the ability to be aware of the student's level of knowledge "($\bar{x} = 4.07$) and (v) "ISH promotes the ability to form independent judgments and conclusions "($\bar{x} = 3.99$).

ISH novelty. The statements about the "attitudes towards ISH" were used to assess the relevance of these statements to the respondent. For the "ISH novelty" indicator, the four highest-rated statements are ranked in the same order as for the "attitudes towards ISH" indicator. However, in the case of "ISH novelty", the statements are rated lower than the statements of the indicator "attitude towards ISH". An exception is the rating of the statement "completion of ISH raises the level of professional competence". With attitudes towards ISH $\bar{x} = 3.61$, however, with the ISH novelty, the average of the evaluation is higher, $\bar{x} = 3.73$. This means that respondents in ISH play an important role in their professional development.

The Paired Samples Correlations method found that there were positive, statistically significant correlations between all scores for the two indicators mentioned above. This means that the assessment of respondents' attitudes towards ISH is directly related to the novelty of ISH and vice versa. The Paired Samples Test method was used to determine differences between samples. The analysis demonstrated a significant correlation among three statements: "ISH promotes the ability to form independent judgments and conclusions" ($p = 0.032 \leq 0.05$), "personalized learning trajectories can be used in ISH performance" ($p = 0.035 \leq 0.05$), and "for students must actively participate in the acquisition of knowledge "($p = 0.023 \leq 0.05$). This means that the assessments of these claims can be applied not only to this sample but to the whole population, meaning to all learners.

ISH work types. Respondents rated five types of ISH work. The following three statements were evaluated highest: (i) "ISH is a homework" ($\bar{x} = 3.77$), (ii) "ISH is a group work on a project that mimics real professional activity" ($\bar{x} = 3.62$), (iii) "ISH is used to learn new topics that have not yet been mastered"($\bar{x} = 3.46$).

ISH factors. Respondents assessed nine factors that could negatively affect ISH. According to the respondents, the following five key factors are mentioned below: (i) "insufficiently developed criteria for ISH assessment" ($\bar{x} = 3.57$), (ii) "lack of resources to perform ISH work on time" ($\bar{x} = 3.52$), (iii) "ignoring students' level of knowledge and learning abilities" ($\bar{x} = 3.43$), (iv) "limited time resources that a student can devote to ISH" ($\bar{x} = 3.36$), (v) "ignoring students' achievements and changes in the learning process "($\bar{x} = 3.25$).

ISH risks. Respondents assessed eleven risk factors that could arise during the execution of ISH. Based on the results of the survey, the risk factors were ranked in the following order from highest to lowest: (i) "lack of motivation to do ISH" ($\bar{x} = 3.55$), (ii) "incorrect ISH planning by the student" ($\bar{x} = 3.24$), (iii) "fear of failure, incorrect assessment of one's abilities" ($\bar{x} = 3.23$), (iv) "there is a risk of spending time studying incorrectly chosen study material" ($\bar{x} = 3.01$), (v) "incorrect choice of informative support by the student" ($\bar{x} = 3.01$), (vi) "incorrectly chosen and incorrectly formulated goal for ISH" ($\bar{x} = 3.00$), (vii) "mismatch between what the teacher expects and the student's real abilities" ($\bar{x} = 3.00$), (viii) "the result does not justify the time spent on learning" ($\bar{x} = 2.92$), (ix) "perfectionism, incorrect optimization during ISH execution" ($\bar{x} = 2.90$), (x)" choice of materials for ISH execution according to the level of knowledge and skills "($\bar{x} = 2.87$), (xi) "incorrect time limits specified for ISH execution" ($\bar{x} = 2.72$).

5.4 Evaluation of the Results

The results of the survey showed the respondents understand that the learner should actively take part in the acquisition of knowledge. This was the highest-rated statement for both the indicator "attitudes towards ISH" and "ISH novelty". Respondents are aware of the importance of ISH. They believe ISH strengthens the knowledge and skills gained in the lessons, promotes the student's level of knowledge, and promotes the ability to make independent judgments and conclusions. This became the basis to include of ISH in the LMPAELS. ISH implementation can be done by implementing LO types in the content model.

Several factors and risks affecting ISH are related to time planning. For example, respondents noted that there is a limited amount of time a student can devote to done ISH; there is a risk of spending time learning the wrongly chosen study material; the obtained result does not justify the time spent on acquisition; incorrect time limits for ISH completion are indicated; and there is a lack of resources for timely execution of ISH work according to the planned time schedule. A solution is to describe properties such as deadline and learning time for the learning object in the LMPAELS. Deadline indicates a date when the LO must be completed/mastered. Learning time allows to plan and control the learning process. LO deadline and learning time are specified by the course teacher.

6 Improved Content Model

The analysis of the results of the LMPAELS evaluation (see Sect. 4) and the survey data (see Sect. 5.4) lead to a decision to improve the existing content model (CM) in the LMPAELS. The original version of it is described in Sect. 3.3. Several additions to the CM were introduced concerning the learning object.

An improved structure of the content model is shown in Fig. 3 by a class diagram. The classes that have not been modified are shown in white. The classes which have been supplemented with new attributes are visualized in grey. Attributes added to the

"Course" class are: "preconditions", "competence" and "outcomes". Attributes added to the "LO" class are: "deadline", "learningTime", "skills" and "knowledge".

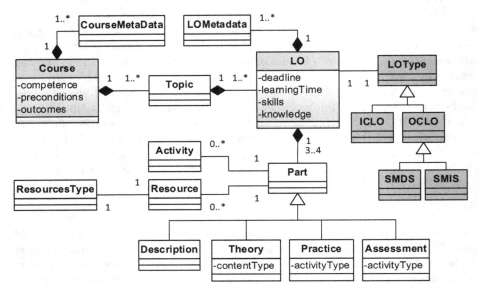

Fig. 3. An improved content model class diagram of the LMPAELS.

In Fig. 3, a dark grey color demonstrates the newly added classes to the CM. "LO-Type" describes the type of the LO depending on the application. Based on LO type they can be divided into two classes: (i) "ICLO" (in-class LO) and (ii) "OCLO" (outside class LO). ICLO represents the learning objects that are meant for studying in the classroom. While OCLO includes ISH activities that can be divided into two types: (i) SMDS (self-managed directed study) and (ii) SMIS (self-managed independent study) (see. Sect 4). SMDS learning objects contain activities that require assessment/grading. While no evaluation is required for SMIS activities and resources.

7 Related Work

This section gives an overview of studies that include learning time in their LOs. The paper [13] offers an approach to maximize learner's scores for a course while satisfying their time constraints. The curriculum is proposed based on the available time and knowledge background. Similar to the LMPAELS, the study course offered by the authors consists of topics which, in turn, contain learning objects. The authors use a two-layer study course graph, where the upper layer contains topics and the lower layer contains corresponding LOs. Each LO is given a duration to complete, and scores to obtain. First, the Depth First Search (DFS) algorithm finds all topic sequences that start with the selected topic. A learning time for each topic and a number of points to be obtained are used as criteria. The output of the DFS is an LO sequence that meets a certain time limit and maximizes scores. Path generation takes place after each successfully mastered topic. If the topic was not mastered, auxiliary LOs are offered that were not there the first time.

Article [5] describes the design of the adaptive educational hypermedia system. The system evaluates the learner's achievements and pays attention to the complete studying process. The authors describe a system model that offers learners a learning path by analyzing learner parameters, such as the best test performance, the time performance, and the reviewed topics. These parameters indicate the level of learning achieved by the learner and determine whether the learners are ready for the next lesson, and whether they need more support in this part of the learning phase. The learner model contains information about learner's learning style, background knowledge and preferences such as learning resource type preferred by the learner, the Internet connection type, the level of interactivity with the learning resource, the level of readiness of the learner and the time the learner spends studying. For each LO, a teacher has attached the required time and grade. At the end of LO accomplishment, it is assessed how the learner has mastered the current LO and how much time has been spent on it. The obtained time and grading are compared with the ones defined by the teacher. If the LO is mastered, the next LO is offered. Otherwise, the same content is offered again, however, with a lower level of complexity.

Studies [13] and [5] use the LO learning time for LO. However, learners have different learning pace. We propose to introduce a deadline for learning the subject for each LO. The learner is able to control their own pace of learning, identify the current situation about following the planned schedule, allow the teacher to evaluate their learning pace in relation to the pace of the group and, if necessary, make adjustments to the curriculum.

8   Conclusions

This study has evaluated the possibilities of the personalized adaptive e-learning system LMPAELS based on the user model in connection with the rapid transformation of digitalization in e-learning and new pedagogical trends.

In this research, a survey among students was conducted with 119 students from three higher education institutions in Latvia taking part in the survey. The results of the survey demonstrated learners are aware of their role in the educational process, that is, they need to play an active role in it. Respondents also recognize the importance and role of independent study hours in the learning process. According to the respondents, the main benefits of ISH are that: it promotes the strengthening of knowledge and skills gained in classes; ISH helps the respondent to realize the actual level of one's knowledge; and, finally, ISH promotes the ability to form independent judgments and conclusions. The most common forms of ISH are homework and group work. The factors and risks affecting ISH are most often related to time planning and lack of resources.

Based on the results of the analysis of the digital transformation process of education and the survey conducted, it was decided to improve the content model of the LMPAELS. Two existing CM classes were expanded with new attributes. The new attributes added to the course description were competence, preconditions, and outcomes. Description of the learning object was expanded with new attributes, such as skills, knowledge, deadline, and learning time. The LO description was also supplemented with learning type, which describes the place of LO in the course topic depending on the deadline. In this research, the LO to be studied in the classroom (ICLO) and the LO characterizing independent work were also described (OCLO). Based on the independent study hours used in higher education, OCLOs were divided into two types: graded LO (SMDS) and LO without grade (SMIS). These additions to the CM allow a more precise description of the entities used in the learning process, such as course, topic, and learning object. By introducing the "deadline" and "type" attributes in the LO, we expanded the possibilities of LO application. This allows the LMPAELS to develop different types of LOs depending on deadline, including the organization of independent study hours. Introduction of deadline and learning time in the LMPAELS learning objects links the learning process of the system with the learning process taking place in-class, where the acquisition of the current topic must end before starting the next topic.

Future work directions include approbation of the improved LMPAELS content model and the development of additional learning resources, with the possibility to implement them as ISH.

References

1. Alsmadi, M.K., Al-Marashdeh, I., Alzaqebah, M., Jaradat, G., Alghamdi, F.A., Mohammad, R.M., et al.: Digitalization of learning in Saudi Arabia during the COVID-19 outbreak: a survey. Informat. Med. Unlock. **25**, 100632 (2021). https://doi.org/10.1016/j.imu.2021.100632
2. Barrit, C., Lewis, D., Wieseler, W.: CISCO Systems Reusable Information Object Strategy Version 3.0. pp. 1-43 (1999)
3. Budiarti, I.S., Triwiyono, T., Panda, F.M.: The development of discovery learning-based module to improve students' scientific literacy. J. Pembelajaran Fisika **9**(1), 73–89 (2021). https://doi.org/10.23960/jpf.v9.n1.202107
4. Bygstad, B., Øvrelid, E., Ludvigsen, S., Dæhlen, M.: From dual digitalization to digital learning space: exploring the digital transformation of higher education. Comput. Educ. **182**, 104463 (2022). https://doi.org/10.1016/j.compedu.2022.104463
5. Colace, F., Santo, M.D., Greco, L.: E-learning and personalized learning path: a proposal based on the adaptive educational hypermedia system. Int. J. Emerg. Technol. Learn. **9**(2), 9–16 (2014). https://doi.org/10.3991/ijet.v9i2.3211
6. Crawford, J., Butler-Henderson, K., Rudolph, J., Malkawi, B., Glowatz, M., Burton, R., et al.: COVID-19: 20 countries' higher education intra-period digital pedagogy responses. J. Appl. Learn. Teach. **3**(1), 9–28 (2020). https://doi.org/10.37074/jalt.2020.3.1.7
7. De Salas, K., Ellis, L.: The development and implementation of learning objects in a higher education setting. Interdiscip. J. E-Learn. Learn. Obj. **2**(1), 1–22 (2006). https://doi.org/10.28945/398
8. Geske, A., Grīnfelds, A.: Izglītības pētījumu aptaujas – no izveidošanas līdz datu apstrādei. LU Akadēmiskais apgāds, Riga (2020)
9. Goodyear, P., Carvalho, L., Yeoman, P.: Activity-centred analysis and design (ACAD): COre purposes, distinctive qualities and current developments. Educ. Tech. Res. Dev. **69**(2), 445–464 (2021). https://doi.org/10.1007/s11423-020-09926-7
10. Kaputa, V., Loučanová, E., Tejerina-Gaite, F.A.: Digital transformation in higher education institutions as a driver of social oriented innovations. In: Păunescu C., Lepik, K.L., Spencer, N. (eds.) Social Innovation in Higher Education. Innovation, Technology, and Knowledge Management, pp. 61–85. Springer, Cham (2022). https://doi.org/10.1007/978-3-030-84044-0_4

11. Limani, Y., Hajrizi, E., Stapleton, L., Retkoceri, M.: Digital transformation readiness in higher education institutions (HEI): the case of Kosovo. IFAC-PapersOnLine **52**(25), 52–57 (2019). https://doi.org/10.1016/j.ifacol.2019.12.445
12. Maļinovska, L.: Studentu patstāvības veidošanās studiju procesā augstskolā. PhD Thesis, University of Latvia, Riga (1997)
13. Nabizadeh, A.H., Gonçalves, D., Gama, S., Jorge, J., Rafsanjani, H.N.: Adaptive learning path recommender approach using auxiliary learning objects. Comput. Educ. **147**, 103777 (2020). https://doi.org/10.1016/j.compedu.2019.103777
14. Nacheva, R., Jansone, A.: Multi-layered higher education E-learning framework. Balt. J. Mod. Comput. **9**(3), 345–362 (2021). https://doi.org/10.22364/bjmc.2021.9.3.08
15. Shahalizade, M., Musavi, S.: The perspective of e-learning in higher education: a systematized review. Interdiscip. J. Virtual Learn. Med. Sci. **12**(3), 149–161 (2021). https://doi.org/10.30476/IJVLMS.2021.89746.1078
16. Sousa, R.D., Karimova, B., Gorlov, S.: Digitalization as a new direction in education sphere. In: E3S Web of Conferences 159, p. 09014. EDP Sciences (2020). https://doi.org/10.1051/e3sconf/202015909014
17. Strekalova, N.B.: Students' individual work: diagnosis and management of study risks. Profess. Educ. Mod. World **8**(1), 1660–1669 (2018). https://doi.org/10.15372/PEMW20180114
18. Vagale, V., Niedrite, L., Ignatjeva, S.: Application of the recommended learning path in the personalized adaptive E-learning system. Balt. J. Mod. Comput. **8**(4), 618–637 (2020). https://doi.org/10.22364/bjmc.2020.8.4.10
19. Vagale, V., Niedrite, L.: Learner group creation and utilization in adaptive E-learning systems. In: Haav, H.M., Kalja, A., Robal, T. (eds.) DB&IS 2014, Frontiers in Artificial Intelligence and Applications, vol. 270, pp. 189–202. IOS Press, Amsterdam (2014). https://doi.org/10.3233/978-1-61499-458-9-189
20. Vagale, V., Niedrite, L.: The organization of topics sequence in adaptive e-learning systems. In: Arnicans, G., Arnicane, V., Borzovs, J., Niedrite, L. (eds.) DB&IS 2016, Databases and Information Systems IX, Frontiers in Artificial Intelligence and Applications vol. 291, pp. 327–340. IOS Press, Amsterdam (2016). https://doi.org/10.3233/978-1-61499-714-6-327
21. Willermark, S., Gellerstedt, M.: Facing radical digitalization: capturing teachers' transition to virtual classrooms through ideal type experiences. J. Educ. Comput. Res. 1–22 (2022). https://doi.org/10.1177/07356331211069424
22. European Commission/EACEA/Eurydice: The European Higher Education Area in 2020: Bologna Process Implementation Report. Publications Office of the European Union, Luxembourg (2020).https://doi.org/10.2797/756192. https://ehea2020rome.it/storage/uploads/e12661a5-715c-4c43-a651-76382b23de42/ehea_bologna_2020.pdf. Accessed 12 Mar 2022
23. Sebillo, A.: Learning to lead I: an overview of European qualification instruments (2016). http://euclidnetwork.eu/wp-content/uploads/2018/07/io3_eutools_final.pdf. Accessed 12 Mar 2022
24. Standards and Guidelines for Quality Assurance in the European Higher Education Area, Brussels, Belgium (2015). https://enqa.eu/wp-content/uploads/2015/11/ESG_2015.pdf. Accessed 12 Mar 2022
25. Study-load: Understanding and managing your studies. https://catoolkit.herts.ac.uk/toolkit/study-load-understanding-and-managing-your-studies/. Accessed 12 Mar 2022

IT Support for Digital Transformation

The Direction of the Future Development of ERP and BPMS: Towards a Single Unified Class?

Marek Szelągowski[1] (ID), Justyna Berniak-Woźny[1] (ID), and Audrone Lupeikiene[2](✉) (ID)

[1] Systems Research Institute, Polish Academy of Sciences, Warsaw, Poland
marek.szelagowski@dbpm.pl
[2] Institute of Data Science and Digital Technologies, Vilnius University, Vilnius, Lithuania
audrone.lupeikiene@mif.vu.lt

Abstract. Enterprise Resource Planning (ERP) systems and Business Process Management Suites (BPMS) are implemented in the organization to increase efficiency, reduce costs, and increase profits. In the case of the implementation of traditionally managed business processes, the scopes of operation of both classes of systems overlap. ERP systems allow for the standardization and improvement of the implementation of repetitive, standardized business processes, and BPMS enables the identification, redesigning, implementation, and monitoring of processes execution. But does the latter still have an application in Industry 4.0 and Industry 5.0, where processes are more complex and diverse? This discussion paper provides an overview of the current state and the direction of development of two classes of information systems (IS) crucial for the management of modern organizations – ERP and BPMS – and compares the critical success factors (CSFs) of both system classes. Based on this comparison, the direction of development of both classes of systems from the point of view of business requirements is determined.

Keywords: Enterprise Resource Planning system · Business Process Management System · Business Process Management Suite · Critical Success Factor · Industry 4.0 · Industry 5.0

1 Introduction

Enterprise Resource Planning (ERP) and Business Process Management Suites (BPMS) are the two classes of information systems (IS) crucial for the management of modern organizations. Both for vendors who create systems and for their users, it is extremely important how both IS classes will develop. The vast majority of organizations that already use ERP systems have to decide whether or not and to what extent BPMS should be implemented or whether their ERP system should be changed to a process-based one. ERP vendors are faced with even more fateful decisions. They have to decide whether to build "process" functionalities into the existing ERP system with a view to preparing integration mechanisms enabling on-demand addition of BPMS elements, including selected hyperautomation techniques, such as process mining, robotic process automation (RPA), or artificial intelligence (AI). For both groups, these are strategic decisions

© The Author(s), under exclusive license to Springer Nature Switzerland AG 2022
M. Ivanovic et al. (Eds.): Baltic DB&IS 2022, CCIS 1598, pp. 111–124, 2022.
https://doi.org/10.1007/978-3-031-09850-5_8

that are difficult to change, essential for the competitive ability of the organization, and involve long-term significant key human resources. As the literature review conducted by the authors has shown, there are no studies showing comparatively the development directions of both IS classes and containing practical recommendations. Thus, this study aims to answer the research question: "Which choice is better for the future: process ERP systems or the flexible, open integration of ERP and BPMS systems?" (In other words: Is the future a single unified class of "process" ERP systems or two separate classes of systems with standardized integration principles?).

The article begins with a discussion on the work methodology. Then, the authors present the results of the literature review relating to the current status and development trends of ERP and BPMS. Section 5 compares the requirements, goals and critical success factors (CSFs) of both system classes. The last part presents conclusions and practical recommendations resulting from the identified business requirements and comparative analysis.

2 Methodology

This discussion paper provides an overview of the current status and development trends of ERP and BPMS and compares the CSFs of both IS classes. The methodology used for the purposes of this paper is the theoretical review, which builds on existing conceptual and empirical research to provide context for identifying, describing, and transferring selected concepts, constructs, or relationships to a higher level (Pare et al. 2015). This type of literature review brings together different work streams (in this case academic and professional) in order to effectively organize previous research, analyze their interrelationships in depth, and identify patterns or similarities that will facilitate the development of new theories (Webster and Watson 2002). Thus, in the next two sections the evolution of the ERP and BPM systems will be presented. In Sect. 5, authors will compare the goals and CSFs for the implementation of ERP and BPMS. Based on that, future development scenarios for both systems will be defined.

3 Enterprise Resources Planning Systems

The use of IS in business began with simple programs or rather record-keeping databases. In a short time, it turned out that they can be successfully used to keep records of not only materials, but also other types of resources, e.g. money, devices, or people. The next step was to extend them with modules for recording operations specific to a given type of resource, e.g. receipts, issues, purchases, sales, employment, or dismissals. This allowed IS to support and monitor various areas of enterprise operation by independent, unrelated area programs, e.g. warehouse, human resources, payroll, or financial accounting programs. The next natural step was to extend the use of IS for material requirements planning (MRP), and then for material resources planning (MRPII) (Katuu 2020). Already at this stage, there was a need for the internal integration of various areas of IS operation, which became the basic distinguishing feature of the next generation

Table 1. ERP systems evolution timetable. Source: Authors own elaboration, based on Katuu 2020, and Rashid et al. 2002.

Date	Class of systems	Characteristics
1950+	Inventory software – databases	Unchanging database tailored to specific user needs. Usually dedicated to inventory
1960	Domain-specific software	Software dedicated to particular functional domains. Operational logic embedded in the software code
1970	Material Requirements Planning (MRP)	Software dedicated to material requirements planning for production purposes. Usually integrating the fields of production, supply, and warehouse management. Operational logic embedded in software code
1980	Material Resource Planning (MRPII)	Software dedicated to planning production and the resources required therefor. Usually integrating data from several functional areas. Limited possibilities of configuring the operational logic
1995	Enterprise Resource Planning (ERP)	Integrated systems supporting the management of the entire organization, consisting of multiple strictly interconnected modules. The possibility to configure the operational logic by way of configuring the system itself
2005	postmodern ERP (Enterprise Resource Planning II)	Integrated solutions supporting the management of the entire organization, consisting of multiple modules integrated within a main ERP system. The possibility to select modules from multiple vendors, configure their operational logic (e.g. by defining the business processes, the integration of activities among many entities) and the scope of the processed information. The possibility to select the principles of licensing and using a given model (e.g. the cloud, mobile devices)

of IS – Enterprise Resource Planning (ERP) systems – enabling consistent management not only of production resources, but also the resources of the entire organization (Table 1) (Gartner IT Glossary – ERP n.d.; Katuu 2020).

Initially, ERP systems, like their predecessors, were monolithic systems with integration mechanisms for elements of various areas rigidly built into the architecture and the IS database (Katuu 2020). In the 1990s and early 2000s, ERP software became the standard and the basis of the organization's systems architecture. But already in the mid-2000s, the weaknesses of this solution began to become increasingly more visible, such as the lack of flexibility, the user's dependence on one supplier, high purchase and use price of the solution, and difficulties in adapting to the user's business processes (Haddara et al. 2015). Business pressure and the emerging technological opportunities resulted in the evolution of ERP systems towards a modular structure with a clearly separated module responsible for consistent integration and data flow between individual modules (Lupeikiene et al. 2014). This opened the possibility of using modules provided by different vendors within one company, and at the same time reduced the dependence of users on one vendor. Recognizing this change, Gartner proposed the introduction of a new class of IS known as "postmodern ERP" (Gartner 2019a; Hardcastle 2014). Their feature is a departure from the monolithic structure of the system in favor of "loosely coupled decentralization" of the administrative and operational modules (Gartner IT Glossary – postmodern ERP n.d.). The goal of a postmodern ERP strategy is to use the best possible applications in each particular area, while ensuring that they adequately integrate with each other when necessary. This approach allowed users not only to choose the best among traditional ERP system modules such as finance, production, or human resources, but also to incorporate many of the hyperautomation technologies not offered by ERP system vendors into the solutions used. Integration with IoT, OCR of texts, reading QR codes, speech recognition, the use of software robots, or decision support by artificial intelligence provided by the best companies in this rapidly developing part of the IT industry are just some of the technologies that can be used as part of postmodern ERP (Gartner 2019b).

According to consulting companies following the development of the ERP systems market, the next step in the evolution of such systems will be the possibility of creating solutions from components integrated according to the needs, with the possibility of combining components provided by different suppliers in one solution (Gartner 2022). This will allow users to choose the best modules available on the market and to quickly expand or adapt their solutions in accordance with the needs of customers and new opportunities offered by vendors (Forrester 2020; Gartner 2021).

Conceptually, ERP systems include the integration of business processes in an organization (Nazemi et al. 2012). However, in practice, even postmodern ERPs remain transactional systems today, i.e. systems for recording and monitoring transactions (operations), and not systems meant to design and execute end-to-end business processes (Gartner 2019b). Recognizing the importance of this limitation, ERP system providers make attempts to integrate with business process management by adding an internal business process modeler (e.g. Dynamics AX – Microsoft or Xpetris – Asseco Business Solutions) or the ability to load and operationalize business process models using the opportunities offered by Business Process Model and Notation from version 2.0 (e.g. SAP).

4 Business Process Management Suites

In the 1990s, it was widely expected that workflow management systems would become the next step in supporting office work, after other tools such as database management systems, spreadsheets, and email systems (van der Aalst et al. 1994). This turned out to be true – workflow management (WFM) and document management (DM) systems work well in organizing people and documents and in automating specific stages of the process, especially in small and medium-sized companies. However, these systems focused on automating selected, fully repeatable workflows with little support for process analysis and optimization or end-to-end process management. The answer to the need for holistic management and greater flexibility of support for implemented processes were Business Process Management Suites (BPMS), which combined information technology and knowledge from management sciences and applied both to operational business processes (van der Aalst 2022; Gartner IT Glossary - BPMS n.d.). BPMS can be defined as an application infrastructure supporting BPM projects and programs. They support the entire execution and improvement life cycle process, from process identification, through modelling, design, implementation and analysis, to continuous improvement (Szelągowski 2019; Dumas et al. 2018).

Business Process Management Suits (BPMS) are being adopted in organizations to increase business process agility across a diverse application landscape (Koopman and Seymour 2020). Their main advantage is the visibility and transparency of the process and the simplified enforcement of organizational rules and principles. Another advantage of implementing BPMS is lower workload in the organization, because process coordination is automated. Countless IT systems are flexibly integrated with a view to supporting work in the organization (Dumas et al. 2018). According to Capgemini (2012), as many as 96% of enterprises that decided to implement business process optimization systems, achieved a significant return on investment, which in the case of 55% of them reached at least 200%. On the other hand, according to the BPTrends report (Harmon and Garcia 2020), 93% of companies are involved in many activities aimed at improving their processes, but only 52% of the companies using BPM software reported that they were satisfied with their specific tool.

BPMS has reached its limits, as it was unable to work with the growing volume of data or the complex decision-making process in real time. With the advent of Industry 4.0, traditional business processes, the management of which assumes the identification, design, implementation, and then implementation thereof in accordance with the optimal model, were systematically replaced by dynamic processes – partially structured (structured processes with ad hoc and unstructured exceptions with predefined fragments) and fully unstructured (where the exact steps to be taken to achieve the goal cannot be defined) (Szelągowski 2019; Kemsley 2011). Organizations must implement an extensive company strategy, coordinate interactions in departments throughout the organization (as well as in external systems), and integrate various platforms such as customer relationship management (CRM), enterprise content management (ECM), and other applications, with a view to facilitating management of different departments, processes, and people. This task is especially important in the era of digital transformation and Industry 4.0, when business processes run through many departments and systems or even organizations, which requires a new approach to their management. Business Process Management Systems, also known as Business Process Management Suites or Business Process Management Software, come in handy here. All these and other challenges have been resolved by the intelligent BPMS (iBPMS) (Gartner 2012).

The evolution of BPM support software systems began with two opposing assumptions:

- case management systems (CMS) – support for processes with an unpredictable flow and a not entirely known, but potentially high intensity of knowledge;

- traditional BPMS – support for processes of known and strictly repeated nature thanks to having all the knowledge necessary to perform the processes prior to execution. It strives to support all process groups, irrespective of their nature, unpredictability, and knowledge intensity (Di Ciccio et al. 2014).

The analysis of the main capabilities of iBPMS and dynamic CMS showed a trend towards a constantly increasing number of overlapping features. At the end of the considered period, both classes of systems enabled the dynamic execution of processes; their adaptation to the operational context; integration with rules processing; access to different sources of data to derive informed decisions in real time; and support of process redesign that emphasizes automation and digitization (Szelągowski and Lupeikiene 2020).

An iBPMS is a type of high-productivity (low-code/no-code) application development platform. An iBPMS enables dynamic changes in operating models and procedures, documented as models, directly driving the execution of business operations. In turn, business users make frequent (or ad hoc) process changes to their operations independently of IT-managed technical assets such as integration with external systems and security administration (Gartner 2015). iBPMS typically include advanced capabilities like enterprise document management, business rules, case management, advanced integration features on a Service-Oriented Architecture (SOA), cloud computing, as well as social collaboration features and responsive mobile user interface (Cheng 2012). Gartner defines the iBPMS market as the group of vendors offering an integrated set of technologies that coordinate people, machines, and things. An iBPMS allows "citizen developers" – most commonly business analysts, but also business end users – and professional developers to collaborate on the improvement and transformation of business processes. Products provide capabilities to optimize business outcomes in real time for a specific piece of work. They also allow new, emergent practices to quickly scale across a function or enterprise. The critical capabilities of the iBPMS platforms are based on six primary use cases (Gartner 2019c):

- composition of intelligent process-centered applications;
- continuous process improvement;
- business transformation;
- digitized processes;
- citizen developer application composition;
- adaptive case management.

BPMS is developing and will probably continue to develop in line with the changing requirements of the business environment. While intelligent business process management platforms take into account aspects of business transformation and digitization, technological improvements and the drive for digital transformation are pushing the evolution of BPM software further (Belev 2018). The aim of the changes is to provide a tool enabling the present effective competition and building a competitive position in the future. In practice, Industry 4.0 and emerging Industry 5.0 require close connection of BPM with the use of various ICT technologies implemented as stand-alone, point-based applications, but increasingly often as elements of comprehensive BPMS packages (van der Aalst et al. 2016). The differentiation of user requirements depending on the nature and context of business processes requires the flexibility of BPMS to integrate various technologies and devices in order to ensure the achievement of the organization's business goals.

5 Goals and CSFs for the Implementation of ERP and BPMS

Conceptually, ERP systems involve the integration of business processes within an organization, with improved order management and control, accurate information on inventory, improved workflow, supply chain management (SCM), and better standardization of business and best practices (Nazemi et al. 2012).

Organizations operating in Industry 4.0 and entering Industry 5.0 use both ERP and BPMS. As recently as 10–15 years ago, the purposes for using these two classes of systems were different. ERP was used to manage the organization's resources and BPMS (or before it, WFM) – to support the implementation of business processes. The requirements and the resulting drivers for the development and architecture of both classes of systems were also different.

Under the digital transformation, the measure of success of an organization is its ongoing efficiency and the development potential of its products and services, as well as the capability to use and develop its own intellectual capital (Nahavandi 2019). Just 10 years ago, the measure of success for implementing BPM according to Dabaghkashani et al. (2012, 727) simply pertained to the simplicity, quality, and flexibility of the business processes in the organization. Industry 5.0 has lessened the emphasis on technology and assumed that the true potential for development is rooted in the collaboration between humans and machines. This approach allows for usage of the rapidly expanding capabilities of machines in conjunction with better-trained experts to support efficient, sustainable and safe production. In the study on the CSFs of implementing ERP systems held by Leyh and Sander (2015), among the 320 respondents, 50% pointed to:

- top management support and involvement (202);
- project management (172);
- user training (167).

In the literature from the last 10 years, there exist multiple publications on the requirements of and CSFs for BPMS. All point to the fact that the success of implementing CSF or BPMS is dependent not on a single system, but on the synergy of several, or even several dozen CSFs (Rosemann and vom Brocke 2015, 110–112). Table 2 contains a comparison of CSFs for both classes of systems. In cases when CSFs with overlapping definitions received different names in particular publications, the "Critical Success Factors" column of Table 2 provides the most common name variant.

The strategic goals of implementing and using ERP and BPMS are unmistakably identical. However, the scopes of use and particular detailed goals, as well as the resulting requirements and CSFs, were different for both classes of systems in the 90's and 2000's. Another differentiating factor were technological limitations, such as the lack of flexibility with respect to internal system integration. The technological changes under

Table 2. Critical Success Factors for ERP and BPM systems.

Core element	Critical success factor	ERP system	BPMS
Strategic alignment	Strategic alignment	Zendehdel Nobari et al. 2022	Bosilj et al. 2018; Gabryelczyk and Roztocki 2018; Syed et al. 2018; Ubaid and Dweiri 2020; Castro et al. 2020; Koopman and Seymour 2020
	Business plan & vision	Gavali and Halder 2020	Kraljić and Kraljić 2017; Syed et al. 2018; Koopman and Seymour 2020
	Business process effectiveness	Hasan et al. 2019; Cieciora et al. 2020	Bosilj et al. 2018; Gabryelczyk and Roztocki 2018; Ubaid and Dweiri 2020
Governance	Top management support	Esteves et al. 2006; Ganesh et al. 2014; Kapur et al. 2014; Nagpal et al. 2017; Hasan et al. 2019; Gavali and Halder 2020; Vargas and Comuzzi 2020	Kraljić and Krallić 2017; Bosilj et al. 2018; Syed et al. 2018; Ubaid and Dweiri 2020; Castro et al. 2020
	Effective organizational change management	Ganesh et al. 2014; Kapur et al. 2014; Nagpal et al. 2017; Zendehdel Nobari et al. 2022; Vanani and Sohrabi 2020; Vargas and Comuzzi 2020	Kraljić and Kraljić 2017; Gabryelczyk and Roztocki 2018; Syed et al. 2018; Ubaid and Dweiri 2020
	Business process improvements implemented	Ganesh et al. 2014; Kapur et al. 2014; Nagpal et al. 2017; Zendehdel Nobari et al. 2022	Kraljić and Kraljić 2017; Brkic et al. 2020
	Continuous monitoring and improvement system	Hasan et al. 2019	Castro et al. 2020; Ubaid and Dweiri 2020

(*continued*)

Table 2. (*continued*)

Core element	Critical success factor	ERP system	BPMS
Methods	Awareness and understanding of BPM	Kapur et al. 2014; Nagpal et al. 2017; Gavali and Halder 2020; Vargas and Comuzzi 2020	Syed et al. 2018; Brkic et al. 2020
	Adequate implementation strategy	Esteves et al. 2006; Ganesh et al. 2014; Vargas and Comuzzi 2020;	
	Appropriate project management	Ganesh et al. 2014; Kapur et al. 2014; Nagpal et al. 2017; Hasan et al. 2019; Gavali and Halder 2020; Zendehdel Nobari et al. 2022; Vanani and Sohrabi 2020; Vargas and Comuzzi 2020	Kraljić and Kraljić 2017; Bosilj et al. 2018; Syed et al. 2018; Castro et al. 2020
Information technology	Realistic consideration of the capabilities and the limitations of the technology to be used	Ganesh et al. 2014; Zendehdel Nobari et al. 2022	Syed et al. 2018
	Architecture (especially flexibility and integration opportunities)	Kapur et al. 2014; Nagpal et al. 2017; Gavali and Halder 2020	Kraljić and Kraljić 2017; Koopman and Seymour 2020
	Data management (data analysis and conversion)	Ganesh et al. 2014; Kapur et al. 2014; Nagpal et al. 2017; Gavali and Halder 2020; Cieciora et al. 2020; Vargas and Comuzzi 2020	Kraljić and Kraljić 2017; Koopman and Seymour 2020
	Careful package/module selection	Ganesh et al. 2014; Kapur et al. 2014; Nagpal et al. 2017; Cieciora et al. 2020; Vargas and Comuzzi 2020	Kraljić and Kraljić 2017

(*continued*)

Table 2. (*continued*)

Core element	Critical success factor	ERP system	BPMS
People	Empowerment		Syed et al. 2018; Ubaid and Dweiri 2020;
	Professional level of employees (project team)	Ganesh et al. 2014; Vargas and Comuzzi 2020	Castro et al. 2020; Koopman and Seymour 2020
	User involvement and participation	Esteves et al. 2006; Ganesh et al. 2014; Vanani and Sohrabi 2020; Vargas and Comuzzi 2020	Syed et al. 2018; Ubaid and Dweiri 2020
Culture	Ogranization culture	Ganesh et al. 2014; Vargas and Comuzzi 2020	Bosilj et al. 2018; Gabryelczyk and Roztocki 2018; Ubaid and Dweiri 2020
	Interdepartmental (inter-parties) communication and collaboration (especially between business and IT)	Ganesh et al. 2014; Kapur et al. 2014; Nagpal et al. 2017; Hasan et al. 2019; Gavali and Halder 2020; Vargas and Comuzzi 2020	Kraljić and Kraljić 2017; Gabryelczyk and Roztocki 2018; Syed et al. 2018; Koopman and Seymour 2020

the digital transformation and, first and foremost, changes to the nature of the business processes creating value for the client, including the growing significance of processes requiring dynamic management, have led to changes in the requirements to and CSFs of the use of both classes of systems. From the perspective of management, the implementation of an ERP system will be considered successful, provided that it reduces the workload, costs, and time, as well as raises quality and the flexibility of executing business processes which create value for the client. At the same time, managers expect implementations of BPMS and its included hyperautomation technologies to ensure the fluidity and flexibility of information exchange and the execution of production-oriented or service-oriented processes, the reduction of the workload, in part thanks to robotization and automation, as well as thanks to providing detailed reporting data analytical information within a set time-frame (Karimi et al. 2007). The difference that is imperceptible to the user in the way of using hyperautomation elements in both classes of systems is that in iBPMS they are a native part of the system, and in postmodernERP they still require integration as an external solution. But from a business point of view, it can be said that the requirements for both classes of systems are the same and probably no one would notice if we changed the names of the functional descriptions of both classes of systems! Therefore, their artificial division and development as systems of two different classes is becoming increasingly meaningless.

The analysis of the CSFs for each of the 6 core elements in Table 2 leads to similar conclusions. In literature from the last 10 years, requirements for both classes of systems are described with the use of the exact same CSFs. Perhaps because of the theoretical approach of BPM, the CSF "Strategic alignment" is more often found in literature devoted to BPMS. And perhaps because of the traditional engineering roots of ERP systems, the CSF "Appropriate project management" is more often mentioned in the context of ERP/postmodern ERP. However, from the perspective of virtually all of the core elements, both classes of systems are described by a single, shared group of CSFs.

6 Conclusions

IS are widely used in the management of organizations to increase their efficiency, speed up operations, and enable simultaneous operations in many places (Katuu 2020). Current user requirements and solutions implemented by IS vendors are fully subordinated to these goals. CSFs allow for detailed analysis and measurement of the degree of completion of these goals. This discussion paper aimed to provide an overview of the current state and the direction of the development of two classes of IS crucial for the management of modern organizations – ERP and BPMS – and to compare from a business point of view the critical success factors of both classes of systems.

As shown, business sets exactly the same goals for both IS classes and their completion is measured by the same CSFs. Until now, the choice of an ERP or BPMS was mainly determined by the size of the organization. But regardless of their size, companies are still in the process of transformation (including digital transformation) and, consequently, require change management, risk management, knowledge management, etc. and they have to manage increasingly dynamic business processes (Szelągowski 2019). As a result of digital transformation, this choice is dictated rather by the nature of business processes and the opportunities offered by information technologies. For this reason, a full answer to the posed study question requires further in-depth research from us to research the possibilities of combining the functionalities of ERP with holistic and dynamic business process management supported by ICT solutions. The overlapping nature of the goals and CSFs of both classes of systems points rather to the emergence of a single class of systems combining in line with the requirements of business as part of the composite architecture the transaction capabilities of ERP systems with the flexibility of iBPMS.

A limitation of this study rests in its theoretical nature and the fact that it focuses only on the requirements of business users. In the course of further studies, the authors intend to broaden their research with an analysis of the architecture of both classes of systems, as well as interviews with the key vendors of both classes of solutions. This will enable them to formulate the final answer to the question on the future of ERP and BPMS.

References

Belev, I.: Software Business Process Management Approaches for Digital Transformation. University of National and World Economy, Sofia, 1/2018, pp. 109–119 (2018)

Bosilj, V., Brkic, L., Tomicic-Pupek, K.: Understanding the success factors in adopting business process management software: case studies. Interdiscip. Descr. Complex Syst. **16**(2), 194–215 (2018). https://doi.org/10.7906/indecs.16.2.1

Brkic, L., Tomicic-Pupek, K., Bosilj, V.: A framework for BPM software selection in relation to digital transformation drivers. Tech. Gaz. **27**(4), 1108–1114 (2020). https://doi.org/10.17559/TV-20190315193304

Capgemini: Global Business Process Management Report (2012). https://www.capgemini.com/wp-content/uploads/2017/07/Global_Business_Process_Management_Report.pdf. Accessed 01 Feb 2022

Castro, B., Dresch, A., Veit, D.: Key critical success factors of BPM implementation: a theoretical and practical view. Bus. Process. Manag. J. **26**(1), 239–256 (2020). https://doi.org/10.1108/BPMJ-09-2018-0272

Cheng, C.: On workflow, BPM, BPMS, iBPMS and mobile phones (part 3) (2012). https://appian.com/blog/2012/on-workflow-bpm-bpms-ibpmsand-mobile-phones-part-3-.html. Accessed 19 Feb 2022

Cieciora, M., Bołkunow, W., Pietrzak, P., Gago, P.: Key criteria of ERP/CRM systems selection in SMEs in Poland. Online J. Appl. Knowl. Manag. **7**(1), 85–98 (2020). https://doi.org/10.36965/OJAKM.2020.8(1)85-98

Dabaghkashani, A., Hajiheydari, B., Haghighinasab, C.: A success model for business process management implementation. Int. J. Inf. Electron. Eng. **2**(5), 725–729 (2012). https://doi.org/10.7763/IJIEE.2012.V2.196

Di Ciccio, C., Marrella, A., Russo, A.: Knowledge-intensive processes: characteristics, requirements and analysis of contemporary approaches. J. Data Semant. **4**(1), 29–57 (2014). https://doi.org/10.1007/s13740-014-0038-4

Dumas, M., La Rosa, M., Mendling, J., Reijers, H.: Fundamentals of Business Process Management, 2nd edn. Springer, Berlin (2018). https://doi.org/10.1007/978-3-662-56509-4

Esteves, J., Pastor, J.A.: Organizational and technological critical success factors behavior along the ERP implementation phases. In: Seruca, I., Cordeiro, J., Hammoudi, S., Filipe, J. (eds.) Enterprise Information Systems VI, pp. 63–71. Springer, Heidelberg (2006). https://doi.org/10.1007/1-4020-3675-2_8

Forrester: Prescriptive Low-Code New Quest to Marry Best Packaged and Custom Apps, 30 October 2020

Gabryelczyk, R., Roztocki, N.: Business process management success framework for transition economies. Inf. Syst. Manag. **35**(3), 234–253 (2018). https://doi.org/10.1080/10580530.2018.1477299

Ganesh, K., Mohapatra, S., Anbuudayasankar, S., Sivakumar, P.: Enterprise Resource Planning. Fundamentals of Design and Implementation. Springer, Cham (2014). https://doi.org/10.1007/978-3-319-05927-3

Gartner: Magic Quadrant for Intelligent Business Process Management Suites, 27 September 2012. ID: G00224913

Gartner: Magic Quadrant for Intelligent Business Process Management Suites, 18 March 2015. ID: G00258612

Gartner: Strategic Roadmap for Postmodern ERP (2019a). ID G00384628

Gartner: Move Beyond RPA to Deliver Hyperautomation (2019b). ID: G00433853

Gartner: Magic Quadrant for Intelligent Business Process Management Suites, 30 January 2019 (2019c). ID: G00345694

Gartner: Top Strategic Technology Trends for 2021 (2021). https://www.gartner.com/smarterwithgartner/gartner-top-strategic-technology-trends-for-2021. Accessed 14 Feb 2022

Gartner: Top Strategic Technology Trends for 2022 (2022). https://www.gartner.com/en/information-technology/insights/top-technology-trends. Accessed 14 Feb 2022

Gartner IT Glossary – ERP: Enterprise Resource Planning (ERP) (n.d.). https://www.gartner.com/en/information-technology/glossary/enterprise-resource-planning-erp. Accessed 08 Dec 2021

Gartner IT Glossary – postmodern ERP (n.d.). https://www.gartner.com/en/information-technology/glossary/postmodern-erp. Accessed 08 Dec 2021

Gartner IT Glossary – BPMS: Business Process Management Suites (BPMSs) (n.d.). https://www.gartner.com/en/information-technology/glossary/bpms-business-process-management-suite. Accessed 08 Dec 2021

Gavali, A., Halder, S.: Identifying critical success factors of ERP in the construction industry. Asian J. Civ. Eng. **21**(2), 311–329 (2019). https://doi.org/10.1007/s42107-019-00192-4

Guay, M.: Postmodern ERP Strategies and Considerations for Midmarket IT Leaders (2016). http://proyectos.andi.com.co/camarabpo/Webinar%202016/Postmodern%20ERP%20strategies%20and%20considerations%20for%20midmarket%20IT%20leaders-%20Gartner.pdf. Accessed 08 Dec 2021

Haddara, M., Fagerstrom, A., Maeland, B.: ERP systems: anatomy of adoption factors & attitudes. J. Enterp. Resour. Plann. Stud. **2015**(2015), 22 (2015). Article ID: 521212. https://doi.org/10.5171/2015.521212

Hardcastle, C.: Postmodern ERP is Fundamentally Different from a Best-of-Breed Approach, 24 June 2014. Gartner Research ID: G00264620

Harmon, P., Garcia, J.: The State of Business Process Management 2020. A BPTrends report (2020). https://www.bptrends.com/bptrends-state-of-business-process-management-2020-report/. Accessed 08 Dec 2021

Hasan, N., Miah, S., Bao, Y., Hoque, R.: Factors affecting post-implementation success of enterprise resource planning systems: a perspective of business process performance. Enterp. Inf. Syst. **13**(4), 1–28 (2019). https://doi.org/10.1080/17517575.2019.1612099

Kapur, P.K., Nagpal, S., Khatri, S.K., Yadavalli, V.S.S.: Critical success factor utility based tool for ERP health assessment: a general framework. Int. J. Syst. Assur. Eng. Manag. **5**(2), 133–148 (2014). https://doi.org/10.1007/s13198-014-0223-8

Karim, J., Somers, T., Bhattacherjee, A.: The impact of ERP implementation on business process outcomes: a factor-based study. J. Manag. Inf. Syst. **24**(1), 101–134 (2007). https://doi.org/10.2753/MIS0742-1222240103

Katuu, S. (2021). Trends in the Enterprise Resource Planning market landscape. Journal of Information and Organizational Sciences, 45(1), pp. 55–75. https://doi.org/10.31341/jios.45.1.4

Katuu, S.: Enterprise resource planning: past, present, and future. New Rev. Inf. Netw. **25**(1), 37–46 (2020). https://doi.org/10.1080/13614576.2020.1742770

Kemsley, S.: The changing nature of work: from structured to unstructured, from controlled to social. In: Rinderle-Ma, S., Toumani, F., Wolf, K. (eds.) BPM 2011. LNCS, vol. 6896, p. 2. Springer, Heidelberg (2011). https://doi.org/10.1007/978-3-642-23059-2_2

Koopman, A., Seymour, L.F.: Factors impacting successful BPMS adoption and use: a South African financial services case study. In: Nurcan, S., Reinhartz-Berger, I., Soffer, P., Zdravkovic, J. (eds.) BPMDS/EMMSAD -2020. LNBIP, vol. 387, pp. 55–69. Springer, Cham (2020). https://doi.org/10.1007/978-3-030-49418-6_4

Kraljić, T., Kraljić, A.: Process driven ERP implementation: business process management approach to ERP implementation. In: Johansson, B., Møller, C., Chaudhuri, A., Sudzina, F. (eds.) BIR 2017. LNBIP, vol. 295, pp. 108–122. Springer, Cham (2017). https://doi.org/10.1007/978-3-319-64930-6_8

Leyh, C., Sander, P.: Critical success factors for ERP system implementation projects: an update of literature reviews. In: Sedera, D., Gronau, N., Sumner, M. (eds.) Pre-ICIS 2010-2012. LNBIP, vol. 198, pp. 45–67. Springer, Cham (2015). https://doi.org/10.1007/978-3-319-17587-4_3

Lupeikiene, A., Dzemyda, G., Kiss, F., Caplinskas, A.: Advanced planning and scheduling systems: modeling and implementation challenges. Informatica **25**(4), 581–616 (2014). https://doi.org/10.15388/Informatica.2014.31

Nahavandi, S.: Industry 5.0 – a human-centric solution. Sustainability **11**(16), 4371 (2019). https://doi.org/10.3390/su11164371

Nagpal, S., Kumar, A., Khatri, S.K.: Modeling interrelationships between CSF in ERP implementations: total ISM and MICMAC approach. Int. J. Syst. Assur. Eng. Manag. **8**(4), 782–798 (2017). https://doi.org/10.1007/s13198-017-0647-z

Nazemi, E., Tarokh, M., Djavanshir, G.: ERP: a literature survey. Int. J. Adv. Manuf. Technol. **61**(9–12), 999–1018 (2012). https://doi.org/10.1007/s00170-011-3756-x

Pare, G., Trudel, M.C., Jaana, M., Kitsiou, S.: Synthesizing information systems knowledge: a typology of literature reviews. Inf. Manag. **52**(2), 183–199 (2015). https://doi.org/10.1016/j.im.2014.08.008

Rashid, M., Hossain, L., Patrick, J.: The evolution of ERP systems: a historical perspective. In: Hossain, L., Patrick, J., Rashid, M. (eds.) Enterprise Resource Planning: Global Opportunities and Challenges, pp. 1–16. IGI Global (2002). https://doi.org/10.4018/978-1-931777-06-3.ch001

Rosemann, M., Brocke, J.: The six core elements of business process management. In: Brocke, J., Rosemann, M. (eds.) Handbook on Business Process Management 1. IHIS, pp. 105–122. Springer, Heidelberg (2015). https://doi.org/10.1007/978-3-642-45100-3_5

Szelągowski, M.: Dynamic BPM in the Knowledge Economy: Creating Value from Intellectual Capital, vol. 71. Springer, Heidelberg (2019). https://doi.org/10.1007/978-3-030-17141-4

Szelągowski, M., Lupeikiene, A.: Business process management systems: evolution and development trends. Informatica **31**(3), 579–595 (2020). https://doi.org/10.15388/20-INFOR429

Syed, R., Bandara, W., French, E., Stewart, G.: Getting it right! Critical success factors of BPM in the public sector: a systematic literature review. Australas. J. Inf. Syst. **22** (2018). https://doi.org/10.3127/ajis.v22i0.1265

Ubaid, A.M., Dweiri, F.T.: Business process management (BPM): terminologies and methodologies unified. Int. J. Syst. Assur. Eng. Manag. **11**(6), 1046–1064 (2020). https://doi.org/10.1007/s13198-020-00959-y

van der Aalst, W.M., Van Hee, K., Houben, G.: Modelling and analysing workflow using a Petri-net based approach. In: de Michelis, G., Ellis, C., Memmi, G. (eds.) Proceedings of the Second Workshop on Computer-Supported Cooperative Work, Petri Nets and Related Formalisms, pp. 31–50 (1994). http://www.padsweb.rwth-aachen.de/wvdaalst/publications/p17.pdf. Accessed 12 Feb 2022

van der Aalst, W.M.: Process Mining and RPA: How to Pick Your Automation Battles? RWTH Aachen University (2022). http://www.padsweb.rwth-aachen.de/wvdaalst/publications/p1154.pdf. Accessed 12 Feb 2022

van der Aalst, W.M.P., La Rosa, M., Santoro, F.M.: Business process management. Bus. Inf. Syst. Eng. **58**(1), 1–6 (2016). https://doi.org/10.1007/s12599-015-0409-x

Vanani, I., Sohrabi, B.: A multiple adaptive neuro-fuzzy inference system for predicting ERP implementation success. Iran. J. Manag. Stud. **13**(4), 587–621 (2020). https://doi.org/10.22059/ijms.2020.289483.673801

Vargas, A., Comuzzi, M.: A multi-dimensional model of Enterprise Resource Planning critical success factors. Enterp. Inf. Syst. **14**(1), 38–57 (2020). https://doi.org/10.1080/17517575.2019.1678072

Webster, J., Watson, R.: Analyzing the past to prepare for the future: writing a literature review. MIS Q. **26**(2), 13–23 (2002)

Nobari, B.Z., Azar, A., Kazerooni, M., Yang, P.: Revisiting enterprise resource planning (ERP) risk factors over the past two decades: defining parameters and providing comprehensive classification. Int. J. Inf. Technol. **14**(2), 899–914 (2022). https://doi.org/10.1007/s41870-020-00502-z

Using Topological Functioning Model to Support Event-Driven Solutions

Sai Teja Deharam[1] and Gundars Alksnis[2(✉)] (iD)

[1] Nellore, Andhra Pradesh, India
[2] Riga Technical University, Riga, Latvia
gundars.alksnis@rtu.lv

Abstract. Identifying, understanding and developing a suitable IT solution that fits business domain is the aim of any enterprise approaching digital transformation. Activities an enterprise performs can be viewed as a sequence of events and responses to them. Event-driven solutions have emerged to emphasize event-driven architecture and management as one of the aspects of the enterprise to capture events and respond accordingly by triggering other events. However, to propose conforming solution is not a trivial task and understanding a problem domain first is important. To understand the problem domain, we consider formalism of Topological Functioning Model which analyses an enterprise from computation independent viewpoint and holistically represents both structural and functional aspects of an enterprise. By using case study approach the paper discusses how using Topological Functioning Model can contribute to obtaining an event-driven solution which conforms with the problem domain of an enterprise and thus fosters its digitalization processes.

Keywords: Event-driven solution · Event-driven architecture · Problem domain analysis · Topological Functioning Model · Computation independent viewpoint

1 Introduction

Information technology systems and enterprises can be viewed as event-driven and real-time. The IT system can be perceived as a sequence of events and responses to them. An event, for example, is a change of state of an object in a system. When an event occurs, it triggers other components or events in the system. As modern IT systems of enterprises to gain value are increasingly using real-time analysis, the notations and methods for producing effective event-driven solutions are in demand [1, 2].

Over time many methods were developed for software design using various modeling languages [3]. Though Unified Modeling Language (UML) is one of finest to design, document, visualize and specify artifacts of a software system, however it lacks in representing problem domain from a computation independent viewpoint [4]. This was one of the reasons for the development of Topological UML based on formalism of Topological Functioning Model. Topological Functioning Model (TFM) helps to analyze a problem domain (e.g., an enterprise as a system) from the computation independent

© The Author(s), under exclusive license to Springer Nature Switzerland AG 2022
M. Ivanovic et al. (Eds.): Baltic DB&IS 2022, CCIS 1598, pp. 125–135, 2022.
https://doi.org/10.1007/978-3-031-09850-5_9

viewpoint. It specifies the functionality of a system in the form of topological space, where functional features of the system are shown in the form of directed graph with cause-and-effect relations among these functional features. By using case study approach the paper discusses how the knowledge of the system's functioning represented with TFM can contribute to obtaining an event-driven solution which conforms with the problem domain of an enterprise and thus fosters its digitalization processes.

The paper is organized as follows. Section 2 introduces principle of TFM and event-driven solutions. Section 3 describes a case study and discusses proposed mappings between elements of TFM and elements of event-driven solution. Section 4 discusses related works of TFM transformations to and from other models. Finally, Sect. 5 concludes the paper summarizing main contributions.

2   Topological Functioning Model and Event-Driven Solutions

2.1   Topological Functioning Model

Understanding the problem domain and developing the conforming solution is a primary goal for any software developer [4]. However, often accurate analysis of the problem domain is not performed carefully in software development. Analysis describes what the solution should be with respect to the problem domain, but the design specified, for example, by UML models show how artifacts of the solution should be implemented. As identified in [4] and [5], UML diagrams are not tailored for analyzing a problem domain from computation independent viewpoint (i.e., the system before the solution). To overcome this, a profile to the UML was developed in which Topological Functioning Model was added and called Topological UML [4].

TFM was originally introduced in 1969 by Jānis Osis with the goal to represent system's functionality in a holistic manner by emphasizing topological (connectedness, closure, neighborhood and continuous mapping) and functional (cause-and-effect relations, cycle structure, inputs and outputs) characteristics. Over the years, due to its fundamental idea, TFM also has been applied to complex systems diagnostics, mechatronics and embedded systems, model-driven software engineering and problem domain modeling [4–6].

Formally, TFM of a system is defined in the form of a topological space [4]:

$$G = (X, \Theta) \tag{1}$$

In the Eq. (1), X represents a finite set of functional features X_{id}, whereas Θ represents the topology that satisfies topological characteristics between functional features of a system. A functional feature represents system's functional characteristic, e.g., a process, a function, a task, an action, an activity. Visually, TFM of a system is represented as a graph where nodes represent the functional features, while arcs correspond to the cause-and-effect relations among them.

A topological space Z represents the functioning of the system which is split into set N to represent the system's inner functional features and set M to represent external functional features that the system interacts with, or which affect system's environment [4]:

$$Z = N \cup M \tag{2}$$

To construct the topological space Z, the information is obtained from various documents, interviews, use cases, ontology and other sources that are related to the problem domain (an enterprise, an organization, etc.). The separation of the system from the topological space Z is done by performing a *closure* operation which is done on a set of inner functional features N [4]:

$$X = [N] = \cup_{\rho=1}^{n} X_{\rho} \tag{3}$$

X_{ρ} is the adherence point of set N and capacity of X is the number of adherence points of N [4]. An adherence point of the set N is a point, each neighborhood of which includes at least one point from the set N.

Every functional feature X_{id} is defined as a tuple containing the necessary elements needed during the construction of TFM [4]:

$$X_{id} = <\text{Id, A, Op, R, O, Cl, St, PreCond, PostCond, E, Es, S}> \tag{4}$$

where:

- Id – Unique identifier
- A – Action of the object O
- Op – Operation that provides functionality defined by the action A
- R – Result of the action A
- O – Object that receives the result or that is used in the action A
- Cl – Class who represents the object O in static viewpoint of the system
- St – the state of the object O after the action A
- PreCond – Set of preconditions
- PostCond – Set of postconditions
- E – Entity responsible for performing the action A
- Es – Indicates if execution of the action A can be automated by software
- S – Subordination (i.e., inner or external functional feature)

However, it is not required that all these fields are used in a particular case.

2.2 Event-Driven Solutions

An event, for example, is a change of a state of an object or in a system. In the world everything can be related to events and its consequences [1, 2]. Most IT systems of enterprises to gain value are transforming to be event-driven and real-time. We are all surrounded by events. Everything we do or plan is connected to events surrounding us. For example, in an elevator one presses destination floor number, and the elevator takes one to the selected floor. Pressing the desired floor number is a simple event one is performing, and the rest happens without one's intervention or knowledge about functioning of elevators. When an event occurs, it brings changes or triggers other components or events in the system to react accordingly. Events are things/processes/steps that trigger a change in the system [7].

The event can be processed in several styles, however, the question is how to understand exactly what type and number of events to consider for a given problem domain, so that the solution performs accordingly to the requirements and restrictions set by the problem domain.

We chose the Solace PubSub+ Platform to demonstrate possible the event-driven solution design, how events flow within the solution, how they are visualized, what events need to be published, what events should be subscribed and how events are managed [7]. This platform can be used to manage event streams and technologies to design and visualize event-driven solutions. An event mesh which supports their respective cloud then is built. After mapping events to applications, one can analyze the IT architecture, the events which are most used and which are rarely used, and model them. One can import and export application domain files that define business areas in the system into the platform. Writing payload schema to the events, the JSON format is used along with the source file and can be understood and easily written by software developer or non-technical user.

3   Case Study

Using a case study approach in the context of State Traffic Department problem domain, we demonstrate an event-driven solution development by using TFM as a source model.

3.1   Problem Domain Description, Analysis and Creation of Topological Functioning Model

Let's assume the following description of a problem domain of traffic violation prevention management:

> When a vehicle driver is causing a traffic rules violation, a camera mounted near the traffic light records the picture of the license plate number. From the license plate number, details of the vehicle owner are gathered, which includes phone number, postal and email address. Then by State Traffic Department an information request form is sent to the owner with the details of the violation – place, type and time. State Traffic Department also asks for confirmation whether the driver causing traffic rules violation was the owner, friend or relative. The owner fills-in the information request form and sends it back to State Traffic Department which is documented for future use.

> Then past violations are checked for the driver. If there is none, a new complaint is opened, and the information about possible fines is sent to the driver. If there already is a violation, then a fine is imposed and information about it is sent to the registered phone number and email address of the driver providing the instructions on how to pay on an Online Payment Portal within deadline. If the violations happened more than twice or the payment were not made within the deadline, then an invitation is sent to the driver for a traffic awareness course on safe driving and about paying a fine.

We assume that in this domain there already are present software applications like camera and object recognition system, and there are applications which are necessary to be built for the solution. They are Safety Driving Application, Online Payment Portal and State Traffic Department Application. When a driver driving a vehicle causes traffic rules violation, camera and object recognition system captures the license plate number of the vehicle issuing a traffic violation record which contains details of the location, type and time of violation along with the license plate number. From the traffic violation record, State Traffic Department Application gathers details about the registered owner, owner's phone number, email and postal address.

State Traffic Department sends an information request form to the vehicle owner, where the location, time and type of violation information is attached and confirmation about the driver is asked in the form. The owner fills-in the form and sends it back to State Traffic Department. The filled-in information request form also contains information about the driver causing traffic rules violation – owner, friend or relative. Personal Profile Management application stores the information about the driver. This application contains all the information and all the future correspondence between the driver causing traffic rules violation and State Traffic Department will take place through this application.

Information request form is documented by State Traffic Department Application for future use. State Traffic Department checks for the past violation record where all the information about the driver's past violations is noted and submits the past violations record to the Safety Driving Application. Safety Driving Application contains all the information about fines, type of violation and how much fine is imposed. By opening new complaint, all the information regarding driver safety is published through this application. After checking the past violation record received from the State Traffic Department, if the violation happens for the first time, Safety Driving Application opens a new complaint, sends a notification about the violation, and informs the driver about fines if the violation will repeat. If the violation happens more than one time, then based on the type of violation, Safety Driving Application imposes fine and sets a deadline for the driver to pay. If it happens more than two times or if the payment were not paid within the deadline, Safety Driving Application sends invitation for a traffic awareness course to the driver along with the fine. Along with the fines, Safety Driving Application also sends instructions about how to pay the imposed fine through Online Payment Portal. The driver follows the instructions and pays the imposed fine and once the fine is paid, the driver closes Online Payment Portal.

The problem domain analysis identified 14 functional features as shown in Table 1. By analyzing cause-and-effect relations between them, the topology has been introduced and the TFM has been created as shown in Fig. 1. Bold lines between nodes 4-7-8-9-10-4 represent the main cycle of functioning. Solid lines between nodes 4-7-8-9-12-16-4 represent fine payment sub-cycle. Nodes 1, 2, 5, 6, 14, 15, 17 and 18 represent the external functional features and are connected by dashed lines.

3.2 Transformation from Topological Functioning Model to Event-Driven Solution

Table 2 summarizes proposed mappings between the elements of TFM and the event-driven solution. A functional feature in TFM forms an event in an event-driven solution. It is because the event, which is referenced by the application, triggers components

Table 1. The specification of TFM functional features for State Traffic Department system.

Id	Functional feature	Action	Result	Object	Precondition	Executor	Subord.*
1	Causing traffic rules violation	Cause	Traffic rules violation	Traffic violation record		Driver	E
2	Capturing license plate number of the vehicle	Capture	License plate number of the vehicle	Camera & Object recognition device	Traffic rules are violated	Camera & Object recognition system	E
3	Gathering details about the vehicle owner	Gather	Owner details from license plate number	Registered vehicle owner	Traffic rules are violated and images are captured	State Traffic Department	I
4	Requesting information	Request	Information request form	Information request form	The owner details are gathered	State Traffic Department	I
5	Receiving information request form	Receive	Information request form	Information request form	If traffic rules are violated	Owner	E
6	Filling-in and submitting information request form	Filling	Information request form	Information request form	The Information request form is received	Owner	E
7	Documenting information request form	Documenting	Information request form	Documented information request form of the driver	The information request form is filled-in and submitted	State Traffic Department	I
8	Checking information on past violations	Check	Violations	Past violations record of the driver	The traffic rules violation is caused	State Traffic Department	I
9	Submitting information on past violations	Submit	Violations	Past violations record of the driver	Past traffic rules violations are checked	State Traffic Department	I
10	Opening a new complaint	Open	New complaint	Personal Profile Management	The driver has no previous violations	Safety Driving Application	I
11	Sending warning notification about possible fines if violation will repeat	Send	Information about possible fines	Personal Profile Management	The traffic rules violation happens for the first time	Safety Driving Application	I
12	Imposing fine and sending instructions	Impose and send	Fine	Personal Profile Management	The driver has more than one violation	Safety Driving Application	I
13	Sending invitation to traffic awareness course on safe driving	Send	Traffic Awareness course	Personal Profile Management	The violation is done more than twice or the payment is not made in time	Safety Driving Application	I
14	Receiving instructions	Receive	Instructions	Personal Messenger	The traffic rules violation is caused more than once	Driver	E
15	Paying fine	Pay	Fine payment	Online Payment Portal	The fine is imposed	Driver	E
16	Receiving payment and closing complaint	Receive and close	Payment received and close complaint	Personal Profile Management	The payment is made	State Traffic Department	I
17	Receiving warning notification	Receive	Warning notification	Personal Messenger	The traffic rules violation happens for the first time	Driver	E
18	Receiving invitation	Receive	Invitation link	Invitation record	The violation is done more than twice or the payment is not made in time	Driver	E

* I – Inner, E – external.

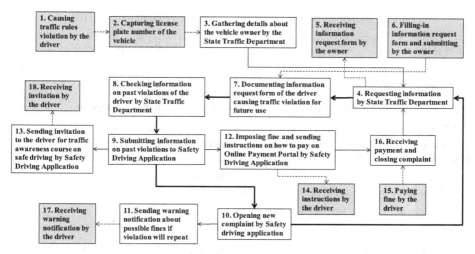

Fig. 1. The Topological Functioning Model of the State Traffic Department problem domain. nodes represent functional features while arrows represent cause-and-effect relations.

and events in other applications. The functional feature also triggers related functional features in TFM. The name of the functional feature forms the name of the event. The event description is the most important element as it represents the main reason or the cause that provides necessary condition to trigger the event. The event description is formed by a physical or business functional feature specification in TFM.

These mappings can be substantiated with the following arguments. An application in the event-driven solution comes from an executor in functional feature. The executor in TFM performs or executes the necessary action with the object. The application in the event-driven solution contains required events which trigger the required action to bring the necessary changes in the system. Cause-and-effect relation in TFM forms publish and subscribe event where one application subscribes or publishes events.

Event schema comes from an object of a functional feature performing the action. Event schemas come from the object of the functional feature. In the case of State Traffic Department: traffic rules violation record, information request form, past violations record. Event schema is specification written inside the object which flows internally to trigger the event. The event schema can be written in several formats – plain text, JSON or binary.

Applying the transformations to TFM shown in Fig. 1 resulting event-driven solution with applications, events, event flows is shown in Fig. 2. In the Solace PubSub+ Platform larger concentric circled nodes represent applications, while smaller green nodes represent events. Event path shows the direction of event flows from one application to another and are shown as directed arcs.

Event flow forms a relationship between the functional features. Logical event mesh is an event mesh where all the events are joined logically and are associated in an event-driven solution. A topological space where all the functional features are logically joined corresponds to the logical event mesh in the event-driven solution.

Table 2. Mappings between elements of event-driven solution and TFM.

TFM element	Event-driven solution element
Functional feature	Event
Name of the functional feature	Event name
A physical or business functional feature specification	Event description
An executor of the functional feature	Application
A cause functional feature in cause-and-effect relation where functional features with different executors take part	Publish event
An effect functional feature in cause-and-effect relation where functional features with different executors take part	Subscribe event
An object or a result of a functional feature	Schema
Cause-and-effect relation between functional features	Event flow
A topological space where functional features are logically joined	Logical event mesh
Objects associated with a particular executor of functional feature	Event tags
An indicator to which functional feature an object belongs	Event topic address

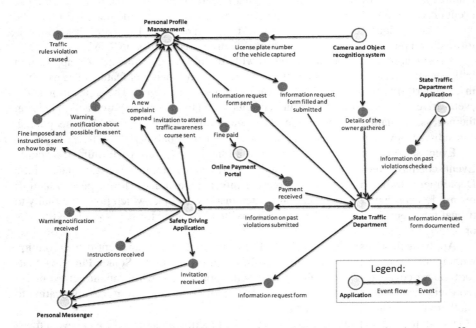

Fig. 2. Event-driven solution with applications, events and their interactions for the state traffic department system.

Event tags are formed as the topological space where the same executor is set for all functional features. Events need to be addressable and should be routable to different applications so that enterprises can reuse events and event-driven applications.

Addressing of an event is done with the help of an event topic. The event topic is information for the systems for making decisions to route particular event. The topic address element in event-driven solution comes from an object of the functional feature in TFM.

There also are elements in the event-driven solution (e.g., version and application type) which doesn't have corresponding mapping elements in TFM and are ignored.

Figure 3 demonstrates the fragment of the TFM how Safety Driving Application receives the driver's past violations record from State Traffic Department Application and then sends notification about opening a new complaint and about possible fines if violations will repeat, and how the fines are imposed, or other activities, which will be sent to the Personal Profile Management Application.

In Fig. 3 the mapping *A* traces to the executor of the functional feature, the mapping *B* refers to the event in the event-driven solution tracing to the functional feature. Finally, the mapping *C* represents the flow of the events in the event-driven solution tracing to the cause-and-effect relation between two functional features.

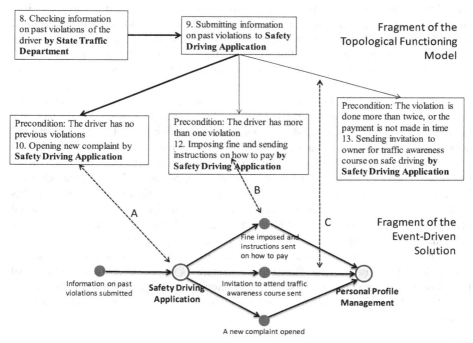

Fig. 3. Mappings from the TFM elements to event-driven solution elements. In the functional features the executors are shown in bold.

4   Related Works

There are several research which involve the use of TFM as a source or destination for transformation to and from other models. For example, the transformation to UML state machine for formal analysis of state changes [8] and the verification of BPMN functional completeness using [9].

In [8] the UML state transitions are analyzed by the functional characteristics of TFM and mappings from TFM elements to the UML state machine elements are proposed. In their approach functional feature object's state is mapped to the state element while the cause-and-effect relation is mapped to the transition of the state machine. Action of the functional feature is mapped to the event, entry or exit action of the state machine. Pre- and postconditions are mapped to guard conditions. Finally, logical relationship between functional features is mapped to fork and join element of the state machine. Later it has been integrated in Topological UML [4].

The authors of [9] verify the completeness of a BPMN model functional completeness. To do this, the BPMN model is transformed to TFM for further analysis. An example is taken and mappings from BPMN elements to TFM elements are introduced, and the completeness of the BPMN model is discussed. The mapping of BPMN elements to other formal notations is not a new concept and also has been mapped to such formal notations like Petri nets, Prolog, Communicating sequential processes, etc. It is concluded that those mappings were limited to deadlocks, thread correctness and data flows. By using TFM, the system's functionality and completeness can be determined holistically. They explain how the functional feature is executed after a trigger. If the trigger is successful, then its termination leads to a successful trigger of the effect functional feature.

In contrast to BPMN, TFM contains just a few however fundamental modeling constructs [9]. BPMN elements are elicited and TFM elements are identified, and mappings between TFM elements and BPMN elements are listed. For example, tasks, events and data come from a functional feature tuple. All elements which have corresponding notion in TFM are mapped, and those which don't have them are ignored. For example, elements like text annotation and conversation link doesn't have corresponding mapping element in TFM. Results of transformation are observed for verification whether the elements follow TFM properties as it is checked for the presence of topological and functional properties. TFM is considered valid if it has no isolated vertices and has a functioning cycle in addition to inputs and outputs, continuous mapping, and all cause-and-effect relations are necessary and sufficient to trigger subsequent functional features [5]. The functioning cycle must contain functional aspects with respect to problem domain. All transformations were done manually, and functioning cycle identification were considered the hardest part as it was not evident how to identify and when to use output and input events.

5   Conclusions

As many industries and enterprises are opting for event-driven solutions to support digitalization processes and there was no prior research on transformation to event-driven solutions from TFM, the paper provided a contribution that ensures solution's conformance with the problem domain.

TFM was chosen as it can represent the functioning of the problem domain (e.g., an enterprise as a system) holistically by emphasizing computation independent viewpoint. TFM allows to capture and emphasize cause-and-effect relations between functional characteristics of the problem domain.

To propose an event-driven solution, a use case approach was considered for a selected problem domain. Functional features were identified, and cause-and-effect relations were identified. TFM was constructed and the event-driven solution was designed in the Solace PubSub+ Platform.

Proposed mappings between TFM elements and event-driven solution elements demonstrate that they contribute to obtaining an event-driven solution which conforms with the problem domain of an enterprise. The scope for future work includes development of automated transformations of proposed mappings to support advanced implementations of event-driven solutions.

References

1. Stopford, B.: Designing Event-Driven Systems. O'Reilly, Sebastopol (2018)
2. A Business Leaders Guide to Event-Driven Architecture by Tiempo Development (2020). https://vdocuments.net/a-business-leaders-guide-to-event-driven-architecture-event-driven-architecture.html. Accessed 8 May 2022
3. Platt, R., Thompson, N.: The evolution of UML. In: Encyclopedia of Information Science and Technology, 3rd edn. IGI Global (2015)
4. Osis, J., Donins, U.: Topological UML Modeling: An Improved Approach for Domain Modeling and Software Development. Elsevier, Amsterdam (2017)
5. Osis, J., Asnina, E.: Topological modeling for model-driven domain analysis and software development: functions and architectures. In: Model-Driven Domain Analysis and Software Development: Architectures and Functions, pp. 15–39. IGI Global, Hershey (2010)
6. Osis, J.: Extension of software development process for mechatronic and embedded systems. In: Proceedings of the 32nd International Conference on Computers and Industrial Engineering, pp. 305–310 (2003)
7. Solace PubSub+ Platform. https://docs.solace.com/Solace-PubSub-Platform.htm. Accessed 8 May 2022
8. Doniņš, U., Osis, J., Nazaruka, E., Jansone, A.: Using functional characteristics to analyze state changes of objects. In: Databases and Information Systems, pp. 94–106 (2012)
9. Nazaruka, E., Ovchinnikova, V., Alksnis, G., Sukovskis, U.: Verification of BPMN model functional completeness by using the topological functioning model. In: Proceedings of the 11th International Conference on Evaluation of Novel Software Approaches to Software Engineering. SciTePress (2016)

Temporal Multi-view Contracts for Efficient Test Models

Jishu Guin[1], Jüri Vain[1], Leonidas Tsiopoulos[1(✉)], and Gert Valdek[2]

[1] Tallinn University of Technology, Ehitaja tee 5, 12616 Tallinn, Estonia
{Jishu.Guin,Juri.Vain,Leonidas.Tsiopoulos}@taltech.ee
[2] Information Technology, Airobot OÜ, Tallinn, Estonia
gert@airobot.ee

Abstract. In this work we focus on practical aspects of test automation, namely reducing the model creation effort for model-based testing by exploiting the multi-view contract paradigm. We take into account explicitly the design views of the system and develop dedicated system test models by views in an incremental manner. The test models formalized as Uppaal Timed Automata refine the requirements of the views and are verified against the view contracts specified in Timed Computation Tree logic. As a novel theoretical contribution we extend the notion of assume/guarantee contracts by introducing temporal modalities. As a second contribution, we demonstrate the feasibility of the approach on an industrial climate control system testing case study. The improvement of testing process productivity is compared to that of developing a monolithic model empirically without extracting views. Finally, we discuss the usability aspects of the method in test development and outline the challenges.

Keywords: Model-checking · Model-based testing · Contract-based design

1 Introduction

Automation in industry has not attained the level of maturity required for a reliable and economically feasible integration testing of cyber-physical systems (CPS). The mainstream methods used in industry for test automation fail to address the complex dynamics caused by the co-existence of multiple aspects of the system like functionality, timing constraints, security and safety requirements, etc. [14]. This demands a method powerful enough to address various design aspects and their integration to produce conclusive result that can assure high standard of quality. Current industrial practice in software assurance still relies on manual testing or limited forms of automated testing, e.g., running test scripts as part of continuous integration process [1, 12]. These methods depend on ad-hoc scenarios that test engineers can design depending on their creativity and in many cases incomplete and ambiguous information in the specification. The tools used for automated tests often execute randomly chosen scenarios using scripts based on combinations of input data. These test scenarios are limited in scope as they fail to achieve thorough test coverage in terms of parameters like execution paths, range of inputs, timing properties, security properties, etc. These parameters have gained

© The Author(s), under exclusive license to Springer Nature Switzerland AG 2022
M. Ivanovic et al. (Eds.): Baltic DB&IS 2022, CCIS 1598, pp. 136–151, 2022.
https://doi.org/10.1007/978-3-031-09850-5_10

importance over time especially in complex CPSs because of the increasing dependability requirements of these systems.

Applying formal verification as an alternative to manual testing is a well-known approach to attain the level of rigour that current CPS development demands. The method we have chosen for verification in this work is Model-Based Testing (MBT) which is one of the approaches for automatically generating test cases from a model of the system under test (SUT) [15]. However, the main obstacle for the widespread industrial adoption of MBT is the effort required to develop the models. In order to facilitate this process, the methodology demonstrated in this paper employs the Contract-based Design (CBD) principle [7] to modularize the specification and provide more tractable and efficient MBT. Additionally, enhanced performance is attained in the verification of the properties of the system as formalized in Uppaal Timed Automata (Uppaal TA) formalism and its specification language Timed Computation Tree Logic (TCTL) [6]. These properties of test model comprise properties of completeness relative to view contracts and compliance with the specification under test. As a novel theoretical contribution we extend the notion of assume/guarantee contracts by introducing temporal modalities expressible in TCTL, because temporal and real-time requirements are often the source of misinterpretation and erroneous implementation and need explicit specification in the contracts [6]. As a second contribution, we demonstrate the feasibility of the approach on an industrial climate control system testing case study. The improvement in productivity of the testing process is revealed by comparing to that attained by developing a monolithic model in a non-modular manner without extracting views. This resulted in higher complexity of the model due to the loss of clear structure that, in turn, led to reduced efficiency in the modeling process and its verification. Finally, we discuss the usability aspects of the method in test development and outline the challenges.

2   Climate Control System

The climate control system used inside premises has four components. Two of them implement user interfaces (UI) - Wall Mount Panel and Mobile application. The third unit, Controller, regulates the climate based on the settings provided by the user via the UI and sensor readings. The fourth component, Server, adds cloud access to the system by providing server supervisor control services for the controller and mobile application. As shown in Fig. 1 the Controller interacts directly with the Server and the Wall Mount Panel. The controller hardware consists of sensors and the climate unit to interact with the physical environment. The user is in the loop via the UI components. The Server which is the System Under Test (SUT) communicates with multiple controllers distributed over various locations forming a distributed CPS. It comprises two server programs. One of them serves the Mobile application over HTTP and the other serves the Controllers over a proprietary protocol using TCP sockets. The case study focuses on testing a part of the Server-Controller communication.

The message interchange between the components has a request-response format. The protocol specification not only covers functional behaviour of the component but also incorporates time constraints. Each controller can initiate the session independently of others after a successful TCP connection is established with the server. This is followed by exchanging five messages to complete the connection procedure. The protocol also supports a number of commands to accomplish various tasks. The five messages that are exchanged between the server and controller consist of header and data fields. The values of data fields must correspond to the protocol specification. The sequence of the message exchange for the connection procedure is: 1) Controller initiates by sending *client_hello*, 2) Server responds with *server_hello*, 3) Controller sends *init*, 4) Server sends *ack_init*, 5) Controller responds with *ack*.

In addition to timing constraints, the server enforces certain fault-tolerance requirements. After successful execution of the connection procedure the components continue the session by exchanging data messages. The key requirements for the test development demonstrated in the paper are - R1) The server disconnects from the client if it fails to receive *client_hello* within first I_{TO} seconds after successful connection. This is a timing requirement. R2) The server disconnects from the client if the *client_hello* message data fields have incorrect values. This is a fault-tolerance requirement and does not involve any timing constraints. R3) The server shall wait for the first M_h bytes from the client for I_{TO} seconds after the TCP connection is established. The client must be able to send M_h bytes in parts within I_{TO} seconds where M_h is as specified in the system specification. R4) The connection procedure shall successfully complete if all aforementioned requirements are satisfied. The next sections provide an account of the approach used to apply the testing method to the system.

3   Preliminaries

3.1   Model-Based Testing

Model-based testing requires a formal model of the SUT composed from system specification. Typically in MBT, the SUT is considered as a black-box which accepts a set of inputs and produces corresponding observable outputs as per the specification [15]. MBT provides the test verdict based on the conformance relation between the observable behaviour of SUT and its model. The test fails when the behaviours of SUT and the model do not match. The test inputs are generated using assumptions on environment that correspond to pre-specified use cases. Typically MBT focuses on input-output conformance (IOCO) testing. However, since CPS requirements generally refer also to timing constraints, stronger conformance relation that covers also timing, namely RTI-OCO [13] relation, is applied in this study. Besides the expressive power another criteria

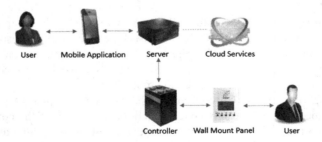

Fig. 1. Components of the climate control system.

of choosing MBT formalism is its relevance for test generation. Model-checking [5] is generally used to generate test cases while the coverage criteria are expressed in terms of properties whose validity is verified at first by model-checker and witness traces used thereafter as symbolic test sequences. The coverage properties can refer to model structural elements such as states and transitions, branching conditions or path expressions.

In general, the coverage properties are extracted from system requirements and expressed in a logic language like TCTL. The model-checking witness traces are used as symbolic test sequences while satisfying the verified property. Executable test cases can be extracted from these symbolic traces and instantiated with explicit tests data values to cover the test goals. This method is called *offline test generation* because it does not require the SUT to be running when test sequences are generated. Converting symbolic traces to executable can also be done *online* by executing the model in random walk mode, which presumes compilation of traces to some test scripting language, e.g., TTCN-3, or running the model against SUT via test adapters. The latter, employed also in our approach, requires transforming symbolic test inputs of traces to executable input format of SUT and the outputs of SUT back to symbolic form for conformance check.

3.2 Uppaal Timed Automata

The time constraints of the SUT advocate the use of Uppaal TA as the preferred modeling formalism. Uppaal TA [6] are defined as a closed network of extended timed automata that are called *processes*. The processes are combined into a single system by synchronous parallel composition. The nodes of the automata graph are called *locations* and directed arcs between locations are called *edges*. The *state* of an automaton consists of its current location and valuation of all variables, including clocks. Synchronization of processes is defined using constructs called *channels*. A channel ch relates a pair of transitions in parallel processes where synchronised edges are labelled with synchronizing input and output actions, e.g., denoted $ch?$ and $ch!$, respectively.

Formally, an Uppaal TA is given as the tuple $(L, E, V, CL, Init, Inv, T_L)$, where L is a finite set of locations, E is the set of edges defined by $E \subseteq L \times G(CL,V) \times Sync \times Act \times L$, where $G(CL,V)$ is the conjunction of enabling constraints, $Sync$ is a set of synchronisation actions over channels and Act is a set of assignments with integer and boolean expressions and clock resets. V denotes the set of variables of boolean and integer type and arrays of those. CL denotes the set of real-valued clocks ($CL \cap V = \emptyset$). $Init \subseteq Act$ is a set of initializing assignments to variables and clocks. $Inv : L \rightarrow I(CL,V)$ maps locations to the set of invariants over clocks CL and variables V. $T_L : L \rightarrow \{ordinary, urgent, committed\}$ maps location types to locations. In *urgent* locations an outgoing edge will be executed immediately when its guard holds. *Committed* locations are useful for creating sequences of actions executed atomically without time passing.

Uppaal TA Requirement Specification Language The requirement specification language (in short, query language) of Uppaal TA, used to specify properties to be model-checked, is a subset of TCTL [6]. The query language consists of path formulae and state formulae. State formulae describe individual states, whereas path formulae quantify over execution paths of the model and can be classified into *reachability*, *safety* and *liveness* [6]. For example, safety properties are specified with formula $A\square\varphi$ stating that first order state formula φ should be true in all reachable states expressed with the pair of modalities $A\square$.

For real-time applications, *time bounded reachability* is one of the most fundamental properties. In Uppaal TA, the reachability of a state which satisfies formula φ from model initial state is expressible using TCTL formula pattern $A\Diamond\varphi$ && $Clock \leqslant TB$, for time bound TB. A special case of time bounded reachability is the reachability of a state when it is considered relative to some other preceding state of the model. This is expressed in TCTL using the "leads to" operator as $ts \leadsto_{TB} rs$, for preceding state ts and reachable from this state rs. In this paper we use time bounded reachability to introduce temporality to formulas of assume/guarantee contracts.

3.3 Contract-Based Design

The CBD paradigm has proven essential for the development of complex systems with many parallel and heterogeneous components adhering to various safety and timing constraints in addition to their basic functionality [7]. Contracts handle components' interface properties representing the *assumptions* on their environment and the *guarantees* (regarding output) of the component under these assumptions. The main advantage of CBD is the explicit identification of responsibilities of the individual components within a complex system. This facilitates component reuse and scalability while addressing correctness and system complexity through components' and their services' operations. The complexity of CPSs requires separation of design concerns by introducing *multi-view* contracts to support compositional design, testing and verification.

The *meta-theory* of contracts introduced by Benveniste et al. [7] defines interface contracts as abstraction subject to contract algebra. A contract C can be defined in terms of an environment in which it operates and of a component that implements it. A contract is said to be *consistent* if there is a component implementing it and *compatible* if there is an environment in which the contract can operate.

For the case study in this paper we are concerned with two main *contract operators* complementing each other. The first one, the *composition* operator between two contracts, denoted by $\otimes$, is a partial function on contracts involving a *compatibility* criterion. Two contracts C and C' are compatible if their shared variable types match and if there exists an environment in which the two contracts properly interact. Working with *Assume/Guarantee* (A/G) contracts being pairs (A, G), the composition $C_1 \otimes C_2 = (A_{C_1 \otimes C_2}, G_{C_1 \otimes C_2})$ of two contracts $C_1 = (A_{C_1}, G_{C_1})$ and $C_2 = (A_{C_2}, G_{C_2})$ is defined as follows:

$$G_{C_1 \otimes C_2} = G_{C_1} \wedge G_{C_2}, \quad A_{C_1 \otimes C_2} = \max\left\{ A \middle| \begin{array}{l} A \wedge G_{C_1} \Rightarrow A_{C_2} \\ A \wedge G_{C_2} \Rightarrow A_{C_1} \end{array} \right. \tag{1}$$

where "max" refers to the order of predicates by implication and $A_{C_1 \otimes C_2}$ is the weakest assumption such that the two referred implications hold. The two contracts C_1 and C_2 are compatible if the assumption computed as above differs from *false*.

The second contract operator required when merging different view contracts is the *conjunction* operator. Conjunction (denoted $\wedge$) of contracts is complementary to composition. Full specification of a component can be a conjunction of multiple viewpoints, each covering a specific aspect (behavioural, timing, safety, etc.) of the intended design and specified by an individual contract.

4   Temporal Multi-view Contracts

For the work in this paper we consider the contracts to be in *saturated form* [7] where the assumptions imply the guarantee.

$$A_{sat} = A, \; G_{sat} = A \Rightarrow G \tag{2}$$

However the contracts of form (2) express static view of functionality without distinguishing different states of the component. To make the temporal aspects explicit we extend the above to a temporal saturated contract where:

$$A_{sat} = A, \; G_{sat} = A \rightsquigarrow G \tag{3}$$

When the explicit timing aspects need to be expressed in the contracts then the "leads to" in (3) is strengthened to *time-bounded leads to* ($\rightsquigarrow_{TB}$) and we get formula (4) where both A and G can be expressed in TCTL.

$$A_{tsat} = A, \; G_{tsat} = A \rightsquigarrow_{TB} G \tag{4}$$

For contract *composition* with saturated contracts, the guarantees of each component are explicitly the assumptions of the other:

$$G_{C_1 \otimes C_2} = G_{C_1} \wedge G_{C_2}, \; A_{C_1 \otimes C_2} = (G_{C_1} \Rightarrow A_{C_2}) \wedge (G_{C_2} \Rightarrow A_{C_1}) \tag{5}$$

In our approach, since we need the contracts to express also temporal and timing properties, we extend the saturated contract composition formula (5) to temporal saturated contract formula (6) by substituting the implication "$\Rightarrow$" with leads to "$\rightsquigarrow$".

$$G_{C_1 \otimes C_2} = G_{C_1} \wedge G_{C_2}, \; A_{C_1 \otimes C_2} = (G_{C_1} \rightsquigarrow A_{C_2}) \wedge (G_{C_2} \rightsquigarrow A_{C_1}) \tag{6}$$

However, this extension does not come for free. Since the distribution law of $\wedge$ and $\rightsquigarrow$ does not hold in temporal contract, formula (6) is not linearly extendable. Nevertheless, extension of formula (5) with "leads to" allows compositional verification by checking the individual conjuncts of (6) independently.

Regarding contract *conjunction* with saturated contracts, assume a contract $C \equiv \wedge_{i=1,n} C_i$ comprising views each of them characterised with its own subcontract $C_i \equiv A_{C_i} \rightsquigarrow G_{C_i}$. Proving conjunction correctness means then proving formula $\wedge_{i=1,n} C_i$ in an incremental, pairwise multi-view manner after proving correctness of each conjunct separately. The operators' applications are exemplified in Sect. 6.

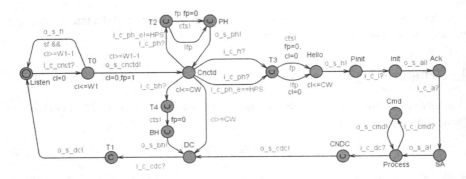

Fig. 2. Uppaal TA empirical model of the Server component - SUT

5   Empirical Approach to Model-Based Test Generation

To demonstrate the advantages of multi-view contracts-based test development compared with empirical approach we present, at first, empirical in this section and multi-view approach in Sect. 6. Figure 2 shows the Uppaal TA model of the server, the SUT of our case study. Due to the space limit the server model captures only the session initialization procedure where different design views manifest themselves clearly. In addition to the i/o behaviour of SUT, the model also introduces some additional channels that do not influence SUT i/o behaviour but assist the testing process.

The SUT model represents behaviours that cover requirements R1-R4 identified in Sect. 2. Location *Cnctd* is reached when the server has established TCP connection with the controller. The outgoing edges from *Cnctd* model the four scenarios being subject to requirements. The transition to location *DC* occurs when the controller fails to send the *client_hello* message within I_{TO} seconds after socket connection is established. Location *BH* is reached if the *client_hello* message is received with incorrect values in its fields. The edge to location *PH* is taken in case of partial reception of *client_hello* message. Finally, the edges to location *Hello* are taken when the *client_hello* message is received successfully by the server. Test case generation step introduces the four corresponding environment models each to test one of these scenarios.

The four test scenarios based on the requirements R1–R4 are implemented at first empirically as separate environment model. In the empirical approach the environment models[1] trigger the scenarios corresponding to four outgoing edges from localtion *Cnctd* of the SUT in a cyclic manner. On completion of each scenario the controller disconnects from the server and the test case selection cycle repeats with same or different scenario. Thus, in each cycle a scenario is selected randomly for execution.

6   Test Model Modularization by Multi-view Design Contracts

This section elaborates modularization principles that allow one to split the large monolithic test models into smaller and conceptually more homogeneous parts.

---

[1] https://www.dropbox.com/sh/22ds5wurmfz3cb9/AABaJGvIlf6MTqbajGyanu7Da?dl=0.

Table 1. Symbols

Symbol	Description
id	Identifier of a controller
$S_{cl}(id)$	State of the controller with identifier id
I_{TO}	Connection timeout for the *hello* message
M_h	Number of bytes in *hello* message
$S_{con}(id)$	State of the dedicated connection on the server side to the controller(id)
$data\_error(id)$	Value denoting occurence of error in the data exchanged with controller(id)
A_{con}	Set of active connections between server and controllers
I_f	Time alloted for fast connection retries
I_s	Short periodicity for faster connection attempts
I_l	Long periodicity for connection attempts

Namely, we apply the multi-view approach by formalizing requirements as view contracts and build the test models by each view individually. This allows compositional verification to assure that each test model representing a view satisfies the view contract and then by merging the view models their conjunction correctness is proved. Furthermore, due to the view contracts partiality their implementation models have generally smaller size compared with holistic non-modular models. Relying on this consideration we introduce design view oriented contracts as an intermediate step to guide the modularization of requirements specification and construction of test models. The derivation of contracts is done in two steps, firstly, a set of requirements is derived from the textual specification and, secondly, a set of view contracts are formulated based on those requirements. This process is manual and does not guarantee a strict bijective relation between the requirements and contracts but provides a traceable relation between their groups. For requirement traceability both the requirement and the contract specifying it, are shown in Tables 2 and 3. Due to space limitations the detailed requirements and contracts[2] are not shown in the paper. The views exemplified in the rest of the paper are *behavioural, timing* and *fault-tolerance*.

6.1 Behavioural View

The behavioural view highlights the functional requirements extracted from the system specification. In order to encode these requirements in the form of contracts, symbols are used to denote certain concepts as described in Table 1.

Contract B_1^c in Table 3 asserts that if the controller, identified by id, is not connected to server, $id \notin A_{con}$, where A_{con} represents the list of connections, then it moves to a state attempting to connect to server, $S_{cl}(id) = connecting$. B_1^c corresponds to requirement R_1^b in Table 2 - "When controller is not connected, it tries to connect". Contract B_1^s denotes the counter part of this transaction on the server side. It states that given the controller is connecting to server, $S_{cl}(id) = connecting$, a transition is made by the server from a connectionless state, $id \notin A_{con}$, to a connected state, $id \in A_{con} \land$

---

[2] https://www.dropbox.com/sh/22ds5wurmfz3cb9/AABaJGvIlf6MTqbajGyanu7Da?dl=0.

Table 2. Requirements

Ref.	Description
R_1^b	When controller is not connected, it tries to connect
R_2^b	When controller is connected, it sends clear text *client_hello* message
R_3^b	After receiving a valid *client_hello*, server responds with *server_hello* message
R_1^f	Controller retries to connect if disconnected
R_2^f	Server disconnects if data received is invalid
R_1^t	The connection is retried every I_s minutes for I_f minutes
R_2^t	The connection is retried every I_l minutes after I_f minutes
R_4^t	Server waits for I_{TO} seconds to receive M_h bytes of *client_hello* message

Table 3. Contracts

R. Id	C. Id	Assume	Guarantee
R_1^b	B_1^c	$id \notin A_{con}$	$id \notin A_{con} \rightsquigarrow S_{cl}(id) = connecting$
(R_1^b)	B_1^s	$S_{cl}(id) = connecting$	$id \notin A_{con} \rightsquigarrow id \in A_{con} \wedge S_{con}(id) = connected$
R_2^b	B_2^c	$S_{con}(id) = connected$	$S_{cl}(id) = connected \rightsquigarrow S_{cl}(id) = chello\_sent$
R_3^b	B_2^s	$S_{cl}(id) = chello\_sent$	$S_{con}(id) = chello\_recv \rightsquigarrow S_{con}(id) = shello\_sent$
R_2^f	F_4^s	$S_{cl}(id) = chello\_sent$	$S_{con}(id) = chello\_recv \rightsquigarrow$
		$\wedge\ data\_error(id)$	$id \notin A_{con}$
R_2^t	T_3^c	$C_g > I_f$	$S_{cl}(id) = wait \rightsquigarrow_{=I_l} S_{cl}(id) = connecting$
$R_2^b,(R_4^t)$	T_4^c	$S_{con}(id) = connected$	$S_{cl}(id) = connected \rightsquigarrow_{<I_{TO}} S_{cl}(id) = chello\_sent$
R_3^b	T_3^s	$S_{cl}(id) = chello\_sent$	$S_{con}(id) = chello\_recv$
		$\wedge \neg data\_error(id) \wedge C_h < I_{TO}$	$\rightsquigarrow S_{con}(id) = shello\_sent$

$S_{con}(id) = connected$, where $S_{con}(id)$ represents the state of the dedicated connection from server to controller(id). The other behavioural contracts formulated in the tables capture the remaining functional requirements. The timing and fault-tolerance aspects of the specification are not considered in this view. However, the contracts reflect the causality aspect of the system which is expressed by the temporal operator "leads to" ($\rightsquigarrow$). In behavioural view contracts ideal lossless communication is assumed, therefore, sent and receive predicates of the same message are counted logically identical.

Behavioural View Model. The behavioural view model is presented in Fig. 3. The controller automaton is on the left of the figure while the server automaton is in the middle. On the right, the automaton that models the connection protocol is depicted. In this view, the server just responds positively to the controller connection requests, i.e., connection loss and data corruption are abstracted away from this view. The states of the corresponding view contracts are encoded as locations in the automata and communication actions between the components are represented with channels. State names follow a

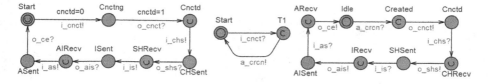

Fig. 3. The behavioural view model of the climate control system.

shorthanded notation in the model. For example, controller state "$S_{cl}(id) = chello\_sent$" maps to location name "CHSent" in the controller model.

Behavioural View Model Verification. In order to verify the model against the specified contracts, we map the contracts to TCTL queries and apply the UPPAAL model-checker. This process is exemplified next with a corresponding pair of contracts for the controller and the server. Contract B_2^c is mapped to TCTL query:

$$(Con.Cnctd \text{ and } C.Cnctd) \; {-}{-}{>} \; C.CHSent \tag{7}$$

stating that when the connection is established, this leads to the state where the controller has sent the *client_hello* message. Contract B_2^s is mapped to query:

$$(C.CHSent \text{ and } Con.CHRecv) \; {-}{-}{>} \; Con.SHSent \tag{8}$$

stating that the server will send the *hello* message after receiving the *hello* message from the controller. Both these queries are satisfied, as well as all other contract queries for this view. Notice the saturated temporal contract *composition* where the guarantee of contract B_2^c is the assumption of contract B_2^s:

$$G_{B_2^c \otimes B_2^s} = ...G_{B_2^c} \wedge G_{B_2^s}...,A_{B_2^c \otimes B_2^s} = ...(G_{B_2^c} \rightsquigarrow A_{B_2^s}) \wedge (G_{B_2^s} \rightsquigarrow A_{B_3^c})... \tag{9}$$

Thus, contract composition compatibility and consistency verification requires model-checking the satisfiability of $G_{B_2^c \otimes B_2^s}$ and $A_{B_2^c \otimes B_2^s}$ by the model where both SUT and environment corresponding view models are composed. Recall that contract assumption strengthens the left hand side of the *leads to*. This does not violate the contract semantics under given modelling assumption - ideal communication.

6.2 Fault-Tolerance View

The climate control system requirements also address scenarios of faulty communication between controller and server. The connection procedure specification as described in Sect. 2 refers to faults related to network link and data fields. Like in behavioural view, the contracts for fault-tolerance view are extracted from requirements. The main difference is that server component's environment is set of controllers that communicate with server via non-ideal media, i.e., the effect of lossy links and data corruption

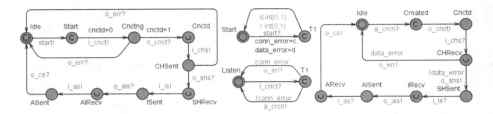

Fig. 4. The fault-tolerance view model of the climate control system.

should be explicitly reflected in the assumptions of the server contracts. Requirement R_1^f specifies that the controller must retry to connect in the event of disconnection. The event may occur due to network failure or transmission of invalid data. R_1^f in effect is the same as requirement R_1^b from the point of view of the controller, i.e., when the controller is disconnected it tries to connect. Since the contract B_1^c maps the reqirement R_1^b for controller and therefore R_1^f, the fault-tolerance view of the component remains unchanged. R_2^f is relevant for the server and augments the server behavioural view with information pertinent to fault-tolerance.

Fault-Tolerance View Model. The fault-tolerance view model is shown in Fig. 4. In addition to the behavioural view model there is an environment component (middle up) which affects, first, how the server (middle low) responds to the controller in case of connection error and, secondly, how the later stages of the connection proceed regarding data error. The controller (left) and connection (right) models are enriched with transitions to handle these fault cases.

Fault-Tolerance View Model Verification. Alike the behavioural view, the fault-tolerance view contract verification is exemplified next with one pair of corresponding contracts for the interacting components. Contract F_4^s is mapped to TCTL query:

$$(C.CHSent \text{ and } data\_error \text{ and } Con.CHRecv) \text{ --> } !cnctd \qquad (10)$$

stating that when the controller has sent the *hello* message and the server has received it with data error, this leads to the server disconnecting. Contract B_1^c is mapped to query:

$$!cnctd \text{ --> } C.Cnctng \qquad (11)$$

stating that when the controller is not connected, it tries to connect.

6.3   Timing View

The timing view of the climate control system addresses scenarios influenced by timing requirements. Timing requirements concern frequency at which the controller retries connections with the server, resetting the clock, and waiting times. R_1^t specifies that the

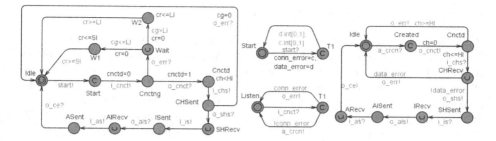

Fig. 5. The timing view model of the climate control system.

controller must retry to connect every I_s minutes for the first I_f minutes after disconnection or start up and R_2^t complements the requirement by stating that connections is retried every I_l minutes thereafter. R_1^t and R_2^t are mapped to contracts T_3^c and T_4^c respectively. The contracts extracted from the timing requirements in addition to those from other views, together provide a set of contracts for the system.

Timing View Model. The timing view model is shown in Fig. 5. Since timing is not orthogonal with other views it can be merged with both behavioural and fault-tolerance view in separate. Since fault-tolerance view is already built upon the behavioural view we superimpose the timing straight on the fault-tolerance view. The timing additions can be seen on the controller (left) and connection (right) model. The rest of the model remains the same. The connection might time out before the controller has sent the *client_hello* message. This is modelled with the upper transitions of both the controller and the connection automaton. In case connection error occurs initially, there is new dedicated part in the controller model involving locations "Wait", "W1" and "W2" handling explicitly the timing requirements for the connection retrials. The rest of the timing requirements are about the time bounded completion of the connection protocol modelled with the clock invariant and clock guards in the lower transitions of the controller and connection automata.

Timing View Model Verification. The timing view contract verification is exemplified next with one pair of related contracts for the interacting components. Controller contract T_4^c is mapped to query:

$$(Con.Cnctd \text{ and } C.Cnctd \text{ and } ch == 0) \rightarrow (C.CHSent \text{ and } ch < I_{TO}) \qquad (12)$$

stating that when the connection has been established this leads to the controller sending the *hello* message in less than I_{TO} seconds. Server contract T_3^s maps to query:

$$(C.CHSent \text{ and } !data\_error \text{ and } ch < I_{TO} \text{ and } Con.CHRecv) \rightarrow Con.SHSent \qquad (13)$$

stating that when the controller has sent the *hello* message without data error in less than I_{TO} seconds, this leads to the *hello* message sent by the server. All contracts for this view are satisfied with the UPPAAL verifier.

6.4 Consistency of Multi-view Contracts

While in general the multi-view contracts consistency has to be verified taking the conjunction of all view contracts, in the incremental approach it suffices verifying only the contract of the last increment that is the strongest, and that entails all the contracts of all preceding increments. Let us show this with an instance of a view contract for the server that was specified for the behavioural view, then was refined to the fault-tolerance view and finally supplemented with timing constraints. Behavioural view contract B_2^s is conjoined with fault-tolerance view contract F_3^s and with timing view contract T_3^s:

$$C.CHSent \ \land \ Con.CHRecv \rightsquigarrow Con.SHSent$$
$$\land \ C.CHSent \ \land \ Con.CHRecv \ \land \ \neg data\_error \rightsquigarrow Con.SHSent \qquad (14)$$
$$\land \ C.CHSent \ \land \ Con.CHRecv \ \land \neg data\_error \ \land \ ch < I_{TO} \rightsquigarrow Con.SHSent$$

The consistency of the rest of the multi-view contracts was verified in the same manner.

7 Comparison of Empirical and Multi-view Contract-Based Testing

In this section, the usability aspects of the test model development method proposed in Sect. 6 is compared with that of empirical approach (Sect. 5). The comparison is based on the experience gathered by practical application of both testing methods on the climate control system (cf. Sect. 2). The following criteria are used for comparison: *Test model construction effort*, *test model correctness verification effort*, *test deployment effort*, *test execution effort*, and *root cause analysis effort*. The comparison results presented in this section are also in line with the identified benefits of the CBD in general when coping with complex systems [7].

Although the empirical MBT approach proves to be useful (defects were found), incorporating large fragments of system behaviour in one monolithic test model increases the effort needed for model construction and validation. In terms of *Test model construction effort*, the CBD approach incorporates an intermediate structuring step to facilitate the creation of models by strictly following the view contracts that guide systematic step-wise model construction. Model development starts with a simple model that is enriched thereafter incrementally with design view specific information. Thus, the modelling is closely driven by the requirements via contracts unlike the text specification of the first approach. Although the system views presented in the case study are incremental, orthogonal views could also be incorporated in the process. e.g., *user authentication* view could be conjuncted at the beginning of each of the developed views before the controller-server connection protocol is started. The *Test model correctness verification effort* is reduced in the CBD approach because only limited amount of information is added in the view model and this requires verifying only the effects introduced by the model increments. Since newly introduced features include also existing ones, the correctness queries of new features are strengthened each time, meaning satisfiability of later query implies also satisfiability of earlier ones, as exemplified in Subsect. 6.4. In case the model includes orthogonal views, the correctness checking is done by applying the conjunction operator in a pairwise manner for scalability [2]. The CBD model verification effort was in average 83 and 98% more efficient compared to the empirical model regarding model-checking time and memory consumed respectively when checking queries corresponding to the main system requirements.

Test deployment effort considers primarily the development of test adapter to assist running the model againt the SUT. The simplicity of the model in the contract-based approach has benefits not only regarding test model development but also in reducing the size of test I/O-alphabet to be implemented in adapters. Our experience has shown that the incremental development of the adapter improves the overall testing efficiency by shortening the adapter development time almost exponentially in the size of symbolic test I/O-alphabet. The testing tool DTRON [3] used in this approach requires only minor changes in time scaling parameter settings to adjust the test execution to physical latency conditions. In terms of the *Test execution effort*, the traces generated from the Uppaal model properties show that the view model properties generate 23% shorter traces in average than the empirical model for the same set of requirements. This has promising implication on the regression test efficiency and testing effort for large set of tests. Due to the incremental nature of building test cases each view related test set incorporates also the tests of the earlier tested views. Beside the validity checking of view implementation correctness, this allows detecting if any of earlier tested features gets corrupted due to newly introduced view features (feature interaction testing). Such feature interaction bugs are usually most difficult to find.

Both testing approaches show that the climate control server fails to comply with requirements R1-R3 (stated in Sect. 2). The results show: (i) As opposed to R1, the server remains connected even if *client_hello* message is received later than I_{TO} seconds after TCP connection is established. (ii) The server fails to disconnect after receiving a *client_hello* message with an incorrect value in one of its field in contrary to R2. (iii) In a scenario where the *client_hello* is sent in parts, the server disconnects the controller before receiving the complete message as opposed to R3. Though the error detection capabilities of applied techniques have shown to be equivalent on the case study, the view contract-based test cases address the violated requirements more clearly. This enlightens the back tracing to what requirements and how they have been violated based on the views, and thus, improving the *Root cause analysis effort*. Error debugging in the code becomes even more straightforward when the code is based on the same design view contracts like the test model.

8   Related Work

The integration of assume/guarantee-based reasoning with automata-based formalisms has aimed at efficient verification through compositional reasoning. Compared to some influential works in the field [10, 11], we use an existing and widely accepted automata-based formalism for verification of real-time systems without technically extending it. We elaborate on how the contract meta-theory [7] corresponds to Uppaal TA via the mapping of system requirements to informal A/G contract patterns and then to TCTL properties that formalize these patterns as temporal saturated contracts. As a new contribution, we also elaborate on temporal multi-view contracts and show how our design multi-view approach covers the two main operators, composition and conjunction. Further, we adopt a more natural contract-based encoding of assumptions and guarantees, while the above works encode the assumptions and guarantees on the models directly.

Specifically, A/G-based testing of software was proposed in [8] where testing was performed on code generated from LTS models. The main difference compared to our work is that we use more expressive Uppaal TA formalism for representing SUT and verifying it against multi-view contracts. More recently, Boudhiba et al. applied MBT with contracts on program call level [9]. Instead, our approach can be applied at any system development phase provided the test interface is well-defined and accessible to test adapters. A MBT approach similar to ours is presented in [2]. The authors proposed the requirement interfaces formalism to model the different views of synchronous data-flow systems. Similar to our approach, they apply an incremental test generation procedure targeting a single system view at a time. Main differences compared to our approach are: 1) Direct encoding of contract assumptions and guarantees on the model, like in [10, 11]; 2) usage of different formalisms targeting different system domains while we apply only Uppaal TA relying on its relevant expressive power regarding CPS; and 3) the use of single modelling formalism instead of multiple domain specific languages allows us to limit to a single tool set, namely UPPAAL, that provides support to almost all required test development steps.

9   Conclusion

The work explores two approaches to MBT used in system verification. In the empirical approach the model is created directly from unstructured requirements specification. The other method exploits contracts as an intermediate step from requirements to models. The merits of the contract-based approach are evident as it makes the model creation and its verification process more structured and reduces the debugging effort due to the incremental nature and explicit correctness conditions expressed in design view contracts. The usability of second approach has been validated on an industrial climate control system testing case study where DTRON tool is used to develop the test adapters. The result of the case study shows the feasibility of this approach in practically all test development phases. One challenge however is the creation of contracts itself from the requirements. As a future work a solution can be explored to reduce the effort by using specification patterns [4] for formulating the contract from requirements.

Acknowledgement. This work has been supported by EXCITE (2014-2020.4.01.15-0018) grant.

References

1. Practitest: The 2022 state of testing report. https://www.practitest.com/state-of-testing/
2. Aichernig, B.K., Hörmaier, K., Lorber, F.L., Nickovic, D., Tiran, S.: Require, test, and trace it. Int. J. Softw. Tools Technol. Transf. **19**, 409–426 (2016)
3. Anier, A., Vain, J., Tsiopoulos, L.: DTRON: a tool for distributed model-based testing of time critical applications. Proc. Estonian Acad. Sci. **66**, 75–88 (2017)

4. Autili, M., Grunske, L., Lumpe, M., Pelliccione, P., Tang, A.: Aligning qualitative, real-time, and probabilistic property specification patterns using a structured English grammar. IEEE Tran. Softw. Eng. **41**(7), 620–638 (2015). https://doi.org/10.1109/TSE.2015.2398877
5. Baier, C., Katoen, J.P.: Principles of Model Checking. The MIT Press, Cambridge (2008)
6. Behrmann, G., David, A., Larsen, K.G.: A tutorial on Uppaal. In: Bernardo, M., Corradini, F. (eds.) SFM-RT 2004. LNCS, vol. 3185, pp. 200–236. Springer, Heidelberg (2004). https://doi.org/10.1007/978-3-540-30080-9_7
7. Benveniste, A., et al.: Contracts for Systems Design: Theory. Research Report RR-8759, Inria Rennes Bretagne Atlantique. INRIA, July 2015. https://hal.inria.fr/hal-01178467
8. Blundell, C., Giannakopoulou, D., Pǎsǎreanu, C.: Assume-guarantee testing. In: Proceedings of the 2005 Conference on Specification and Verification of Component-Based Systems, pp. 1–5. SAVCBS 2005, Association for Computing Machinery, New York, NY, USA (2005). https://doi.org/10.1145/1123058.1123060
9. Boudhiba, I., Gaston, C., Le Gall, P., Prevosto, V.: Model-based testing from input output symbolic transition systems enriched by program calls and contracts. In: El-Fakih, K., Barlas, G., Yevtushenko, N. (eds.) ICTSS 2015. LNCS, vol. 9447, pp. 35–51. Springer, Cham (2015). https://doi.org/10.1007/978-3-319-25945-1_3
10. David, A., Larsen, K.G., Legay, A., Nyman, U., Wąsowski, A.: ECDAR: an environment for compositional design and analysis of real time systems. In: Bouajjani, A., Chin, W.-N. (eds.) ATVA 2010. LNCS, vol. 6252, pp. 365–370. Springer, Heidelberg (2010). https://doi.org/10.1007/978-3-642-15643-4_29
11. David, A., Larsen, K.G., Nyman, U., Legay, A., Wasowski, A.: Timed i/o automata: a complete specification theory for real-time systems. In: Proceedings of the 13th ACM International Conference on Hybrid Systems: Computation and Control, pp. 91–100. HSCC 2010, Association for Computing Machinery, New York, NY, USA (2010). https://doi.org/10.1145/1755952.1755967
12. Dias-Neto, A.C., Matalonga, S., Solari, M., Robiolo, G., Travassos, G.H.: Toward the characterization of software testing practices in South America: looking at Brazil and Uruguay. Softw. Qual. J. **25**(4), 1145–1183 (2016). https://doi.org/10.1007/s11219-016-9329-3
13. Larsen, K.G., Mikucionis, M., Nielsen, B.: Online testing of real-time systems using Uppaal. In: Grabowski, J., Nielsen, B. (eds.) FATES 2004. LNCS, vol. 3395, pp. 79–94. Springer, Heidelberg (2005). https://doi.org/10.1007/978-3-540-31848-4_6
14. Törngren, M., Sellgren, U.: Complexity challenges in development of cyber-physical systems. In: Lohstroh, M., Derler, P., Sirjani, M. (eds.) Principles of Modeling. LNCS, vol. 10760, pp. 478–503. Springer, Cham (2018). https://doi.org/10.1007/978-3-319-95246-8_27
15. Utting, M., Pretschner, A., Legeard, B.: A taxonomy of model-based testing approaches. Softw. Test. Verif. Reliabil. **22**(5), 297–312. https://doi.org/10.1002/stvr.456

Features of Quantified Products
and Their Design Implications

Kurt Sandkuhl[1,2]([⊠]) (iD)

[1] Institute of Computer Science, University of Rostock, Rostock, Germany
kurt.sandkuhl@uni-rostock.de
[2] Jönköping University, Jönköping, Sweden

Abstract. Digital transformation of industrial areas resulted in new products and services that build upon innovative technologies and enable new kinds of business models. Quantified products (QP) are such a kind of new product category that exploits data of on-board sensors. A quantified product is a product whose instances collect data about themselves that can be measured, or, by design, leave traces of data. This paper aims at contributing to a better understanding what design dependencies exist between product, service and ecosystem. For this purpose, we combine the analysis of features of QP potentially affecting design with an analysis of QP case studies for validating the suitability and pertinence of the features. Main contributions of this paper are (1) two case studies showing QP development, (2) a set of features of QPs derived from the cases and (3) a feature model showing design dependencies of these feature.

Keywords: Quantified products · Feature modelling · Design implications · Design dependencies

1 Introduction

Digital transformation of many industrial areas has resulted in new products and services that build upon innovative technologies, as for example Internet-of-Things (IoT), machine learning (ML) and high-speed near real-time data transfer on mobile networks (5G). These new products/services enable new kinds of business models [1] by exploiting data from product operations and data-driven services. In this context, the specific focus of this paper is on innovations related to physical products as data sources and basis of new services. Many physical products, like manufacturing machinery, vehicles or household devices, are equipped with control units, sensors and actuators that capture and provide access to relevant data.

In previous work, we proposed the concept of quantified products as sub-category of smart connected products (see Sect. 3). A quantified product is a product whose instances collect data about themselves that can be measured, or, by design, leave traces of data (cf. Sect. 3.1). One example for a quantified product are quantified vehicles [2].

Quantified product design, development and operation has been found to include three different aspects: physical product, data-driven services and ecosystems management. This paper aims at contributing to a better understanding what design dependencies

M. Ivanovic et al. (Eds.): Baltic DB&IS 2022, CCIS 1598, pp. 152–163, 2022.
https://doi.org/10.1007/978-3-031-09850-5_11

exist between product, service and ecosystem. The research question for this paper is: *In the context of QP development, what are relevant features to consider during design and what dependencies between these features must be taken into account?*

For this purpose, we combine the analysis of features of QP potentially affecting design with an analysis of QP case studies for validating the suitability and pertinence of the features. Main contributions of this paper are (1) two case studies showing QP development, (2) a set of features of QPs derived from the cases and (3) a feature model showing design dependencies of these feature.

Section 2 describes our research approach. Section 3 covers the theoretical background and related work. Section 4 presents the first industrial case study to motivate our work and to identify features affecting QP design. The validation of the features is subject of Sect. 5 and based on the second industrial case. This section also discusses design implications. Section 6 summarizes the findings.

2 Research Method

This paper is part of a research project aiming at technological and methodical support for quantified product design and development. It follows the paradigm of design science research [3] and concerns the requirements analysis and first steps towards designing the envisioned artefact, a methodology integrating the lifecycles of physical product, data-driven services and ecosystems services. This paper builds on previous research on QP lifecycle management [4] and addresses the research question presented in the introduction.

The research approach used is a combination of descriptive case study and conceptual modelling. The motivation for using case studies as empirical basis is the lack of scientific work on quantified products. In previous work [4], we conducted a systematic literature analysis with the conclusion that hardly any work consists in the field. Literature search in Scopus, IEEE Xplore, AISeL and ACM DL when preparing this paper confirmed this finding. Thus, we need to explore the nature and phenomenon of QP in real-world environments designing and developing QP, which is possible in case studies.

Based on the research question, we identified industrial case studies suitable to shed light on QP development. The analysis of the first case study follows the intention to provide a hypothesis of features relevant for design. A second case study is used to validate the identified features and lead to a second version of the set of features. By modelling the identified features with the technique of feature modelling, we contribute to structuring them and finding dependencies. According to [5] the case studies in this paper are exploratory, as they are used to explore development approaches and design features of QP.

3 Background and Previous Work

3.1 Quantified Products (QP)

Work on QP is related to various research streams of the past years with a focus on turning data into value. Service sectors start to "collect data on everything" [6] to achieve automation and increased efficiency. Smart connected products (SCP) are not only a category of IoT products but also represent a business model category characterized by IT- and data-based services [7]. In individual lifestyle the term of Quantified Self [8] is used when people collect physical and biometric data to "quantify" their life. The term quantified vehicle adapts this idea for the automotive industry as a complete ecosystem for using data for data-driven services [9].

Products are often equipped with sensors, e.g., for capturing geographic positions, energy consumption, usage profiles or other information pertinent to operation and maintenance of the product. Such products also collect additional data, which could be of interest for third parties. For instance, suppliers want to know how their components are used in the field [10]. In case of cars, insurance companies want to know how the insured person drives [11] and traffic planners how roads are used by vehicles [12].

For the definition of the term quantified product, we differentiate between product data traditionally captured during product lifecycle management (PLM) and data collected by manufactured individual copies of a product, which we refer to as product instances: "A Quantified Product is a product whose instances collect data about themselves that can be measured, or, by design, leave traces of data, including operational, physical, behavioural, or environmental information for the purpose of data analysis and (optional) data sharing and services." [4]

Often enterprises quantify the products by (a) collecting data not only from a single device but the entire fleet of products operating in the field, (b) using this data for monitoring and real-time control in a management system for the fleet, and (c) offering aggregated data on marketplaces.

Implementation of QP is accompanied by substantial changes in the companies' PLM of QP, as different kinds of products and their lifecycles have to be coordinated:

- the actual physical product,
- services built upon data from connected physical products and services exploiting data from a complete fleet of products,
- data-driven services using the fleet data for ecosystem services, possibly in combination with other services.

Coordination of these different lifecycles requires both organizational, structural, and technical solutions.

3.2 Variability Modelling and Feature Models

Variability modelling has its origin in software product line research and generative programming [19]. Complex software systems offer a rich set of functions and features to their users, but cause challenge to their developers: how to provide high flexibility with many possible variants for different application contexts and at the same time restrict the systems' complexity in order to achieve maintainability? Variability modelling offers a contribution to control the variety of the variants of systems by capturing and visualizing commonalities and dependencies between features and between the components providing feature implementations. Since more than 20 years, variability modelling is frequently used in the area of complex software systems and technical systems. Among the variability modelling approaches, feature models are considered as in particular relevant for QPs.

A feature is a "distinctive and user-visible aspect, quality, or characteristic of a software system or systems" [13]. The purpose of a feature model is to capture, structure and visualize the commonality and variability of a domain or a set of products. Commonalities are the properties of products shared among all the products in a set, placing the products in the same category or family. Variability are the elements of the products that differentiate and show the configuration options, choices and variation points that are possible between variants of the product, aimed to satisfy customer needs and requirements. The variability and commonality are modelled as features and organized into a hierarchy of features and sub-features, sometimes called feature tree, in the feature model. The hierarchy and other properties of the feature model are visualized in a feature diagram. Feature diagrams express the relation between features with the relation types mandatory, optional, alternative, required and mutually-exclusive.

Different methodical approaches in the field and the exact syntax of feature diagrams were analysed and compared in [14] and an overview to methods for feature model development is provided in [21]. Both papers show a focus on notations and approaches specialized for certain application fields, i.e., there is no generally accepted feature model development method.

3.3 Data-Driven Services and Ecosystems

In general, the utilization of data and data analysis is expected to offer new ways for growth and competitive advantage in many industrial and service sectors [15]. The increasing data availability opens opportunities for the creation of entirely new services [16], data-driven business models and possibilities of data analytics [17]. In the context of QPs, data-driven services exploit sensor and operational data provided by instances of products or entire product fleets, i.e., the data transmitted to a data-driven service, for example via an IoT platform. This data has its own value on data marketplaces and data-focused business models. Data marketplaces are expected to transform the data economy by providing an infrastructure for trading data and data-related services" [18].

A digital ecosystem "is an interdependent group of enterprises, people and/or things that share standardized digital platforms for a mutually beneficial purpose" [20]. Thus, data-driven service ecosystems are shaped by organizations involved in service delivery and their mutual relationships. Such ecosystems use sensor and context data from QPs in an integrated manner for enabling new business models.

4   Case Study A

During the last five years, we actively participated in several industrial projects that aimed at introducing new kinds of products and services in manufacturing enterprises. Several of these projects resulted in solutions that can be regarded as QPs, including SCP and data-driven services. One of these cases is described in this section (case study A); another case in Sect. 5 (case study B). In both case studies, we collected documents, field notes taken during work with the companies, minutes of meetings and interviews with company representatives, models of processes, information structures and business models, and other relevant information.

4.1 Case Study Description

Case A originates from a research project conducted together with a leading producer of outdoor and garden products for the end-consumer and business market (lawn mowers, chainsaws, robotic lawn mowers, garden tractors, trimmers, watering systems). The research project was positioned in the business line "outdoor products" and focused the shift from conventional products (without connectivity to the Internet) to networked ones (QPs). The aim of the business line was to create an ecosystem of products and services that is based on a joint application architecture and service infrastructure. The ecosystem is expected to support different profit centres within the business line with their services and products, as well as services from external partners.

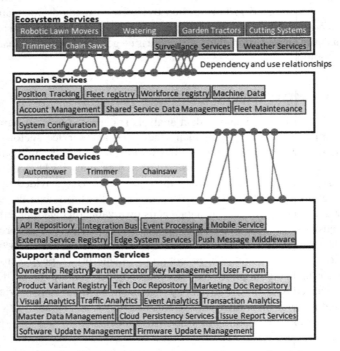

Fig. 1. Simplified IT and service architecture of case A.

Most products have built-in electronics or embedded systems and networking and communication capabilities based on a common services architecture and infrastructure (see Fig. 1). The built-in electronics and connected infrastructure services are usually used for controlling mechatronic components and collecting data when the product is in use. This includes, e.g., performance parameters, status information of product components, information from the product's application environment or service information.

The integration into the infrastructure is used for communicating usage statistics, license information, information about maintenance needs or location data to product owner and/or vendor's back-office.

Table 1. *Data* collected by the QP "automower"

Attribute	Accuracy/Resolution	Description
GPS coordinate	16 ft accuracy, recorded every minute	Position of the mower robot
Start and end of charging	Day, hour, minute, seconds	Charging duration
Start and end of operation	Day, hour, minute, seconds	Operation time
Battery level	Recorded every 10 s	Battery level development
Speed of the mower	In km/h, recorded every 10 s	Speed differs based on quality requirements of the cutting
Rotation speed of cutting device	Rotations/second with same energy supply	Basis for calculation resistance of grass type
Vertical and horizontal position	recorded every 10 s	Basis for calculation of "pollution" of grass area

One of the QPs in the business line is a robotic lawn mower called "automower". The automower of an end-consumer provides operations data to a base station (see Table 1 for examples) and receives software updates or schedules from it. The base station is cloud-based through the customer's Internet. Business customers, such as housing companies or garden service providers, often operate a fleet of robotic mowers, sometimes with additional products, such as trimmers or garden tractors. In this case, fleet management functionality offers that even workers can be equipped with devices capturing their working hours and routes. The case company offers the required fleet management services and data collection for their business customers through a cloud-based platform, e.g. operating, supervising and planning garden and park maintenance.

Since many of the products require similar networking and communication functionality, the process of QP development included the design and implementation of reusable services and infrastructure components of both, the "quantified" product and the (fleet management) back-office. One of the development steps was an alignment between different product lines in terms of networking functionality, communication, and service provision. This resulted in the service architecture and infrastructure depicted in Fig. 1. Another step consisted of the definition of domain services and integration services for preparing an ecosystem architecture. Integration services offer a middleware for fleets of devices in the field with event processing, push messages, API to common services and other integration possibilities. Based on the integration services, specific services for domains, such as fleet management or workforce management, can be implemented. Ecosystem services provide functionality to other services in the ecosystem based on the domain and common services.

As for the data-driven services, there are device-level services (e.g. theft protection of automower for end consumer) and fleet-level services (e.g. fleet management for housing companies), and additional shared services for other divisions of the enterprise. This creates an enterprise-internal ecosystem approach.

4.2 Feature Identification

The process of developing a feature model has to start by exactly defining the application field or system under consideration (scoping). In case A we started to analyse the case material guided by the question what features, i.e., distinctive user-visible characteristics (see Sect. 3.2), a quantified product needs to have. "Users" in case A would be the internal product managers for the QP in the case company and external customers supposed to use the QP, data from the QP or services built upon these data.

The next step was the identification of the actual features that characterize the defined scope, which in our case are the features of the QPs visible in case A. All features have to be made explicit and were noted down with a short description documenting there meaning. Before looking at dependencies of features, for each feature we captured the components used to implement the features. These implementations for each feature helped to identify dependencies and additional characteristics for the particular feature.

In case A, we have to distinguish between use of data collected during operation of individual product instances (device-level services), and also on aggregation level across all instances (fleet-level services). Device-level services target the operators or owners of the device, whereas fleet-level services in addition also include data-driven services for third parties that often abstracted from device-level and only offer aggregations, combination or selection of the data. On device-level, information can be captured regarding the actual device (like battery level, energy consumption of certain components, mowing speed) and regarding the "context" of the device (like temperature, weather conditions or the terrain). The context information also is of interest on fleet level and some third-party services.

In the final step, we documented the dependencies between features visible in the previous step and the inter-relations between components and implementations implicated by the features. Table 2 summarizes the identified features on device-level, fleet-level and data-driven service level.

Table 2. Identified *Features of QP*

Device-level	Fleet-level	Service-level
Access to real-time information of individual device	Access to real-time information aggregated for fleet	Definition of services tailored to application domain
Recording of information during operations	Recording of fleet information during operations	Fleet and device-level visualization of recorded data
Configure what information to be captured (real-time or recorded)	Configure fleet information to be captured (real-time or recorded)	Fleet and device-level visualization of real-time data

(continued)

Table 2. (*continued*)

Device-level	Fleet-level	Service-level
Modify sensors on device	Access to context information aggregated for fleet	Fleet and device-level visualization of context data
Access to context information	Recording of context information	
Recording of context information		

5 Case Study B

The objective of this section is to validate the features of QP identified in case study A, modify them if necessary and investigate their implications for QP design. Section 5.1 introduces the case study B as such, Sect. 5.2 addresses validation of the features and Sect. 5.3 the implications for design.

5.1 Case Study Description

The second QP case study is an industrial case from air conditioning and cleanroom technologies (ACT). The case study company, a medium-sized enterprise from Northern Germany, is designing, developing, installing and operating large ACT facilities. For energy optimization purposes and as a basis for predictive maintenance, additional sensors and control systems have to be integrated into the ACT facilities and connected to a network. This results in an IoT solution that also offers the opportunity of new business services. Complexity and size of such facilities for industrial and public buildings are growing more and more. Inspections of air handling units in operation often reveal significant deviations from the planed energy consumption in the design phase. Furthermore, in the course of automation, the amount of data is increasing strongly. The direct and indirect processes of air handling units can no longer be operated in an energy-efficient or optimal way without intelligent data processing. The need for solutions with self-optimization based on machine learning and intelligent control of the facilities is therefore high.

The envisioned IoT solution in case study B is supposed to implement diagnosis support of possible optimizations in air handling units as well as for the operational processes of the case study company. This requires processing of large amounts of time-series data from different sources in the facility. The IoT solution has to be integrated into the case company's operational processes to support new types of services.

In an ACT facility, different technical devices are combined that are integrated into a control flow and together provide the desired AC functionality. Examples for such devices are ventilators, recuperators, humidifiers, heating or cooling units, and air filters. Some of the devices are by design equipped with sensors for capturing energy consumption, temperature, revolution speed or other relevant parameters; other devices have to be equipped with additional sensors during the development of the IoT solution.

These sensors provide information that is evaluated on facility-level to determine energy consumption, anomalies or error situations.

ACT facilities can be grouped according to their functionality, which often corresponds to the type of buildings they were designed for and are installed in. The ACT groups relevant for the case study company are hospitals, manufacturing buildings, shopping centres and educational organizations. For all ACT facilities within a group, evaluation of the collected facility-level information is relevant during planning and operations, for example for dimension planning, i.e., deciding on the required performance class.

5.2 Feature Identification

The identification of features for case study B followed the same steps as for case A (Sect. 4.2). Comparing case A and B, the first observation is that the features in case B also can be sorted into levels, but the levels have to be named differently if we follow the terminology used by the companies in their different application domains: the device-level in case A corresponds to the facility-level in case B. Furthermore, the fleet-level in case A corresponds to the group-level in case B. To normalize the terminology in an application-independent way, we propose to use "product instance level" (instead of device or facility) and "product class level" (instead of fleet or group).

On product instance level all features from case study A also are relevant for case study B, which is illustrated in Table 3.

Table 3. Product instance-level feature comparison

Feature	Application in case A	Application in Case B
Access to real-time information of individual device	GPS position of automower for anti-theft protection	Energy consumption of ventilation for anomaly detection
Recording of information during operations	Energy consumption and other values for predictive maintenance	Air flow, temperatures and other values for predictive maintenance
Configure what information to be captured (real-time or recorded)	Adapt to differences of customer types	Adapt to differences of ACT type
Modify sensors on device	Finer granularity for professional product group	Lower resolution for ACT with modern control units
Access to context information	Temperature, weather, terrain	Outdoor temperature
Recording of context information	Analysis of energy consumption of ACT in different terrains	Analysis of energy consumption of ACT in outdoor temperature conditions

5.3   Implications of Features on QP Design

The implementation of a feature requires certain technical functionality on product instance or product class level. On product instance level, this functionality has to be taken into account during the design phase of the physical product development, as it can affect the weight, material, size or components to be used in the product. In this paper, we will focus on the components only, not on all design parameters.

There usually is no one to one match between a feature and the component implementing it as one feature might require several technical functionalities implemented by different components and components also depend on each other. For the two case studies, we started from the common set of features and analysed how these features were technically implemented in the cases. We found components in both cases with similar or even identical functionality, but completely different implementation. An example is the communication unit allowing for transmitting data from product instances to the cloud. In case study A there is a WIFI module connecting to the base station and in case study B there is a LoRaWAN module for connecting the ACT facility with the cloud. As the term "component" usually is associated with a concrete implementation, we use the term "building block" instead. Building blocks are providing a defined functionality, possibly in different variants, contributing to implement features.

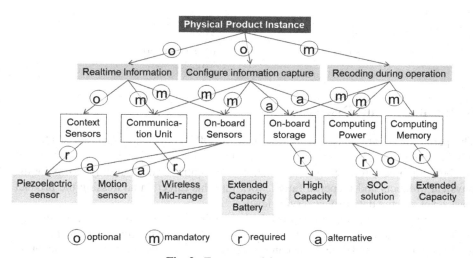

Fig. 2. Feature model excerpt

Our analysis resulted in a feature model identifying the relationship between features (blue boxes) and building blocks (white boxes) and the dependencies between building blocks (see Fig. 2). And it also resulted in a list of building blocks common for both cases with their required variants (see Table 4).

Table 4. Building blocks for implementing QP features

No	Building block	Possible variants
1	On-board sensors	Fixed set; fixed + configurable set; dynamic set
2	Context sensors	Depending on required functionality. Example: temperature, position, other connected devices
3	Communication unit	Cable-based interface; wireless, low range; wireless, high range
4	On-board sensor integration approach	Wireless; internal bus; direct (system on chip)
5	On-board sensor information computing	Adaptive; fixed; none
6	Battery constraints	High capacity; extended capacity; regular capacity
7	Reliability of sensors	High (double sensors); normal
8	On-board computing memory	(defined in storage size)
9	On-board storage capacity	(defined in storage size)
10	Heartbeat required	Yes/no
11	Firmware update	Yes/no
12	On-board computing power	(defined in performance metrics´, e.g. MIPS)

6 Summary and Discussion

The paper aimed at contributing to the field of QP by analysing features of QP, the implications of these features for product design and the dependencies between features and building blocks for their implementation. We identified such building blocks for the physical products and prepared future work into this direction addressing the product class level and the data-driven service level.

The biggest limitation of our work is the empirical basis in only two case studies. Although the case studies were carefully selected to represent the construct under investigation, QP features and design, we cannot assume completeness or general applicability of our work. Future research will have to address this shortcoming by conducting more case study and empirical research.

References

1. Blixt Hansen, E., Bøgh, S.: Artificial intelligence and internet of things in small and medium-sized. J. Manuf. Syst. **58**, 362–372 (2021)
2. Kaiser, C., Stocker, A., Viscusi, G., Fellmann, M., Richter, A.: Conceptualizing value creation in data-driven services: the case of vehicle data. Int. J. Inf. Manag. **59** (2021). https://doi.org/10.1016/j.ijinfo-mgt.2021.102335

3. Bichler, M.: Design science in information systems research. Wirtschaftsinformatik **48**(2), 133–135 (2006). https://doi.org/10.1007/s11576-006-0028-8
4. Sandkuhl, K., Shilov, N., Seigerroth, U., Smirnov, A.: Towards the quantified product – product lifecycle support by multi-aspect ontologies. In: IFAC 14th Intelligent Manufacturing Systems (IMS) Conference. Tel Aviv, March 2022 (2022). Accepted for publication in the proceedings
5. Yin, R.K.: The abridged version of case study research. Handb. Appl. Soc. Res. Methods **2**, 229–259 (1998)
6. Mayer-Schönberger, V., Cukier, K.: Big Data: A Revolution That Will Transform How We Live, Work, and Think. Houghton Mifflin Harcourt, Boston (2013). ISBN: 0544002695 9780544002692
7. Porter, M., Heppelmann, J.: How smart, connected products are transforming competition". Harv. Bus. Rev. **92**(11), 64–88 (2014)
8. Swan, M.: The quantified self: fundamental disruption in big data science and biological discovery. Big Data. **1**(2), 85–99 (2013)
9. Kaiser, C.: Quantified vehicles: data, services, ecosystems. Ph.D. dissertation. Rostock University (2021)
10. Farahani, P., Meier, C., Wilke, J.: Digital supply chain management agenda for the automotive supplier industry. In: Oswald, G., Kleinemeier, M. (eds.) Shaping the Digital Enterprise, pp. 157–172. Springer, Cham (2017). https://doi.org/10.1007/978-3-319-40967-2_8
11. Tselentis, D.I., Yannis, G., Vlahogianni, E.I.: Innovative insurance schemes: pay as/how you drive. Transp. Res. Procedia **14**, 362–371 (2016)
12. Kong, X., Song, X., Xia, F., Guo, H., Wang, J., Tolba, A.: LoTAD: long-term traffic anomaly detection based on crowdsourced bus trajectory data. World Wide Web **21**(3), 825–847 (2018)
13. Kang, K.C., Cohen, S.G., Hess, J.A., Novak, W.E., Peterson, A.S.: Feature-oriented domain analysis (FODA) feasibility study (No. CMU/SEI-90-TR-21). Carnegie-Mellon University Pittsburgh, Software Engineering Institute (1990)
14. Thörn, C., Sandkuhl, K.: Feature modeling: managing variability in complex systems. In: Tolk, A., Jain, L.C. (eds.) Complex Systems in Knowledge-Based Environments. Theory, Models And Applications, vol. 168, pp 129–162. Springer, Berlin (2009). https://doi.org/10.1007/978-3-540-88075-2_6
15. Davenport, T., Harris, J.: Competing on Analytics: Updated, with a New Introduction: The New Science of Winning. Harvard Business Press, Boston (2017)
16. Manyika, J., et al.: Big data: the next frontier for innovation, competition (Vol. 5, No. 6). and productivity. Technical report, McKinsey Global Institute (2011)
17. Hartmann, P.M., Zaki, M., Feldmann, N., Neely, A.: Capturing value from big data – a taxonomy of data-driven business models used by start-up firms. Int. J. Oper. Prod. Manag. **36**(10), 1382–1406 (2016). https://doi.org/10.1108/IJOPM-02-2014-0098
18. Spiekermann, M.: Data marketplaces: trends and monetisation of data goods. Intereconomics **54**(4), 208–216 (2019). https://doi.org/10.1007/s10272-019-0826-z
19. Czarnecki, K., Eisenecker, U.: Generative Programming. Addison-Wesley, Reading (2000)
20. Gartner Group: Seize the Digital Ecosystem Opportunity. Insights From the 2017 CIO Agenda Report (2017). https://www.gartner.com/imagesrv/cio/pdf/Gartner_CIO_Agenda_2017.pdf. Accessed 7 May 2022
21. Li, L., et al.: A survey of feature modeling methods: historical evolution and new development. Robot. Comput. Integr. Manuf. **61**, 101851 (2020)

Artificial Agents and Smart Systems for Digital Business

Retail Self-checkout Image Classification Performance: Similar Class Grouping or Individual Class Classification Approach

Bernardas Ciapas$^{(\boxtimes)}$ and Povilas Treigys

Institute of Data Science and Digital Technologies, Vilnius University,
Akademijos str. 4, 08663 Vilnius, Lithuania
{bernardas.ciapas,povilas.treigys}@mif.vu.lt
http://www.mii.lt

Abstract. Top-end image classifiers cannot predict with sufficient accuracy in some domains due to variety of reasons: too many classes, unevenly distributed classes, frequently changing classes, too few training samples. On the other hand, predicting a cluster of a few similar classes is often acceptable in applications, such as retail self-checkout picklist assistant or entire species kingdom classification in random environments such as Google Lens.

This article investigates strategies for predicting clusters of similar classes. The main research topic is to compare classification-into-clusters metrics of individual class classifier vs. classifiers trained on clustered classes.

Public datasets representative of food retail store self-checkout area do not exist to the best of authors' knowledge; performance of well known computer vision algorithms on self-checkout images in unknown. This study attempts to fill the gap: it was performed on self-collected image set of barcodeless products from a retail store.

This article compares different ways to measure image class similarity, which drives the order of grouping classes into clusters. Authors measure class similarity using Self Organizing Maps (SOM) cluster purity, distance between samples embeddings of a classifier neural network, error contribution in a confusion matrix. Authors compare classifiers trained on individual-class-labelled data and cluster-labelled data. All the comparisons measure metrics (accuracy, f-score) of classifying into clusters.

The main finding of this article is that having determined clusters of similar classes, it is not worthy training on cluster-labelled data. Instead, classifiers trained on individual classes perform better when classifying into clusters-of-similar-classes.

Keywords: Retail products image similarity · Retail products class clustering · Retail products classification performance · Grouping accuracy impact

© The Author(s), under exclusive license to Springer Nature Switzerland AG 2022
M. Ivanovic et al. (Eds.): Baltic DB&IS 2022, CCIS 1598, pp. 167–182, 2022.
https://doi.org/10.1007/978-3-031-09850-5_12

1   Introduction

Visually similar classes present a challenge and an opportunity in computer vision tasks. The classes being similar usually results in more errors between these classes in a confusion matrix of a multi-class classifier that negatively affects the model accuracy. In some domains, where class similarity is high and/or data for training is limited, predicting a Top 1 class is unpractical due to lower boundary on accuracy drawn by applications.

Some applications do not always require the exact class to be recognized as a top 1, but often narrowing down the list of possible classes to a few similar ones is good enough. For example, in retail self-checkouts a picklist assistant can narrow down a list of products to choose from to a few similar ones. This is even desirable by retailers provided the accuracy of several presented products to choose from exceeds the accuracy of showing the top 1 product.

Often taxonomy of classes is unknown, or class similarity has little correlation with class proximity in taxonomic hierarchy. For example, among retail self-checkout products, red apples are more similar to tomatoes than red apples are to green apples, even though red apples and green apples might be in the same product category. Different candy sorts differ among themselves as much as they differ from other product categories: candies similarity to other products is mostly determined by the wrapping paper.

When classification of individual classes in unpractical, one must find a way to find class "clusters" - groups of classes such that classes within clusters are more similar than classes in different clusters. Resulting class clusters become labels for classifying images into these clusters. The class assignment to clusters must be done in a way to maximize accuracy of image classification into these "class clusters".

The goal of this research is investigate "class clustering" mechanism such that metrics of classification into these "class clusters" are maximized. This research investigates two aspects of classifying into "class clusters": first, determining class similarity; second, whether it is beneficial to train "cluster" classifiers.

Determining class similarity drives the order of class assignment into clusters. As opposed to classic clustering tasks that produce "data clusters", grouping classes into clusters cannot be achieved by using such clustering techniques as K-means or similar. Once classes are grouped into clusters, there is no metric (such as purity) to measure the quality of the clusters. Authors of this paper measure quality of data classification into these "class clusters".

The second aspect of this research is to investigate usefulness of training cluster classifiers - classifiers that predict class clusters instead of individual classes. Cluster classifiers are trained on data labelled with cluster ID rather than individual class. Authors compare performance of cluster classifiers with performance of individual class classifiers.

Drawing upper boundary on number of classes, merged into a cluster, depends on application. For example, a self-checkout picklist assistant may display 3–10 items for a customer to choose from. Authors of this research refrain from optimizing number of clusters.

The findings of this research applies to domains where 1) Top 1 image classification accuracy does not meet minimum requirements and 2) predicting a few similar classes is useful. One example is retail self-checkout picklist assistant for barcodeless products. Another example is species classification of entire animal or plant kingdom in random environments, such as Google Lens.

The following terms are used throughout the article:

- Class cluster - a group of individual classes (1 or more) that are deemed similar by one of the similarity techniques; a target category in a cluster classifier; each individual class is assigned to one and only one class cluster.
- Group of classes - used as a synonym for "class cluster".
- Individual Class - a target category in a classifier, representing a single product offered by a retailer. Examples: plum tomatoes, big oranges, persimmons, bananas. Used interchangeably with terms "Class", "Product".
- Metrics hypothetically merged - given an individual class classifier and similar class clusters, evaluate accuracy, f-score as if classification errors between classes in the same cluster were correct predictions.
- Metrics actually merged - given class clusters, and dataset labelled with individual class ID, change labels to cluster ID and train a classifier. Evaluate accuracy, f-score of classifier-into clusters.
- Taxonomic hierarchy - a pickist menu tree in retailers' self-checkout menu for selection of barcodeless products. Menu tree usually represents biological hierarchy. E.g. individual product category "plum tomatoes" is a leaf of category "all tomatoes", which is a branch of a higher-level category "Vegetables".
- Taxonomic Proximity - number of steps required to traverse between 2 products in Taxonomic hierarchy graph.

This article is structured as follows: Methods section describes techniques used to determine class similarity, details for constructing cluster classifiers; Results section shows statistics of inter-class similarity, compares the classification performance of various similarity techniques and individual vs. cluster classifiers; Conclusions section summarizes the main findings of this article.

2 Literature Review

Image similarity. Ranking technique in [14] learns image similarity by training a network on triplets that consist of 3 images: query, positive (similar) and negative (dissimilar). It relies on a self-created dataset, where similar candidates are google image search results. It then calculates image pairwise similarity using an extensive list of features among images of the same search query results, whereas similarity of images between different query results is set to 0. Using this method for our research presents an issue: since we are trying to learn inter-class similarity, it does not make sense to label pairwise similarity of images of different classes to be 0. Image similarity is drawn from image description in [12]. Such a description is not available in self-checkout image sets. Concept of similarity descriptor is presented in [15]. It uses pre-trained famous classifiers to draw feature maps of deep layers. The authors first train a neural network in order to choose the most proper deep layer to use as a feature set for image similarity. Then feature map histograms are used to measure image similarity by calculating Earth Mover's distance. We also use pre-trained classifier to draw feature maps for further comparison. Instead of building a complex network to choose the deep layer, we use the pre-last dense layer: the cited paper shows little difference in performance by using different layers of classifiers. Using convolutional layer intensity histograms for comparison helps to eliminate proximity dimension. We have the proximity element eliminated already by using pre-last fully connected layer.

Determining class similarity requires some generalization based on similarity of image samples. Average of all samples of a given class is used to calculate a "class vector" in [8]. Cosine similarity between class vectors is used as a measure for class similarity. They use linear discriminant analysis (LDA) to come up with a feature space for calculating class vectors. We realize that samples within the same class may be quite different (e.g. a "Snickers" candy has 2 views depending whether it's put front side up or down), therefore calculating a class average may not be representative of a class. Instead, we use sample-to-sample comparison. Like the authors of the cited paper, we use cosine similarity between embeddings. To come up with a lower-dimensional space of image embeddings, we use pre-last fully connected layer instead of LDA: we do not consider this a significant difference as long as class-specific information is preserved within embeddings. A technique proposed in [9] is for class-to-image comparison by training a Siamese-like network that takes extracted class and image features. Although a promising technique to identify if an image belongs to a specific class, it doesn't provide a way to compare how similar 2 classes are.

Image clustering techniques in [3,11,13] group images by exploiting some deep layer's embeddings. The resulting image clusters, however, do not map into groups of classes ("class clusters"): clusters usually contain images from multitude classes, and images of a class are dispersed over multitude clusters. This means that image clustering cannot be used directly to measure class proximity, but may be used as the first step following by some post processing to determine class similarity. Clustering categorical datasets usually use purity metric to determine quality of clusters; subsequently cluster purity improvement by merging classes can be measured to determine class proximity. Self Organizing Maps (SOM) [5] is a clustering technique that preserves inter-cluster proximity: data points that are close in high dimensional spaces are assigned to cluster centroids that are close in 2D space. Since our paper investigates inter-class proximity, we choose SOM to be one of the alternatives to group classes into clusters.

Hierarchical classification tasks present a challenge of picking the right classification strategy. Two ubiquitous strategies are local classifiers and multilabel classifiers. Local classifiers in [10] can be split into classifiers-per-level (LCL), classifiers-per-parent-node (LCPN) and binary classifiers-per-node (LCN). Each local classifier strategy requires multiple classifiers to be trained and used during inference - a potential obstacle for not so powerful devices, such as self-checkout computers. Our task can be thought of as a hierarchical classification task of 2 levels, where leaf nodes are groups of products; therefore, the task converges to a classic multi-class classification problem. Multilabel classification tasks such as [1, 6, 16] use multiple labels for every data point - one label per hierarchy level. Loss function of multilabel classifiers requires setting weights between levels. Our task can be thought of as a multilabel classification task of 3 levels - root level, class group level and individual product level - where weight of leaf (individual products) level is 0, and weight of class group level is 1.

Specifics in retail self-checkout images include unevenly distributed classes, many images containing poorly visible products due to semi-transparent bags, etc. It's discussed in detail in [2].

3   Methods

3.1   Experiment Design

The dataset used in this experiment (Fig. 1, *Individual Products Data Set*) is a collection of product images collected in a food retail store at self-checkout by a camera placed above the self-checkout scales area. Photos were taken by exploiting a self-checkout event of having the scales settled (usually, one product is placed on scales at that time). The set consists of 26,637 images that belong to 194 classes. The classes are products not labelled with barcodes sold in retail stores: various vegetables (tomatoes, carrots), fruits (bananas, oranges), candies. Distribution of images among classes is extremely uneven: the biggest classes contain 3282 (bananas), 2760 (carrots), 2181 (lemons) samples, whereas the smallest classes (rarely purchased candies) contain only 3 samples.

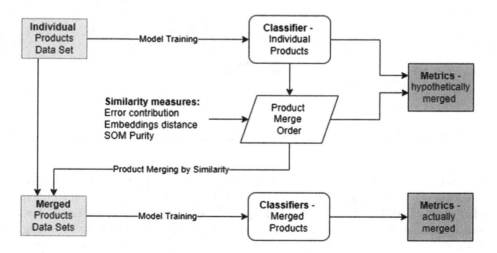

Fig. 1. Comparing Actual vs. Hypothetical metrics of merged similar classes

This research presumes existence of an individual class classifier trained on the dataset described above (Fig. 1, *Classifier - Individual Products*). Authors made a classifier using architecture described in Fig. 4 (detailed description in [2]) and got preliminary results: 83.0% accuracy and 55.4% f-score on the test set of the above dataset.

Inter-class similarity is determined using three different methods (details below in this chapter): "Error contribution", "Embeddings distance", and "SOM purity". Based on class similarity using each of the 3 methods, an agglomerative clustering scheme is produced - that is the order of how classes are merged into clusters by similarity (Fig. 1, *Product Merge Order*).

Datasets labelled with cluster ID (Fig. 1, *Merged Products Data Sets*) are produced from the initial dataset of individual products using agglomerative clustering schemes of class similarity. Although a separate cluster-labelled dataset can be produced for each number of clusters in the range [2;n-1] (n - number of individual classes), but the authors limit number of cluster-labelled datasets for performance reasons. The logic behind choosing the number of clusters to train classifiers on is discussed later in this section.

Using datasets labelled with cluster IDs, classifiers are trained (Fig. 1, *Classifiers - Merged Products*) that predict cluster of classes that the image belongs to. The architecture of all the classifiers is identical except for the last softmax layer (which differs in number of neurons only). The cluster classifier architecture is also identical to the individual product classifier.

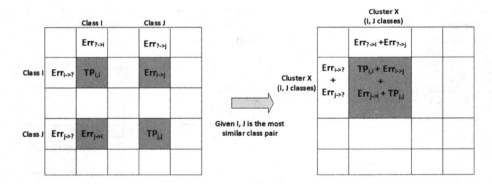

Fig. 2. Calculating confusion matrix based on hypothetical class merge

Metrics - hypothetically merged. Individual product classifier's Top 1 predictions are the basis for individual classifier's confusion matrix (Fig. 2, Left). Given class clusters (In Fig. 2, classes I, J belong to cluster X), confusion matrix of classification into clusters (Fig. 2, Right), row/column X is produced by summing rows/columns that represent classes [I, J]. Essentially, this treats Top 1 predictions of either class [I, J] of individual classifier as correct if true class is either of classes [I, J], and incorrect otherwise. Confusion matrix of classification into clusters (Fig. 2, Right) is the basis for other metrics of hypothetically merged classes: accuracy, f-score.

Metrics - actually merged. Given class clusters, images of classes that belong to the same cluster, are merged into the same folder before training (essentially labelling the dataset with cluster IDs instead of individual class ID). Cluster classifier is trained on dataset labelled with cluster ID. Confusion matrix of a cluster classifier in the basis for other metrics of actually merged classes: accuracy, f-score.

Authors compared metrics for classification-into-clusters of:

- A) individual products classifier (Fig. 1, *Metrics - hypothetically merged*);
- B) cluster classifiers (Fig. 1, *Metrics - actually merged*).

3.2   Inter-class Similarity

Class merge order is determined by class similarity: more similar classes are merged earlier. However, similarity between classes is subjective: measuring class similarity using different techniques yields different results. Authors chose 3 distinct ways to measure similarity between classes, later used to determine class merge order:

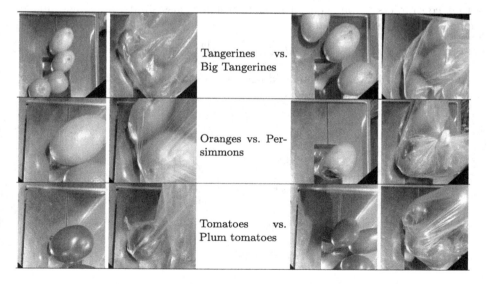

Fig. 3. Representative samples of the biggest error-contributing class-pairs in a confusion matrix

- Biggest error contributors;
- Self-Organizing Maps (SOM) purity improvement;
- Embeddings distance.

Biggest error contributors. Higher number of errors between two classes in a classifier's confusion matrix implies these classes are more similar. Authors used validation set's confusion matrix to determine inter-class similarity. Figure 3 shows representative samples of the Top-3 most similar class-pairs using "biggest error contributors" method. These class-pairs indeed seem similar to the human eye: different size tangerines, oranges and persimmons, different sorts of tomatoes.

Embeddings distance. Measuring image similarity by direct pixel comparison is unpractical due to high dimensionality of image data. In addition, even slight variation in object's position yields high difference between pixels in two images. Instead of direct pixel comparison, any higher-level, lower-dimensional features is preferable for comparing images. Authors used their own classifier - that yielded 83% accuracy - to extract higher-level features. The high accuracy of the classifier implies that enough information about classes is carried in all the layers of the classifier network.

Authors chose pre-last dense layer for comparing image similarity for several reasons. First, deeper layers in sequential networks carry higher-level feature information. Second, deeper dense layers usually have lower dimensionality, which is preferred for performance reasons. Third, last layer (softmax) carries individual class probabilities, which implies that using last layer embeddings of an ideal classifier would yield equal similarity between any pair of classes - that contradicts to our goal of measuring inter-class similarity. Single image embeddings vector took shape:

$$embeddings \in \mathbb{R}^{128}$$

Figure 4 depicts how image embeddings were extracted from the classifier for inter-class similarity measurement.

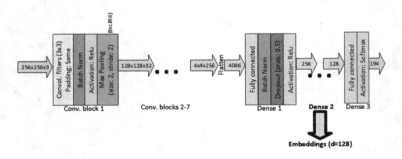

Fig. 4. Embeddings for inter-class distance measurement [2]

Authors used cosine distance to measure similarity between image embeddings. Using other distance types (Euclidean, Manhattan) showed very similar results, therefore authors settled for a single distance type (cosine) for all experiments.

$$Mat\_Emb\_Dist_{i,j} = \frac{1}{m_i * m_j} \sum_{k=1}^{m_i} \sum_{l=1}^{m_j} distCosine(E_k, E_l) \qquad (1)$$

where:

$Mat\_Emb\_Dist \in \mathbb{R}^{n*n}$

n – number of classes in the dataset

m_i – number of samples in the class i

$Mat\_Emb\_Dist_{i,j}$ – Mean distance between all samples in class i and class j

Finally, mean distances between all class pairs were calculated by averaging distance between all images in class A and all images in class B (where A≠B), as shown in Formula 1. This resulted in a half-matrix of mean distances among all classes. Figure 5 shows top 3 class pairs that have the lowest inter-class distance.

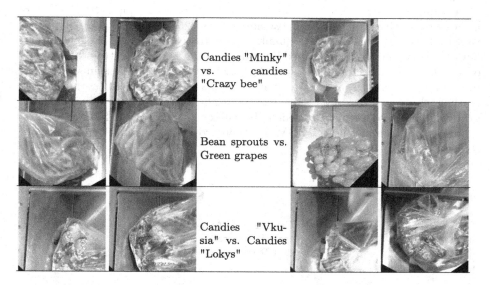

Fig. 5. Representative samples of smallest mean distance between image embeddings having class pairs

SOM purity improvement. SOM is a clustering technique that groups similar data points together; as opposed to other clustering techniques, SOM preserves an inter-cluster grid, where nearby cluster centroids imply more similar data points attached to them - an important factor in our investigation of class similarity. Ideal SOM trained on an image set of various classes should result in a) images of the same classes falling under the same cluster; b) images of different classes falling under different clusters, provided there are at least as many clusters as there are classes. Although training SOM on real data rarely results in such clusters, but images of similar classes tend to fall under the same clusters more frequently than images of dissimilar classes. Therefore, merging two similar classes should result in bigger cluster purity (Formula 2) improvement than merging two classes that are not similar.

$$Purity = \frac{1}{N} \sum_{i=1}^{k} max_j |c_i \cap t_j| \tag{2}$$

where:

N – number of samples in the dataset
k – number of SOM clusters
c_i – i-th cluster
t_j – classification which has the max count for cluster c_i formula defined in [7]

Training SOM on an image set requires a few hyper-parameters. First, input data should be decided on: like for most clustering techniques, direct clustering of image pixels of high dimnesionality ($d = 256 \times 256 \approx 64K$) is irrelevant performance-wise and data-quantity-wise. Instead of image pixel clustering, authors chose the classifier embeddings from Fig. 4 as input to train SOM. Second, SOM grid size should be selected. In order for different class images to fall under different cluster, at least as many clusters as there are classes must exist. Authors chose grid size of 15 × 15, making ~225 clusters (a little less if hexagon grid cells are used), which exceeded the number of classes (194). Top-3 pairs' representative samples using "SOM purity improvement" similarity measure are shown in Fig. 6.

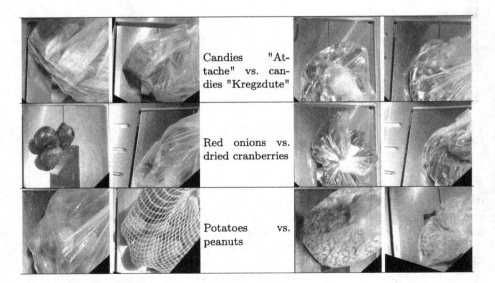

Fig. 6. Representative samples of the class-pairs that improve SOM purity the most if merged

3.3 Choosing Number of Clusters

Drawing upper bound on number of classes within a cluster usually depends on applications and is not part of this research. However, investigating performance of classifiers trained on "class clusters" requires choosing number of clusters. Although it is possible to train cluster classifiers on each number of merged classes in the range $[2; n - 1]$ (n = number of classes), but such a task requires enormous amount of resources. Since the goal was to investigate in what order merged classes yield the best classification results, it makes sense to choose number of clusters to be at the intersection points of important metrics using hypothetical classification results. Authors chose these metrics to be accuracy and f-score. It also makes sense to choose local maxima points of f-score - meaning that smaller number of classes from local maxima yields lower f-score, making the classifier of next-smaller number of classes inferior in terms of both f-score and number of classes.

All the class grouping experiments were followed by training cluster classifiers. Authors measured both accuracy and f-score (accuracy represents the real-world class disbalance in the self-checkout domain).

Authors used Nvidia GeForce GTX 1080 GPU and 64 GB RAM having computer for all the experiments. The deep learning frameworks were Keras 2.4.1-tf, CUDA 11.2. Authors trained all models for 100 epochs unless validation accuracy did not improve for the last 10 epochs. Adam [4] optimizer was used with learning rate $1e-3$.

4 Results

This section has two parts: first, the findings of using various techniques for class similarity are presented; second, classification-into-clusters is summarized for different techniques of similarity and for individual vs. cluster classifiers.

Table 1. Top 5 class pairs having most errors in a confusion matrix

Class A	Class B	Errors %
Tangerines	Big tangerines	6.5%
Oranges	Persimmons	5.1%
Tomatoes	Plum tomatoes	3.0%
Bananas	Apples golden	2.6%
Bananas	Lemons	2.5%

Most errors contributing class pairs are depicted in Table 1. The column "Errors %" represents false predictions both ways (Class A instead of class B and vice versa) as a percentage of total errors in a confusion matrix. Almost 20% of all errors are caused by 5 class-pairs - a significant percentage in a confusion matrix of size 194×194 (194 - class count in self-checkout dataset).

Table 2. Top 5 class pairs having the lowest inter-class mean distance between image embeddings

Class A	Class B	Normalized similarity
Candies "Minky"	Candies "Crazy bee"	8.3
Bean sprouts	Green grapes	6.8
Candies "Vkusia"	Candies "Lokys"	6.7
Candies "Murkiny"	Candies "Verze"	5.9
Candies "Murkiny"	Candies "Kregzdute"	5.7

Embeddings distance similarity technique is summarized in Table 2: it shows the top 5 class-pairs that have the lowest mean inter-class distance (i.e. highest inter-class similarity, where $similarity = \frac{1}{distance}$).

SOM purity improvement technique suggested the class pairs that improve cluster purity the most when merged. Original (before merging) SOM cluster structure is shown in Fig. 7. Circle sizes are proportional to the number of samples in those clusters. The biggest class of every cluster is shown in blue, whereas every color within a cluster represents a different class. Color angle is proportional to class' number of samples in a cluster. Although most clusters contain

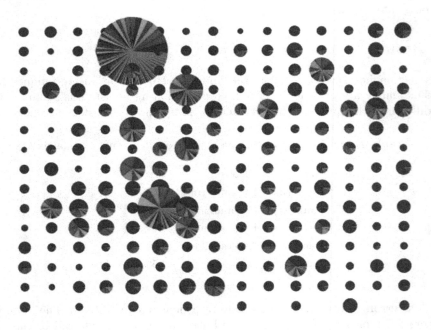

Fig. 7. SOM cluster structure. Circle size represents number of samples. Colors indicate different classes within clusters, blue being the most-frequent class (Color figure online)

mostly images of a single class, but the biggest clusters appear to consist of multitude classes.

All three similarity techniques - biggest error contributors (Fig. 3), smallest mean distance between embeddings (Fig. 5), most SOM purity improvement (Fig. 6) - suggested the most similar pairs to appear similar to the human eye, although all three techniques suggested different class pairs in the top of the similarity list.

Authors limited number cluster-classifiers as described in the Methods section. Figure 8 depicts the choice for number of clusters using accuracy intersection point (top-left), f-score intersection points (top-right) and f-score local maxima (bottom).

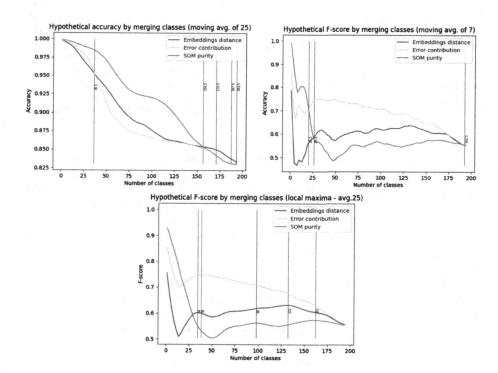

Fig. 8. Choosing number of merged classes in 3 ways: intersection of accuracy, f-score, and local f-score maxima

The main result of this research is comparing the following:

- Different techniques to determine visual class similarity. Based on similarity, classes are merged into "class clusters" and classification metrics are measured;
- Classifiers trained on individual classes vs. classifiers trained on "class clusters", where classes are merged into clusters by similarity.

Table 3. Accuracy using various methods for merging classes into clusters

Num. classes	Hypothetical merge			Actual merge		
	Embeddings distance	Error contribution	SOM purity	Embeddings distance	Error contribution	SOM purity
20	0.982	0.987	**0.992**	0.965	0.983	0.981
26	0.965	0.976	**0.990**	0.929	0.954	0.977
36	0.952	0.964	**0.985**	0.900	0.953	0.957
38	0.952	0.962	**0.984**	0.937	0.908	0.974
132	0.860	0.858	**0.890**	0.844	0.850	0.863
156	0.854	0.853	0.855	**0.862**	0.839	0.847
162	**0.854**	0.848	**0.854**	0.843	0.806	0.825
170	**0.852**	0.845	0.843	0.850	0.822	0.828
187	**0.842**	0.831	0.831	0.837	0.831	0.814

Table 4. F-score using various methods for merging classes into clusters

Num. classes	Hypothetical merge			Actual merge		
	Embeddings distance	Error contribution	SOM purity	Embeddings distance	Error contribution	SOM purity
20	0.557	0.702	**0.731**	0.373	0.491	0.383
26	0.584	**0.748**	0.562	0.421	0.597	0.318
36	0.618	**0.749**	0.534	0.435	0.633	0.335
38	0.610	**0.744**	0.528	0.516	0.534	0.371
132	0.635	**0.681**	0.552	0.597	0.659	0.450
156	0.607	**0.649**	0.573	0.606	0.630	0.528
162	0.606	**0.634**	0.575	0.578	0.595	0.545
170	0.601	**0.610**	0.575	0.566	0.587	0.516
187	0.563	**0.569**	0.562	0.525	0.553	0.528

Table 3 compares accuracy of classification into "class clusters". Best accuracy is achieved using "SOM purity" merging technique for smaller number of "class clusters", but "Embeddings distance" merging technique outperforms the rest when number of classes is high (>160). In all cases except one, individual class classifiers outperformed "class cluster" classifiers.

Table 4 compares f-score of "class cluster" classification. In all cases except one, "Error contribution" merging technique outperformed the rest. Individual classifiers always performed better that "class cluster" classifiers.

Figure 9 shows the margin between various methods of merging classes into clusters (different colors); between individual classifiers (lines) and "class cluster" classifiers (dots); accuracy (left) and f-score (right). Merging classes using "SOM purity" technique generally outperforms other methods when accuracy optimization is key (e.g. in retail self-checkouts, where class distribution is uneven). Merging classes using "Error contribution" technique generally outperforms other methods when f-score optimization is key.

Individual classifiers outperform "class cluster" classifiers with few exceptions (lines above same-colored dots).

In addition to 3 techniques of merging classes described in this article, authors present results of individual classifier using "barcode structure" class merging (red line in Fig. 9). This merging technique underperforms all other proposed merging techniques. This suggests that higher-level category (e.g. all apples; fruits) predictors in retail stores would not work as well as predictors of similarity-based class clusters.

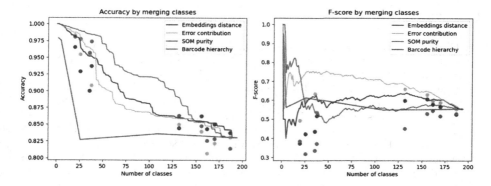

Fig. 9. Actual vs. Hypothetical metrics by merging similar classes (dots represent metrics of actually merged datasets)

Application of trained classifiers in retail stores. Inference of trained classifiers was tested on a self-checkout-like computer with 2 GB RAM, no GPU, 2 GHz CPU. Inference of an image took up to 100 ms, having the classifier model pre-loaded into RAM. A single classifier model takes less than 50 MB of disk space and requires to be placed on an inference computer. These requirements are acceptable for most self-checkout computers. Class similarity analysis and choosing the upper limit for number of classes, followed by creating clusters of similar classes, should be done outside of store computers, similar to our described infrastructure.

5 Conclusions

The results of this research apply to domains where training individual class classifiers and using them to predict a single class does not achieve required accuracy, such as where image class similarity is high, or there is insufficient training data.

The experiments in this research showed inconclusive results for the class similarity method to be used when merging classes into clusters. The best similarity measure depends on count of "class clusters" and on performance metric used (accuracy vs. f-score). Using "Error contribution" similarity method improved f-score by $9.9\% \pm 9.1\%$ over "SOM purity" and $7.8\% \pm 6.4\%$ over "Embeddings distance". Although "SOM purity" similarity method generally improved accuracy by $1.2 \pm 1.5\%$, its significance waned having higher number of clusters.

Authors of this paper have experimentally shown that classifiers trained on individual classes that predict "class cluster" usually outperform classifiers trained on "class clusters". Accuracy of individual classifiers was $1.8\% \pm 1.5\%$, f-score was $10.3\% \pm 9.0\%$ higher than of cluster-classifiers. Average retail self-checkout computers are powerful enough to run trained classifiers for inference.

References

1. Chen, H., Miao, S., Xu, D., Hager, G.D., Harrison, A.P.: Deep hierarchical multi-label classification of chest X-ray images. In: International Conference on Medical Imaging With Deep Learning, pp. 109–120. PMLR (2019)
2. Ciapas, B., Treigys, P.: High f-score model for recognizing object visibility in images with occluded objects of interest. Baltic J. Mod. Comput. **9**(1), 35–48 (2021)
3. Ji, X., Henriques, J.F., Vedaldi, A.: Invariant information clustering for unsupervised image classification and segmentation. In: Proceedings of the IEEE/CVF International Conference on Computer Vision, pp. 9865–9874 (2019)
4. Kingma, D.P., Ba, J.: Adam: A method for stochastic optimization. arXiv preprint arXiv:1412.6980 (2014). https://arxiv.org/abs/1412.6980
5. Kohonen, T.: The self-organizing map. Proc. IEEE **78**(9), 1464–1480 (1990)
6. Kolisnik, B., Hogan, I., Zulkernine, F.: Condition-CNN: a hierarchical multi-label fashion image classification model. Expert Syst. App. **182**, 115195 (2021)
7. Manning, C., Nayak, P.: Introduction to Information Retrieval-Evaluation (2013)
8. Negi, P.S., Mahoor, M., Others: Leveraging Class Similarity to Improve Deep Neural Network Robustness. arXiv preprint arXiv:1812.09744 (2018)
9. Park, K., Kim, D.H.: Accelerating image classification using feature map similarity in convolutional neural networks. Appl. Sci. **9**(1), 108 (2019)
10. Pereira, R.M., Costa, Y.M.G., Silla, C.N.: Handling imbalance in hierarchical classification problems using local classifiers approaches. Data Mining Knowl. Disc. **35**(4), 1564–1621 (2021). https://doi.org/10.1007/s10618-021-00762-8
11. Ren, Y., Wang, N., Li, M., Xu, Z.: Deep density-based image clustering. Knowl. Based Syst. **197**, 105841 (2020)
12. Shen, Y., Feng, Y., Fang, B., Zhou, M., Kwong, S., Qiang, B.h.: DSRPH: deep semantic-aware ranking preserving hashing for efficient multi-label image retrieval. Inf. Sci. **539**, 145–156 (2020)
13. Tsai, T.W., Li, C., Zhu, J.: Mice: mixture of contrastive experts for unsupervised image clustering. In: International Conference on Learning Representations (2020)
14. Wang, J., et al.: Learning fine-grained image similarity with deep ranking. In: Proceedings of the IEEE Conference on Computer Vision and Pattern Recognition, pp. 1386–1393 (2014)
15. Wang, L., Rajan, D.: An image similarity descriptor for classification tasks. J. Visual Commun. Image Represent. **71**, 102847 (2020)
16. Wehrmann, J., Cerri, R., Barros, R.: Hierarchical multi-label classification networks. In: International Conference on Machine Learning, pp. 5075–5084. PMLR (2018)

From Smart Life to Smart Life Engineering: A Systematic Mapping Study and Research Agenda

Elena Kornyshova[1]([⊠]), Rebecca Deneckère[2], Eric Gressier-Soudan[1], John Murray[3], and Sjaak Brinkkemper[4]

[1] Conservatoire National des Arts et Métiers, Paris, France
{elena.kornyshova,eric.gressier_soudan}@cnam.fr
[2] Université Paris 1 Panthéon Sorbonne, Paris, France
rebecca.deneckere@univ-paris1.fr
[3] San José State University, San Jose, CA, USA
john.murray@sjsu.edu
[4] Utrecht University, Utrecht, Netherlands
S.Brinkkemper@uu.nl

Abstract. The development of new digital technologies and their omnipresence impact the everyday life of people and intend to contribute to a so-called Smart Life. Numerous Smart Life applications and technologies relate directly to individuals and their life (Smart health, Smart buildings, Smart cities, etc.), but also indirectly through professional applications (Smart manufacturing, Smart grids, Smart farming, etc.). We assert that these applications have common foundations, and several design principles could be established to contextualize the development of Smart Life applications, thus, to introduce the field of Smart Life Engineering. We foresee the domain of Smart Life and Smart Life Engineering as an independent research domain that would contribute to the sharing or reuse of efforts to develop and maintain Smart applications. However, there is no common agreement on the concept of Smart Life and the associated methods and technologies. Thus, this paper provides a systematic view of the existing literature on Smart Life and its decomposition into sub-domains using systematic mapping study and presents a research agenda for Smart Life and Smart Life Engineering.

Keywords: Smart life · Smart life engineering · Smart technologies · Systematic mapping study · Research agenda

1 Introduction

The term *Smart* is an old English word that originated in the 13–14th century with the meaning quick, active, and clever in relation to sharp humor or words [1]. Since then, it became a synonym for intelligent, quick, and fashionable [2]. In the early 1970s, the adjective Smart began to be used to mean devices that behaved as if they were guided by intelligence. With the emergence of ubiquitous wireless computing, we can really

M. Ivanovic et al. (Eds.): Baltic DB&IS 2022, CCIS 1598, pp. 183–200, 2022.
https://doi.org/10.1007/978-3-031-09850-5_13

speak of *smartification* in many domains [3]: all kinds of devices and human activity get equipped with computational and intelligent features: Smart phone, Smart city, Smart energy, Smart car, and Smart manufacturing.

The rise of Smart applications and technologies in different scientific domains articulates a need for a more encompassing understanding of *Smart* that can function as a fundamental theoretical concept: what does it mean? And also, what does it not mean? The concept of Smart object was already introduced in 1998 by Kallman and Thalmann [4]. Recently all these terms seem to be bundled under the umbrella topic of *Smart Life*. However, there is no precise definition of what Smart Life entails. Many papers exist and contribute to expanding the knowledge about parts of this field, but there is still no clear explanation of what it is called exactly *Smart Life* and, by extension, what can then be called *Smart Life Engineering (SLE)*. Engineering of Smart Life applications is now widespread in many domains. But the extent to which the engineering of Smart Life applications differs from regular information systems remains not investigated.

Numerous works exist to present research agendas in Smart-related fields. For instance, Smart cities future research is given in [5–8], but the whole number of the related research papers is about 40. The same for Smart grids, Smart home, and many other Smart fields.

The main research goal is *to define and characterize Smart Life and Smart Life Engineering and to summarize the existing work on this topic*. Smart Life is a concept emerging from a plethora of studies on Smart cities, Smart devices, Smart energy, and so on. However, there is no real consensus about the scope and contents of this new domain. In [9], we suggested a taxonomy of contemporary Smart applications and analyzed their evolution. In this work, on top of a clear definition of Smart Life, we will identify research topics, methods, and technologies used in this domain to describe and delineate the different elements of SLE. In addition, we define a Smart Life research agenda to identify the key issues remaining in this field.

We present our research method mainly based on a Systematic Mapping Study methodology in Sect. 2, and in Sects. 3 and 4 we detail and discuss the obtained findings with regards to the Smart Life definition, Smart Life topics, and technologies used in this field. We end the paper with a set of research directions in a Smart Life and Smart Life Engineering research agenda in Sect. 5, and we conclude the paper in Sect. 6 with prospects of our research.

2   Research Method

The lack of a theoretical framing in the domain of Smart Life motivated us to conduct a Systematic Mapping Study (SMS) [10]. SMS relies on well-defined and evaluated review protocols to extract, analyze, and document results. We selected this type of research methodology as it is a useful product to describe the existing research in a particular field of study and allow the identification of knowledge gaps, which will help in the definition of a specific research agenda for this new field of study. We follow the process presented in [10] with a five-step review that includes the definition of research questions, the conducting search for primary studies, the screening of papers, the keywording of abstract, and finally the data extraction and mapping of studies. The review is completed by an evaluation of each step's outcome.

Step 1: Definition of research questions. The goal of a systematic mapping study is to provide an overview of a particular research area. The need for this review has been outlined in the introduction and we identify the research questions to help in shaping the review protocol.

Our research goal is to systematize the existing work about Smart Life and characterize Smart Life and Smart Life Engineering. To attain the main research goal, we defined three following research questions (RQ):

RQ1. How can Smart Life be defined?

RQ2. What are the different topics in application domains covered by Smart Life?

RQ3. What methods and technologies are used for various Smart Life applications?

Step 2: Conducting a search for primary studies. This step is composed of the selection of the primary studies with the identification of search key terms, guided by the main research question. In order to avoid excluding any studies in this emerging context, we only used the search string TITLE-ABS-KEY("Smart Life"), thus the search term "Smart Life" applied on title, abstract, and keywords. We extracted initially 121 studies from the years 2011 to 2021 (incl.) from the Scopus API (which includes databases from Elsevier, Springer, ACM, IEEE, etc.). The year 2011 was chosen as the term "smart life" began to appear more often in the literature at that time. Seven papers were identified as secondary sources and were used to describe the existing state of the art on Smart Life.

Steps 3 and 4: Screening of Papers and Keywording of Abstract. Since we used our primary search criteria on title and abstract, this resulted in the selection of some irrelevant studies (primarily in the health domain) which we then deleted from our dataset, using our inclusion/exclusion criteria, which led us to use 71 sources in our SMS[1]. The inclusion and exclusion criteria are presented in Table 1.

To complete the answer to RQ2, we conducted another study to obtain the largest set of Smart topics and their evolution. As the number of papers in Scopus with the keyword "Smart" is more than 126 000, we reduced the search to the state-of-the-art- and research agenda-related articles to obtain 2410 sources with DOIs. Based on the title and, if needed, on the abstract, we excluded 69 sources not relevant to Smart Life topics papers, obtaining 2341 papers[2]. Table 2 presents the inclusion and exclusion criteria for this additional study.

Step 5: Data extraction and Mapping of studies. In this last step of the SMS study, we analyze the results obtained, answer the research questions, and draw some conclusions about Smart Life (see Sect. 3). Firstly, we analyzed the obtained sources according to years, paper type, and field of science. For RQ1, we checked the papers to discover the existing definitions of Smart Life and summarized the found concepts. For RQ2, we identified Smart topics and classified them. During the additional study, we identified topics for all papers and classified them into macro-topics regarding to their

---

[1] The complete list of the papers of this SMS is given in Appendix A, available at http://cri-dist.univ-paris1.fr/smart-life/Appendix%20A%20-%20SMS%20on%20Smart%20Life.pdf. All sources from this list have their references starting with "A".

[2] The complete list of these papers is available at http://cri-dist.univ-paris1.fr/smart-life/Appendix%20B%20-%20Smart%20SoA%20and%20Research%20Agenda%20by%20topic.pdf.

Table 1. Inclusion/exclusion criteria for the study on Smart Life.

Selection criteria	Criteria description
Inclusion criteria	Title/Abstract/keywords include key term "smart life": Search string TITLE-ABS-KEY("smart life") The paper is published after 2011 From the abstract it is clear that a contribution towards Smart Life is made
Exclusion criteria	The source is not a research paper (blog, presentation, etc.) The source is secondary (literature review only) The source is not in English or French

Table 2. Inclusion/exclusion criteria for the study on Smart topics.

Selection criteria	Criteria description
Inclusion criteria	Title includes the term "smart" and at least one of the terms "research agenda", "state-of-the-art", "review", or "survey": Search string: TITLE(smart) AND (TITLE("research agenda") OR TITLE("State-of-the-art") OR TITLE(review) OR TITLE(survey))
Exclusion criteria	The source is not a research paper (erratum, retracted, etc.) The source is related to an abbreviation SMART, like, for instance, SMART (stroke-like migraine attacks after radiation therapy) syndrome The source mentions the term «Smart», which is used in its ordinary sense, like "working smart and hard"

nature. For RQ3, we extracted the used technologies and methods in the field of Smart Life.

In order to minimize the impact of the validity threats that could affect our study, we present them with the corresponding mitigation actions, as preconized in [11]:

Descriptive Validity: It seeks to ensure that observations are objectively and accurately described. At this end, we unified the concepts and criteria we used in the study, and we structured the information to be collected with a data extraction form to support a uniform recording of data and to objectify the data extraction process.

Theoretical Validity: It depends on the ability to get the information that it is intended to capture. We started with a search string and applied it to a library including the most popular digital libraries on computer sciences and software engineering online databases. A set of inclusion and exclusion criteria have been defined. Two researchers studied the papers. They were working independently but with an overlap of studies to identify potential analysis differences. We combined two different search methods: an automatic search and a manual search (backward and forward snowballing), to diminish the risk of not finding all the available evidence. The choice of English sources should be of minimal impact concerning the discard of other languages.

Generalizability: This validity is concerned with the ability to generalize the results to the whole domain. Our set of research questions is general enough to identify and classify the findings on Smart Life, its topics, and technologies.

Interpretive Validity: This validity is achieved when the conclusions are reasonable given the data. To this end, at least two researchers validated every conclusion.

Repeatability: The research process must be detailed enough in order to ensure it can be exhaustively repeated. We detailed this protocol sufficiently to allow us to repeat the followed process. The protocol as well as the results of the study are presented in this paper, so other researchers can replicate the process and corroborate the results.

3 Results of the Systematic Mapping Study

In this section, we sum up the results obtained during SMS. The initial study of the relevant sources on Smart Life shows the growing interest in this topic. We can observe the almost continual increase since 2011 and completely regular progression since 2016 of the number of papers on Smart Life (See Fig. 1).

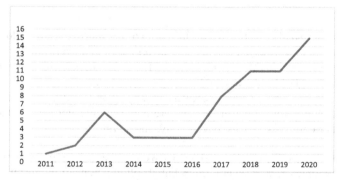

Fig. 1. Growth of the number of papers on Smart Life (without 8 papers for the first half of 2021 for data consistency).

Paper Type. We categorized these papers according to the type of research approaches introduced by Wieringa et al. [12] (See Table 3). We can see that a third of the papers are validation research papers (35,2%), presenting novel techniques with an experimental setup. Another third represents philosophical papers (32,39%) dealing with new ways of looking at existing things by structuring the field in one way or another. The last third contains all the other types of research, with a good representation of solution proposals and very few evaluation, opinion, or experience papers.

Fields of Science. We characterized the papers with regards to the fields of science publishing on Smart Life. For this purpose, we used the classification FOS (Fields of Science and Technology) of OCDE [13] as the most recognized classification of the scientific fields. When dealing with multi-disciplinary journals or conferences, we picked the field based on the paper content. The results are given in Table 4.

Table 3. Categorization in paper contribution types.

Research approach type	Number of papers	Ratio (%)	References
Validation research	25	35,2%	[A12][A13][A15][A16][A19][A21][A27][A28][A31] [A35][A38][A40][A41][A43][A44][A45][A51][A56] [A58][A6][A64][A65][A69][A70][A9]
Evaluation research	2	2,81%	[A10][A29]
Solution proposal	16	22,53%	[A1][A11][A17][A25][A26][A3][A4][A49][A54] [A57][A60][A62][A63][A66][A68]
Philosophical papers	23	32,39	[A14][A18][A2][A20][A22][A23][A30][A32][A33] [A34][A39][A46][A48][A5][A50][A52][A53][A55] [A59][A61][A67][A7][A71]
Opinion papers	4	5,63%	[A24][A36][A42][A47]
Experience papers	1	1,4%	[A37]

The most published research works in the area of Smart Life are fields related to ICT (computer and information science and information engineering). However, other fields are also interested in this research topic. During the characterization, we observed that the current Field of Study and Technology categorization does not take several new technologies into account. For instance, sensors appear in this classification only with relation to medical fields, however, sensors are now omnipresent and are used in civil engineering, agricultural sciences, psychology, and so on.

Smart Topics. Smart Topics. Several topics were extracted from the first SMS (see Table 5). Some topics appear several times but absolutely none of them stand out of this set with a spectacular proportion of references. We can then conclude that this domain covers many fields of research and is still evolving with new terms appearing regularly.

Existing State-of-the-Art Works. To analyze the state-of-the-art of this domain, we first studied the seven secondary research papers. Most of them mention smart life but focus on different sub-topics of this field. In [14], the authors present a systematic literature review on Internet-of-Things (IoT) application for energy consumption and discuss future research directions. [15] details a state-of-the-art perspective on Security in IoT. The third work [16] contains a state-of-the-art overview of IoT usage for Smart cities and classification of smart technologies that were applied. [17] presents a thorough catalog of computer technologies from the viewpoint of artificial intelligence. In [18], the concept of machine to machine (M2M) is studied to define the current research on this field, describe its technical features and present the key aspects under which M2M technologies can function. The last paper specifies an integrative study about IoT, an operational view, their benefits, and corresponding problems [19].

Table 4. Fields of science and technology.

Field of science and technology	Number of papers	Percentage	References
Natural sciences	**34**	**47,9%**	
Biological sciences	1	1,4%	[A22]
Computer and information science	30	42,3%	[A1][A3][A4][A5][A7][9]][A12] [A14][A15][A17][A24][A25][A29] [A30][A32][A33][A35][A36][A39] [A43][A44][A49][A55][A57][A58] [A64][A65][A66][A67][A70]
Mathematics	1	1,4%	[A11]
Physical science	2	2,8%	[A48][A6]
Engineering and technology	**30**	**42,3%**	
Electrical engineering, Electronic engineering, information engineering	20	28,2%	[A8][A10][A16][A18][A19][A20] [A23][A26][A27][A28][A37][A40] [A41][A45][A52][A54][A56][A60] [A68][A69]
Environmental engineering	3	4,2%	[A2][A51][A59]
Material engineering	5	7,0%	[A13][A21][A31][A34][A42]
Mechanical engineering	2	2,9%	[A46][A61]
Medical and Health sciences	**1**	**1,4%**	
Medical biotechnology	1	1,4%	[A50]
Social sciences	**6**	**8,4%**	
Economies and business	2	2,8%	[A53][A63]
Media and communication	4	5,6%	[A38][A47][A62][A71]

Only one retrieved paper [20], entitled "Smart Technologies for Smart Life", deals with a problem corresponding to our purpose. In this paper, the author describes a state-of-the-art synopsis focused on Smart technologies. She gives several definitions, lists different concepts related to Smart technologies by year, and suggests a classification of Smart technologies in general. From the additional study on Smart topics, we then identified a systematic literature review on Smart systems [21]. In this work, the authors concentrate on the concept of smartness, enumerate several related definitions, and provide a set of primary characteristics of Smart systems.

So summarizing, we may truthfully state that none of the existing works focuses on the definition, systematic review, or future trends in the field of Smart Life.

4 Findings

We detail the findings in the following sub-sections according to the defined RQ.

Table 5. Topics identified from smart life related literature.

Number of references	Topics
6	Smart home [A22][A41][A43][A44][A57][A8]
5	Smart HCI [A15][A19][A35][A38][A70], Smart city [A17][A20][A55][A59] [A67], Smart communication [A1][A11][A50][A64][A7]
4	Smart service [A30][A32][A46][A49], Smart device [A23][A31][A4][A56]
3	Smart localization [A12][A6][A66], Smart application [A14][A39][A62]
2	Smart appliance [A25][A42], Smart environment [A21][A69], Smart health [A36][A60], Smart manufacturing [A10][A53], Smart monitoring [A40][A63], Smart sensor [A13][A51], Smart transport [A48][A52], Smart vehicle [A18] [A26], Smart object [A33][A58]
1	Smart assistant [A68], Smart bin [A27], Smart building [A2], Smart carpet [A3], Smart family [A71], Smart farming [A37], Smart life cycle management [A61], Smart luggage [A54], Smart market [A28], Smart mirror [A45], Smart product [A16], Smart project [A47], Smart sound [A65], Smart system [A24], Smart textile [A34], Smart university [A29], Smart web [A5], Smart navigation [A9]

4.1 Smart Life Definition

In the existing literature, the concept of Smart Life is often linked to the Internet of Things (IoT). IoT has made revolutionary changes in human life and enables the exchanges of information in a wide variety of applications such as Smart buildings, Smart health, Smart transport, and so on, which can be unified into a single entity referred to as Smart Life [15, 22]. A step beyond is in [23], where this new entity of IoT is characterized as a new lifestyle. Smart Life connects all IoT microdevices and microsensors under wireless communication grids [24]. This widely spread idea of a connection of all embedded devices around us to the internet has the potential to change our lives and the world, to enable us to live a Smart Life in a Smart world [19]. IoT then becomes an indispensable technology to improve the quality of life for human beings [25, 26] and people want to live a Smart Life [27].

However, Smart Life is not reduced to IoT. The key concept of Smart Life is the data use and processing to improve our living. Each artefact processing data is smart even if it is not connected. In addition, "Being smart" should not be confused with "being digital" as infrastructures and technologies are the means, not the end, enabling a set of services that affect deeply life [28]. IoT objects and devices collect every possible data about a user, but their final goal is to make intelligent use of such data to support this user [29]. These intelligent devices will drive people into Smart Life, becoming the new innovative direction of the internet [30].

In a thorough analysis of the studied literature, we did not find any consistent definition of Smart Life. Even the notion of smart is understood rather differently between sub-fields and even inside fields. For instance, different notions of Smart object could be found in [31, 32], but there is no common agreement on the notion of Smart object. In this paper, we try to overcome this drawback by analyzing the development of the notion of Smart Life with regards to its structure and the definition of different smartness degrees to better specify the concept of Smart.

Smart Life Structure. From the structure point of view, we foresee Smart Life using the systemic approach [33]. The core element of Smart Life is a so-called Smart Artefact, the term we selected to avoid intermingling with already established terms such as a Smart object or Smart thing. Smart artefacts correspond to any standalone device with a program and a capability to store and process data. Smart artefacts of the same or similar functional usage form a Smart Application. Smart applications could be identified at different levels of granularity from detailed and concrete (e.g., a Smart lighting system including several sensors about the home environment and people positions in a home) to more global ones (such as a Smart home application covering different aspects: lighting, heating, windows management, and so on). Smart artefacts could belong to two or more Smart applications, like Smart lighting systems could be found in Smart home, Smart factory, or Smart city. Each Smart application is a system of Smart artefacts, which means that it should have at least one emergent property [34]. Emergent properties correspond to features of the whole system and that system elements do not have, like all components of a car should be put together in a certain manner so this car could run. Smart life, in its turn, is composed of various Smart applications, thus Smart Life is a system of systems. In its simplest form, Smart Life is a combination of at least two Smart applications, that requires coordination based on the input and analysis of emergent properties. This system-oriented vision of Smart Life is illustrated in Fig. 2.

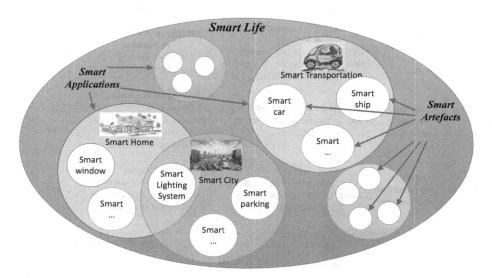

Fig. 2. System-oriented vision of smart life.

Smartness Degree. To understand better the nature of Smart Life, we go in deep into the definition of the term "Smart". We define the degree of smartness depending on data integration and processing type. The first axis reflects different levels of consideration of data coming from the environment and users. Data complexity varies from the embedded sensors data (immediate environment) to data from the distant environment in addition to the sensors data, and, finally, to data on users' well-being and state. The second axis shows how data are processed from non-AI processors to AI based processors (expressing the processor complexity). We distinguish three degrees of smartness: *smart, intelligent, and sentient*.

- **Degree 1 of Smartness – Smart:** is a capability to process data and to adapt its functioning.
- **Degree 2 of Smartness – Intelligent:** is a capability to process data and to adapt its functioning with the usage of AI (smart + AI).
- **Degree 3 of Smartness – Sentient:** is a capability to process data coming from users about his/her feelings, emotions, physical state, and so on. The notion of sentience came from the field of animals' rights protection and is quite new to the field of ICT. It is already used to qualify the evolution of artificial intelligence of machines [35] or to introduce requirements for human-aware information systems and technologies [36].

To illustrate this proposal, we position the smartness degrees according to the two axes (data complexity and processing complexity) and give some examples (Fig. 3).

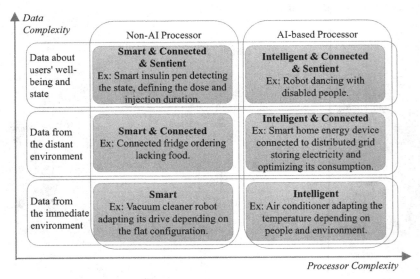

Fig. 3. Smartness degrees according to data and processor complexity.

We can summarize the main definitions of our proposal as follows:

- **Smart Artefact** is any autonomous and stand-alone artefact provided with a data processor when data is obtained, stored, processed, and used to trigger actions of the artefact in the environment. A Smart artefact could be connected or not. For example, a Smart artefact can be a Smart watch, Smart window, Smart toy, Smart antenna, and so on.
- **Smart Application** is a system of connected Smart artefacts, and possibly other Smart applications. Thus, it corresponds to a set of artefacts with a common goal. For instance, a Smart city application can be composed of a Smart parking application, a Smart energy application, and so on. A Smart home can be composed of a Smart TV, a Smart fridge, a Smart assistant, and so on. A Smart application should contain at least two Smart artefacts.
- **Smart Life** is defined as the domain that embraces all Smart applications and Smart artefacts for the purpose of an enriched experience from the personal, societal, environmental and enterprise perspectives [9]. Smart Life can be seen as a societal domain that unifies all in initiatives to apply Smart artefacts and applications in any setting. We also use the term of Smart Life as a comprehensive scientific research domain that includes all research areas with studies into Smart technology, artefacts, and applications.
- **Smart Life Engineering** as the use of scientific principles to design, build, implement and evolve Smart Life applications. SLE can therefore be seen as overlapping with the domain of Information Systems Engineering, but it also has a broad set of links with research domains in Wireless Network Technology, Artificial Intelligence, Urban Geography, Logistics, Medical Technology, etc.

Note, that in these definitions, the perspective of the distributed ownership or multi-stakeholder arrangements does not appear. Smart Life usually deals with a variety of technologies, a variety of development approaches, a multitude of modeling and coding. Furthermore, the individual or human perspective is not included. We relate these viewpoints in Sect. 5 when describing the research agenda.

4.2 Smart Life Topics

A set of topics was considered on the 71 SMS papers. The "smart" term is used for a lot of many different things, but our study was not including enough papers to be consistent on this specific question. As a result, we made another study to identify which are exactly the "smart" topics, not restraining ourselves only to the Smart Life topics but more generally to the "smart" term. Based on the titles analyses, we identified 775 different formulations of Smart topics quite detailed like Smart grid, Smart energy, Smart energy system, Smart energy management system, etc. To deal with this huge number of topics, we grouped them by macro-topics (i.e., we grouped the above-mentioned energy-related topics with several others within a macro-topic "Smart grid, Smart microgrid, Smart energy, Smart meter". Another example is "Smart transportation, Smart road, Smart bridge, Smart mobility, Smart vehicle" including Smart airport, Smart train, Smart ship, etc. The evolution of Smart macro-topics is shown in Table 6.

As a reminder, this additional study contains papers only on state-of-the-arts and research agendas, thus, the current quantity and growth of these research themes are

Table 6. Large Study on Smart Topics.

Macro-topic	1986	1990	1996	1998	1999	2000	2001	2002	2003	2004	2005	2006	2007	2008	2009	2010	2011	2012	2013	2014	2015	2016	2017	2018	2019	2020	2021	2022	Total
smart application																						1	1	1	1	1	1		6
smart charging																							1	1	1	1	1	1	6
smart city														1	1			3	2	5	9	19	33	42	93	77	85	5	375
smart clothing, smart shoes															1	1						1		3	1	7	1	1	16
smart contract																							2	4	8	13	22	2	51
smart device, smart object, smart well								1		1	2		3	1	2	1	1	5	6	6	5	9	14	26	17	19	16	1	137
smart drug, smart drug delivery						1												2				1	1		2	2	5		14
smart environment, smart water management						1										2		2	2	2	2	4	3	6	10	14	16		64
smart factory, smart manufacturing and other business-related smart topics	1	1						1					1			2		2	2	4	2	6	10	23	34	41	34	2	166
smart farming, smart agriculture																				1	1	2	9	5	12	20	36	2	88
smart grid, smart microgrid, smart energy, smart meter										1				1		8	14	34	35	33	48	80	57	76	88	91	89	1	656
smart healthcare													2	1				1	4	4	2	1	5	5	22	28	31		106
smart home, smart building														3	6	1	3	4	10	5	8	19	15	30	35	51	39	1	230
smart learning, smart education																				1		3	1	5	7	5	5		27
smart lighting system																			1					1	1		2		5
smart material, smart structure, smart surface, smart textile			2	2	1		2	2	1		1	3	2	2	3	5	2	4	5	6	6	9	5	16	28	27	35	1	170
smart methodology																							1		1				2
smart phone														1		1	1	1	1	2	2	1	1	2	3	4	2		22
smart sensor															1	1	1	1	1	1	1		2	2	2	1	8		22
smart service																									1	1	2	2	6
smart society, smart world, smart growth												1	1			1		1		2	1	3	2	8	7	4	4	1	36
smart space exploration																								1					1
smart sport																								1	2	1	1		5
smart survey															1		1						1		1	1	2		7
smart system													1	1			1			1		1	1	1	4	1	2		14
smart technology	1							1						1	1	1			1	1	1	1	1	2	3	2	2		19
smart tourism															1			2							4	5	2		14
smart transportation, smart road, smart bridge, smart mobility, smart vehicle															1	1	1		2	2	2	1	1	3	9	11	14		48
smart university, smart campus																						1	2	2	3	3	6		17
smart waste management																							1	2	4	4			11
Total	2	1	2	2	2	4	2	5	1	2	3	6	11	11	17	18	25	63	71	72	94	160	172	266	401	438	473	17	2341

impressive. As we can see, the most popular topics are Smart energy-, Smart city-, and Smart home-related. This study allowed us to identify very specific emerging Smart artefacts, like Smart toys, Smart socks, Smart guns, but also Smart applications like Smart earth, Smart space exploration, Smart fishery, Smart pest management, and so on.

The situation presented in Table 6 drastically confirms a need for a systematization of knowledge in order to make life smarter.

4.3 Smart Life Technologies

As IoT is the core of Smart Life, a lot of diverse technologies are used in this field. Smart objects of course (devices, sensors, and so on), but also some single-board computers. Networks are envisioned in different ways to improve the data communication with GPS, 5G, or even NFC protocol. Sometimes the data collection is handled on social media instead of Smart objects and some specific software can help in the process. Table 7 shows the repartition of these technologies in our study papers.

Different kinds of deep learning or machine learning techniques are used, such as regression algorithms [A17] [A60], standardization methods [A48], neural networks [A35], clustering [A57], Hidden Markov models [A69], recommendation systems [A65] or decision support tools [A58] to cite the widely known ones.

Table 7. Smart technologies.

Type	References
Smart objects and sensors	Smart phones [A35][A21][A65][A10][A68][A12]; Devices [A62][A56][A49][A26]; Specific sensors [A3][A39][A6] [A51][A54][A27][A41]; Bluetooth beacons [A66][A12]; Cameras and robot sensors [A9][A15]; RFID [A38]
Single-board computers (arduino and raspberry)	[A21][A45][A41][A9]
Networks and protocols	5G [A50]; Wireless sensor network [A8]; GPS [A66][A62][A12]; NFC [A66][A12][A8]
Social media / Social networks	Social media [A60][A8]; Context [A65][A8]
Software	Applications [A14][A62][A68][A43]; Blockchain [A7]

5 Smart Life and Smart Life Engineering Research Agenda

In the research agenda, we define four perspectives for Smart Life and Smart Life Engineering research: technological, methodological, organizational, and societal (See Fig. 4). Different research agendas in particular Smart technologies or applications can be found in other works, for instance [5, 5] for Smart cities, e.g.

Technological Challenges. Smart applications generate all sorts of data that is of interest to other applications (it does not make sense to build a central data archive). The necessity to manage a huge amount of data implies multiple issues: How can secure and privacy-aware access to data be granted and obtained for various applications? How can high-level information wishes be expressed in distributed queries over a variety of applications? An appropriate distributed infrastructure should be defined accordingly.

In addition, Smart applications require devices, resources, and energy, which are scarce and need careful implementation and a recycling perspective. Thus, other questions should be highlighted: Can we identify Smart Life methods for Green IT and ensure sustainable development?

Thus, we define the following SLE technological challenges: developing shared but secure and privacy-aware access to data, developing efficient distributed infrastructure, considering Green IT, considering sustainability, and so on.

Methodological Challenges. Smart Life is already applied in a lot of projects, sometimes successfully, sometimes not. The Information Systems Engineering field has brought about many strong conceptual modeling techniques (class diagrams, process models, object-orientation, state-transaction graphs). What conceptual modeling techniques provide the most effective modeling of Smart applications? Situational Method Engineering [37] focuses on formalizing the use of methods for systems construction using organization-, project-specific and context-aware methodological approaches. Would these approaches be suitable for Smart Life applications? Would it be possible to use these methods to provide a real-time adaptation of Smart Life applications?

Next to scientific reporting, a huge variety of application projects have been reported in the popular press and industrial magazines. What are the key factors of success? How can we objectively obtain the essential contributions of contextual factors in different cases? Early estimations of explicit and implicit values of Smart applications projects are often vague and debatable. How different value-modeling techniques can assist in Smart Life projects quantification?

In this manner, a first list of methodological challenges for SLE comprises: defining common methods for SLE, defining quality criteria and value models, providing context awareness of SLE, providing real time adaptation, etc.

Organizational Challenges. When multiple Smart applications build up a large-scale Smart Life experience, there is a variety of stakeholder groups (e.g., citizens, entrepreneurs, city officials) that have different interests in the data, products, and services sharing. How can multi-stakeholder policies be organized and communicated? How can governmental and democratic representations assist in the elicitation of views and strategies for the future?

Smart artefacts and applications in real-life settings are usually owned by different stakeholders, who have their own budgets, plans, and Information and Communication Technologies infrastructures. Bringing these parties together in various Smart Life projects requires careful communication and planning across organizations. How agile engineering approaches can engage distributed owners in a SLE project? How investments in facilities and resources can be shared in complex beneficiary dependencies, where long-term costs and benefits are not balanced among stakeholders?

We then define the following preliminary set of organizational challenges for SLE: defining policies for smart applications governance, defining policies for distributed ownership engagement, defining policies for data, products, and services sharing, etc.

Societal Challenges. The propagation of Smart Life applications raises questions related to ethics and well-being issues. The issue of system accessibility is becoming critical. While organizations are promoting guidelines for making some websites more usable by people with disabilities, almost no attention is being paid to other types of smart products and embedded systems. How can we build Smart systems that will reason coherently over the type of ethical dilemmas that we humans have to deal with?

Engineering of Smart Life artefacts and applications should not only provide means to attain their main functional purposes, but also contribute to users' well-being. Many current technologies cause addiction or depression, for instance, social media induce the FOMO (Fear Of Missing Out) syndrome (discussed in [38]) which could increase the risk of becoming depressive. How the well-being of users can be considered during all engineering phases starting from requirements elicitation?

The most important SLE societal challenges include ensuring machine ethics, developing Smart Life applications consciousness, providing sentient systems, providing system accessibility, and so on.

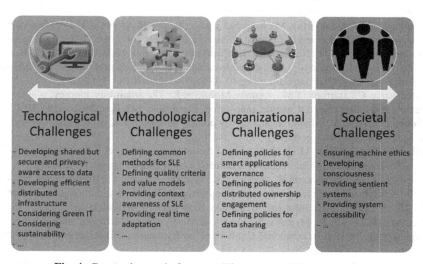

Fig. 4. Research agenda for smart life and smart life engineering.

6   Conclusion and Future Works

In this paper, we studied the existing literature on Smart Life using the Systematic Mapping Study methodology and we investigated this field in order to systematize the existing knowledge. We discovered a very large, and continuously growing, set of Smart topics ranging from very established (like Smart energy, Smart material, Smart city, and so on) to emerging ones (like Smart airport, Smart toy, or Smart gun) and from very practical (like Smart waste bin system and Smart self-power generating streetlight) to more conceptual (like Smart earth and Smart world). We believe that a huge scientific effort should be made to optimize these fields to make life smarter. For us, this effort should be done through the definition of common methods, techniques, and tools, thus by the development of a new field, Smart Life Engineering. Thus, we elaborated a research agenda towards this field.

In our future research, we foresee focusing on methodological aspects of SLE. Our first goal will be to identify different opportunities for optimizing the research effort between different fields and sub-fields of Smart Life.

References

1. Online Etymology Dictionary (2021). www.etymonline.com
2. Oxford Dictionary, Oxford University Press (2021). www.oxfordlearnersdictionaries.com
3. Schuh, G., Zeller, V., Hicking, J., Bernardy, A.: Introducing a methodology for smartification of products in manufacturing industry. Proc. CIRP **81**, 228–233 (2019)
4. Kallman, M., Thalmann D.: Modeling objects for interaction tasks. In: Arnaldi, B., Hégron, G. (eds) Computer Animation and Simulation Eurographics, pp. 73–86. Springer, Vienna (1999). https://doi.org/10.1007/978-3-7091-6375-7_6
5. Gopinath, B., Kaliamoorthy, M., Ragupathy, U.S., Sudha, R., Nandini, D.U., Maheswar, R.: State-of-the-art and emerging trends in internet of things for smart Cities. In: Maheswar, R., Balasaraswathi, M., Rastogi, R., Sampathkumar, A., Kanagachidambaresan, G.R. (eds.) Challenges and Solutions for Sustainable Smart City Development. EICC, pp. 263–274. Springer, Cham (2021). https://doi.org/10.1007/978-3-030-70183-3_12
6. Echebarria, C., Barrutia, J.M., Aguado-Moralejo, I.: The smart city journey: a systematic review and future research agenda, innovation. Eur. J. Soc. Sci. Res. **34**(2), 159–201 (2021)
7. Bohloul, S.M., et al.: Smart cities: a survey on new developments, trends, and opportunities. J. Indust. Integr. Manage. **05**(03), 311–326 (2020)
8. Ali, H., Qazi, R., Shah, M. A.: Smart cities: methods, encounters & hunt for future – survey. In: 25th International Conference on Automation and Computing, pp. 1–6 (2019)
9. Kornyshova, E., Deneckere, R., Sadouki, K., Gressier-Soudan, E., Brinkkemper, S.: Smart Life: review of the contemporary smart applications. In 16th International Conference on Research Challenges in Information Science, Barcelona, Spain (2022)
10. Petersen, K., Feldt, R., Mujtaba, S., Mattsson, M.: Systematic mapping studies in software engineering. In 12th International Conference on Evaluation and Assessment in Software Engineering, vol. 17 (2008)
11. Pinciroli F., Justo J., Zeligueta L., Palma M.: Systematic Mapping Protocol - Coverage of Aspect-Oriented Methodologies for the Early Phases of the Software Development Life Cycle (2018)
12. Wieringa, R., Maiden, N.A.M., Mead, N.R., Rolland, C.: Requirements engineering paper classification and evaluation criteria: a proposal and a discussion. Requir. Eng. **11**(1), 102–107 (2006)
13. Revised field of science and technology (FOS) classification in the Fracasti manual, OCDE (2007)
14. Wang, D., Zhong, D., Souri, A.: Energy management solutions in the Internet of Things applications: technical analysis and new research directions. Cogn. Syst. Res. **67**, 33–49 (2021)
15. Harbi, Y., Aliouat, Z., Harous, S., Bentaleb, A., Refoufi, A.: A review of security in internet of things. Wirel. Pers. Commun. **108**(1), 325–344 (2019). https://doi.org/10.1007/s11277-019-06405-y

16. Kim, T., Ramos, C., Mohammed, S.: Smart City and IoT. Futur. Gener. Comput. Syst. **76**, 159–162 (2017)
17. Yamane, S.: Deductively verifying embedded software in the era of artificial intelligence = machine learning + software science. In: 2017 IEEE 6th Global Conference on Consumer Electronics, GCCE 2017 (2017)
18. Severi, S., Sottile, F., Abreu, G., Pastrone, C., Spirito, M., Berens, F.: M2M technologies: Enablers for a pervasive internet of things. In: EuCNC 2014 - European Conference on Networks and Communications (2014)
19. Baruah, P.D., Dhir, S., Hooda, M.: Impact of IOT in current era. In: Proceedings of the International Conference on Machine Learning, Big Data, Cloud and Parallel Computing: Trends, Prespectives and Prospects, COMITCon 2019, pp. 334–339 (2019)
20. Mizintseva, M.F.: Smart technologies for smart life. In: Popkova, E.G., Sergi, B.S. (eds.) "Smart Technologies" for Society, State and Economy. LNNS, vol. 155, pp. 653–664. Springer, Cham (2021). https://doi.org/10.1007/978-3-030-59126-7_73
21. Romero, M., Guédria, W., Panetto, H., Barafort, B.: Towards a characterisation of smart systems: a systematic literature review. Comput. Indust. **120**, 103224 (2020)
22. Benhaddi, M.: Web of goals: a proposal for a new highly smart web. In: Proceedings of the 19th International Conference on Enterprise Information Systems, vol. 2, pp. 687–694 (2017)
23. Chen, Y.S., Chou, J.C.L., Chen, W.R.: Long-term strategic development application by a two-stage expert-based AHP model for the internet plus era: a leading TFT-LCD manufacturer case. J. Appl. Sci. Eng. **21**, 361–374 (2018)
24. Lee, S.H., et al.: Enhanced electrochemical performance of micro-supercapacitors via laser-scribed cobalt/reduced graphene oxide hybrids. ACS Appl. Mater. Interfaces. **13**, 1–18 (2021)
25. Cho, Y., et al.: Sustainable hybrid energy harvester based on air stable quantum dot solar cells and triboelectric nanogenerator. J. Mater. Chem. A. **6**, 1–6 (2018)
26. Ho, Y., Sato-Shimokawara, E., Wada, K., Yamaguchi, T., Tagawa, N.: Developing a life rhythm related human support system. In: IEEE International Symposium on Industrial Electronics, pp. 894–899 (2015)
27. Sharma, K., Tayal, S.: Indian smart city ranking model using taxicab distance-based approach. Energy Syst. **22**, 1–18 (2019). https://doi.org/10.1007/s12667-019-00365-9
28. Coccoli, M., Guercio, A., Maresca, P., Stanganelli, L.: Smarter universities: a vision for the fast changing digital era. J. Vis. Lang. Comput. **25**, 1003–1011 (2014)
29. Yoon, I., Ng, G., Dong, X., Duan, H., Aggarwal, A., Shah, R., Ku, G.: SuperCaly: smart life assistance by integrating a calendar app with location tracking, media organization and social connection. In: 2017 IEEE 7th Annual Computing and Communication Workshop and Conference, CCWC 2017 (2017)
30. Fu, J.: Intelligent hardware somatosensory design. In: Proceedings - 2016 6th International Conference on Instrumentation and Measurement, Computer, Communication and Control, IMCCC 2016, pp. 331–334 (2016)
31. González García, C., Meana-Llorián, D., Pelayo García-Bustelo, B.C., Cueva Lovelle, J.V.: A review about smart objects, sensors, and actuators. Int. J. Interact. Multimed. Artif. Intell. **4**(3), 1–4 (2017)
32. Liu, X., Baiocchi, O.: A comparison of the definitions for smart sensors, smart objects and Things in IoT. In: IEEE 7th Annual Information Technology, Electronics and Mobile Communication Conference (IEMCON), pp. 1–4 (2016)
33. Thagard, P.: Computational Philosophy of Science. MIT Press, Cambridge (1993)
34. Nikolaev, M. Y., Fortin, C.: Systems thinking ontology of emergent properties for complex engineering systems, In: Journal of Physics: Conference Series, vol. 1687, p. 012005 (2020)
35. Husain, A.: The Sentient Machine: The Coming Age of Artificial Intelligence. Scribner, USA (2017)

36. Kornyshova, E., Gressier-Soudan, E.: Introducing sentient requirements for information systems and digital technologies. In: EMCIS 2021, Dubai, United Arab Emirates (2021)
37. Henderson-Sellers, B., Ralyte, J., Agerfalk, P.J., Rossi, M.: Situational Method Engineering. Springer, Heidelberg (2014). https://doi.org/10.1007/978-3-642-41467-1
38. Kreps, D., Rowe, F., Muirhead, J.: Understanding digital events: process philosophy and causal autonomy. In: HICSS 2020, Maui, Hawaii, USA, pp. 1–10 (2020)

Shared SAT Solvers and SAT Memory in Distributed Business Applications

Sergejs Kozlovičs[(✉)]

Institute of Mathematics and Computer Science, University of Latvia,
Raiņa bulv. 29, Riga 1459, Latvia
sergejs.kozlovics@lumii.lv

Abstract. We propose a software architecture where SAT solvers act as a shared network resource for distributed business applications. There can be multiple parallel SAT solvers running either on dedicated hardware (a multi-processor system or a system with a specific GPU) or in the cloud. In order to avoid complex message passing between network nodes, we introduce a novel concept of the shared SAT memory, which can be accessed (in the read/write mode) from multiple different SAT solvers and modules implementing the business logic. As a result, our architecture allows for the easy generation, diversification, and solving of SAT instances from existing high-level programming languages without the need to think about the network. We demonstrate our architecture on the use case of transforming the integer factorization problem to SAT.

Keywords: SAT · Distributed applications · Software architecture · Integer factorization

1 Introduction

The Boolean satisfiability problem (SAT)[1] problem has many practical applications such as circuit design, model generation and verification, planning, software package management, program analysis, and other constraint satisfaction problems [7,9,13,22]. SAT is a problem within the NP complexity class, since for every satisfiable Boolean formula there is a proof verifiable in polynomial time.[2]

A problem X is called **NP-complete** if it is in NP, and every other problem from NP can be reduced to X in polynomial time. SAT is known to be NP-complete. Thus, SAT is a "silver bullet" for solving all problems of the NP class. However, finding the most direct low-degree polynomial reduction to SAT can be a challenge. Even if some problem from NP is not known to be NP-complete (such as integer factorization or graph isomorphism), reducing it to SAT can be a reasonable temporary measure until a specific efficient algorithm is found (if it exists).

---

[1] Given a Boolean formula F, determine whether there exists an assignment for all Boolean variables used in F such that F evaluates to `true`.

[2] For SAT, the proof could consist of assignments for the variables and a polynomial algorithm for evaluating the SAT formula.

© The Author(s), under exclusive license to Springer Nature Switzerland AG 2022
M. Ivanovic et al. (Eds.): Baltic DB&IS 2022, CCIS 1598, pp. 201–216, 2022.
https://doi.org/10.1007/978-3-031-09850-5_14

While no polynomial algorithm is known for SAT, and we do not know whether it exists (the $P = NP$ problem), numerous techniques have been proposed to solve SAT efficiently. They include heuristics, conflict-driven clause learning, backjumping, random restarts, message passing, and machine learning [6,18,19]. As a result, state-of-the-art SAT solvers are able to find variable assignments for SAT instances with tens of thousands of variables and clauses, meaning that many practical SAT applications are now tractable.

While some solvers are optimized to run on a single-core CPU (e.g., Glusoce and GSAT), others take advantage specific of hardware, e.g., HordeSAT utilizes multiple CPU cores [3,4,11]. At IMCS[3], we have developed our own solver QuerySAT, which uses graph neural networks internally and requires a GPU[4] for better performance [21].

Solvers that use branching (e.g., MapleSAT[5] and Lingeling[6]) can be used together with parallel solvers that can diversify a single SAT instance into multiple subtasks to be executed in parallel. Besides, multiple different solvers can be launched in parallel on the same SAT instance, hoping that one of them will find the solution faster. Furthermore, we can combine solvers, resulting in hybrid ones, e.g., we can replace the query mechanism in our QuerySAT with a third-party solver.

Since SAT solvers are computationally intense and often require specific hardware, we consider the task of making SAT solvers available as a shared resource deployed either to the dedicated on-premise hardware on to the cloud servers. In this paper, we cover the following tasks:

1. Integrating SAT solvers (as a shared resource) into distributed business software.
2. Optimizing the communication between multiple parallel SAT solvers (e.g., for diversification and learned clause exchange).

Our idea is to introduce the shared SAT memory, which can be accessed from all involved modules (SAT solvers and business software components).

The following section provides the terminology and introduces the web kernel concept, an OS kernel analog for distributed applications. The web kernel will act as the communication broker between SAT solvers, business logic units, and SAT memory. We continue by providing essential implementation details. In particular, we show how to implement SAT memory and manage SAT solvers on multiple shared hardware units. In Sect. 5, we provide a usage scenario based on integer factorization. Finally, we discuss related work and sketch further research directions.

---

[3] Institute of Mathematics and Computer Science, University of Latvia.

[4] Such as Nvidia T4 16 GB GPU (used in our experiments).

[5] MapleSAT has multiple configurations. It is based on MiniSAT [10]; see https://sites.google.com/a/gsd.uwaterloo.ca/maplesat/maplesat.

[6] https://github.com/arminbiere/lingeling.

2   Definitions

A **distributed application** is a program that runs on more than one autonomous computer that communicate over a network. Usually, it consists of two separate programs: the back-end (server-side software) and the front-end (client-side) software. However, multiple server and client nodes are also possible.

The **web computer** is an abstraction that simplifies the development of distributed applications by providing the illusion of a single target computer [15,16]. The web computer factors out the network and multi-user/multi-process management. As a result, distributed applications can be created like traditional desktop applications, i.e., by focusing on just one program, one target computer, and one user.

The web computer consists of the following main parts:

- **data memory** (or web memory), which is shared among network nodes (e.g., the client and the server); since it is constantly being automatically and transparently synchronized, each network node can access web memory as if it was directly attached;
- the **instruction memory** (or code space), where executable/interpretable code is placed; the particular code is delivered only the nodes being able to execute/interpret it (e.g., Java and Python code is installed at the server-side and executed there, while JavaScript code can be delivered and executed at the client browser as well as at the server-side by means of a JavaScript engine such as node.js);
- **web processors**, which are software modules that can execute certain types of instructions from the code space;
- **web I/O devices**, which can be either physical devices (e.g., printers) directly attached to particular physical nodes and available via specific APIs, or virtual devices implemented as software running either on a single node or in a cluster (e.g., databases or file systems).

Notice that due to security considerations, the web computer separates instruction memory from data memory. Thus, it corresponds to the Harvard architecture (as opposed to von Neumann architecture). That protects server-side code from being able to execute code from the shared data memory, which the client can modify (and we should not trust the client) [2].

Although the web computer still requires multiple physical network nodes to operate, web applications do not access them directly but via the intermediate layer, making the single computer illusion possible. Since this intermediate layer acts as an operating system analog, its reference implementation is called *webAppOS* (available at http://webappos.org).

The **web kernel** is the abstraction layer used by webAppOS applications to access web memory, to invoke code from the instruction memory (the code will be executed by some web processor), and to access web I/O devices (Fig. 1). The web kernel factors out the network communication and provides the illusion that all web computer components are located at the same network node as the

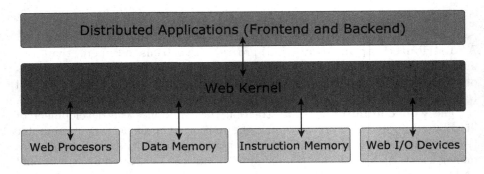

Fig. 1. webAppOS web kernel as an abstraction that factors out the network

calling application code. Since code invocations may require network communication, they are called **web calls**. Web calls are enqueued and forwarded to the corresponding web processors by the web kernel. All web calls are asynchronous (however, the async/await capabilities of modern programming languages can be used as a syntax sugar to simplify asynchronous code).

In fact, web memory is a graph-like structure for storing objects, their states (attributes), and the links between these objects. Besides, web memory also stores the meta-level information (object classes, inheritance relations, etc.). Thus, web memory resembles the OOP memory used by the Java virtual machine. In web memory, multiple inheritance is supported.

The code space, in its turn, stores executable code as **web methods**, which are either functions or methods (depending on a programming language). Each web method is identified by an implementation-agnostic fully-qualified name (e.g., `ClassName.methodName`). Thus, a web call is specified by a fully-qualified method name, the web memory slot, the web object reference in that slot (a `this` or `self` analog), and a JSON object as an argument. Each web call must also return a JSON object (at least an empty JSON `{}`, if no result is expected). Errors (including network errors) are returned in the `error` field.

Different methods of the same class can be written in different programming languages (we call that approach **per-method granularity**). Obviously, there must be web processors (among all nodes) that are able to execute different types of code used in the given webAppOS application.

Since methods can be executed by different web processors (which can be located on different network nodes), it is not possible to implement static linking. The process or substituting a particular web call with the corresponding method implementation is called **web linking**. Due to dynamic and distributed nature of web linking, we use the **duck typing** mechanism to define the *implements* relationship between web objects and interfaces.[7]

---

[7] If interface I is a set of web methods $m_1, m_2, \ldots$, and the object o is included in web memory classes $C_1, C_2, \ldots$, then o implements I, iff $\forall m_i \exists C_j$: $\mathrm{ClassName}(C_j).\mathrm{methodName}(m_i) \in$ Code Space.

Each webAppOS application can be used by multiple users, and each user can have multiple concurrent sessions with the same application. Each such application instance is called a **web process**; it has a dedicated web memory slot identified by **webPid** (in essence, UUID).

Web I/O devices are implemented as code libraries that define device-specific classes and provide implementations for the device-specific methods. For real hardware, these methods access the device via native drivers or OS calls; for virtual devices, they provide software implementation. Since web I/O devices are shared among all web processes, there is a dedicated web memory slot called the **root web memory**, where web I/O devices (with their states) are stored. Thus, device-specific methods can be invoked via the web kernel in the same way as invoking ordinary web calls. Internally, however, device-specific web calls are implemented like software interrupts—they take precedence over ordinary web calls in web processors. This is done intentionally since we may need to interrupt the previous command sent to the device or to release the device for other users as soon as possible.[8]

The web kernel is already available as part of webAppOS. In our architecture, it will act as the communication broker between SAT solvers, business logic units, and the SAT memory, all of which can be located at different network nodes.

3   Integrating SAT Solvers

Each SAT solver is integrated as a virtual web I/O device (i.e., implemented as a software unit). In the root web memory, different types of SAT solvers are represented as subclasses of the SatSolver superclass, while each particular solver instance is represented as an object of the corresponding subclass. Typically, the number of solver instances will correspond to the number of free CPU cores (i.e., not occupied by web processors); however, the solver type and the required hardware (e.g., GPU) can also affect the number of solvers at each node. In any case, all available solvers among all nodes can be easily detected by traversing the root web memory.

3.1   Per-Solver Concurrency

The SAT instance can be a standalone SAT problem, a subtask of a larger problem, or its diversified variant. Since solving SAT is a computationally intensive task, we intentionally limit each solver to processing only one SAT instance at a time. However, since the solver can be invoked by different users concurrently, it has to be implemented in a thread-safe way, returning an **error** attribute when necessary.

Each solver must implement the following web methods (=web I/O device interrupts):

---

[8] This implies that web I/O devices must be implemented in a thread-safe way.

- `solve({satMemoryUrl, timeout, diversification})`—starts the solver on a SAT instance stored in the given SAT memory using the given diversification guidelines (the SAT memory is discussed in the next section, while diversification is discussed in the following subsection).
  The solver gets the clauses from the SAT memory, diversifies itself, solves the SAT instance, and returns the `result` attribute equal to `SAT`, `UNSAT`, or `UNKNOWN`. The latter value is returned when neither the satisfying variables assignment, nor the contradiction could be devised (e.g., for heuristics-based or randomized solvers). The `UNKNOWN` value is also returned when the solver has been interrupted. In case of `SAT`, the variable assignments are returned in the `model` attribute (a JSON array).
  Suppose the solver is already solving another SAT instance. In that case, the `solve` method must return the `BUSY` flag in the `error` attribute or wait at most `timeout` seconds for the solver to become available.
- `pause({})`—requests the solver to interrupt the search as soon as possible with the ability to resume the search (e.g., the call stack has to be maintained);
- `resume({})`—resumes the previously interrupted search;
- `cancel({})`—interrupts the search for good for the SAT instance currently being processed. As a result, the currently running `solve` web call must return `UNKNOWN`.

We assume that in case of any error (e.g., when a non-paused solver is requested to `resume`, or when the memory/CPU limits have been exceeded), the `error` attribute is returned. Besides, since the web calls above are web I/O device interrupts, `webPid` of the caller web process is always implicitly passed. That allows the solver to verify, for example, whether the `pause` web call originated from the same web process that had invoked `solve`,—a helpful security precaution.

3.2   Diversification

The following diversification settings can be passed to the `solve` web call. We borrowed them from the HordeSAT portfolio-based solver and transformed them to the JSON syntax to comply with the requirements of the web kernel [4]. Each solver type can implement diversification differently.

- `rank`—the index of this particular solver among all solvers working on the current SAT problem; as a trivial example, `rank` could be used to initialize the random number generator seed;
- `size`—the number of solvers working on the current SAT problem;
- `phases`—an optional JSON object with attributes named xi, e.g., `x5`, $1 \leq i \leq \#$(SAT variables); for variable x_i, `phases[xi]` denotes the Boolean value to try first during the search (the variable "phase").

Notice that although each solver in the root web memory is treated as a single instance, it can rely on multiple parallel solvers (e.g., multiple GPU subprograms) inside. Such "internals solvers" are not visible to the web kernel and cannot be diversified in the way described above.

3.3   Joining Parallel Solvers

A solver can divide the task into subtasks (e.g., by applying diversification from Sect. 3.2) and solve them in parallel via `parallelize`, a built-in web call provided by the web kernel. The `parallelize` web call takes a list L of child web calls and invokes them in parallel (when possible). In our case, L consists of the `solve` web calls with diversified arguments corresponding to the subtasks.

Technically, `parallelize` stores a counter in web memory and appends the `join` method (also built-in) invocation to each web call from L. The `join` method increments the counter and stores the return value of the child web call. When the counter reaches the length of L, `parallelize` returns the list of child return values, which can be processed by the parent solver.

The sequence diagram in Fig. 2 shows how diversification and parallelization are applied when solving a SAT instance. The initial `solve` web call is invoked with a single argument, a SAT memory URL, where the SAT instance has been previously stored. The web kernel searches for a suitable `SatSolver` instance and forwards the call to it. The SAT solver decides to diversify the task by splitting it into two subtasks: $solve_1$ and $solve_2$. The subtasks are invoked in parallel via the `parallelize` web call, which appends the `join` call to each subtask. Each subtask is executed by an idle SAT solver (as soon as one becomes available). A `join` web call is invoked when each subtask finishes. When both `join`-s have been invoked, the web kernel combines the return values of the subtasks and returns them as a result of the `parallelize` web call. Based on the result, the initial solver computes the global solution and returns it.

4   Implementing the SAT Memory

Like SAT solvers, each SAT memory instance is also represented as a virtual web I/O device. The reason for such design choice is to avoid introducing a new memory type, which could complicate the web kernel architecture. Unlike web memory, SAT memory is not used in all web processes. Besides, depending on the normal form used to represent the clauses (e.g., CNF or ANF), there could be different types of SAT memory[9]. In addition, certain web methods (such as converters between normal forms) may need multiple types of SAT memory at the same time.

---

[9] In this paper, we cover CNF only.

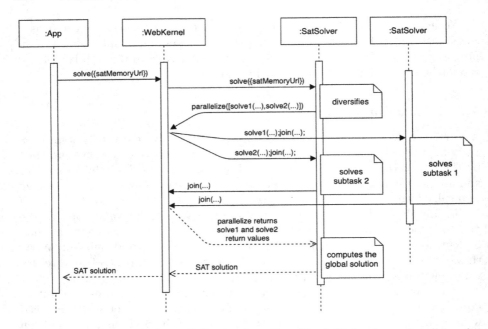

Fig. 2. Diversification and parallelization in action. The initial `solve` web call is split into two web calls, `solve1` and `solve2`, which are then executed in parallel via the `parallelize` web call.

In this section, we focus on SAT memory with clauses given in the conjunctive normal form (CNF) since it is used in the DIMACS file format, a *de facto* standard supported by the majority of SAT solvers. Besides, it is used at SAT competitions[10].

SAT memory instances with CNF clauses are represented as instances of the `SatCnf` web class in the root web memory. Unlike instances of `SatSolver`, which are preconfigured in advance, `SatCnf` objects can be created and deleted dynamically. Such an approach resembles the process of attaching and detaching external data storage (e.g., USB drives) to the PC.

The CNF SAT memory consists of free variables $x_1, x_2, \ldots, x_n$ and CNF clauses in the form $(l_1, l_2, \ldots, l_k)$, where each $l_i, 1 \leq l_i \leq n$, is an integer representing a literal:

$$x_{l_i} \text{ if } l_i > 0$$
$$\neg x_{l_i} \text{ if } l_i < 0$$

The number of free variables can be increased at runtime. Additional variables can be introduced, for example, to avoid exponential formula growth while converting Boolean formulas to CNF (resulting in an equisatisfiable formula, not equivalent). Besides, specific formula fragments can be easier expressible by introducing helper variables.

---

[10] https://satcompetition.github.io.

SatCnf objects are created by specifying the initial number of Boolean variables.

The SatCnf web class implements the following web methods (in a thread-safe way):

- addVariable({}) - adds a new free variable and returns its index (a positive integer);
- addClause({clause}) - adds a new CNF clause as an array of integers $(l_1, l_2, \dots)$ representing literals, where $1 \le |l_i| \le \#$(free variables). In order to avoid duplicate clauses, we sort literals before adding the clause. However, a Bloom filter could also be used instead.
- clauses({}) - returns the array of clauses currently stored in the SAT memory, e.g., [[1,-2,3],[4,-5]];
- fork({detach}) - returns a new SatCnf instance that retains the clauses of the current SAT memory with the ability to add new clauses to the forked SAT memory only.[11] If detach=true, further changes to the original SAT are not reflected in the fork. Otherwise, the fork will share free variables with the origin and will get clause updates.
  Forks are helpful for defining SAT subtasks that can be passed to solve. For example, specific variable assignments can be added as single-literal clauses. Learned clauses (in CDCL-based solvers) can also be added to the forked memory.

Notice that we do not have methods to read and write the assignments of the variables in SAT memory. Although counter-intuitive, that protects SAT memory from possible collisions between different variable assignments by different solvers (if the solution is not unique, or in case of a partial solution).

While the methods above are convenient to constructing the initial SAT instance, invoking them via web calls involves certain serialization/deserialization overhead, which is undesirable when multiple solvers access SAT memory. That would also negatively impact portfolio-based solvers, which need to exchange learned clauses at runtime.

In order to minimize the web kernel overhead, we introduce *direct access* to SAT memory, resembling the DMA[12] feature in traditional hardware computing systems. We implement it by means of web sockets[13].

Web sockets of a SAT memory instance can be accessed by the address available in the directUrl attribute. All web socket connections are managed by an internal hub of the SatCnf class. When a new variable or clause is added via one web socket, the hub forwards them to other web sockets. This way, new variables and clauses can be efficiently exchanged between all other nodes using the same SAT memory.

---

[11] Technically, in order to avoid copying of clauses, the common part with the original SAT memory is factored out and stored only once.

[12] Direct memory access.

[13] The extension of the HTTP protocol for highly-efficient bi-directional communication via the network.

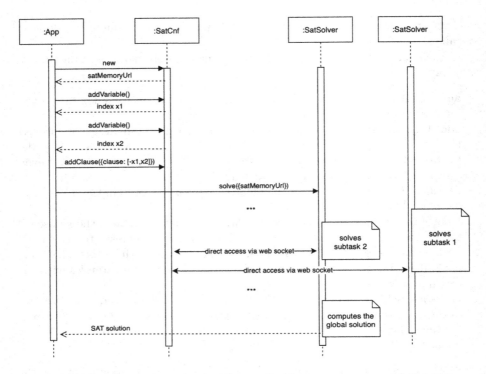

Fig. 3. SAT memory usage example. The application creates a new `SatCnf` instance and fills it with SAT variables and clauses by invoking traditional web calls. Solvers, however, access `SatCnf` directly via web sockets.

In a nutshell, the protocol used in web sockets uses binary messages corresponding to the `SatCnf` methods. However, `addVariable` and `addClause` can be both sent and received. When received, the client shall treat them as variable and clause synchronization messages from other solvers.

In addition to the `addVariable` message, we introduce also the messages (sent by the client) for:

- locking variables (thus, the last used variable index stays fixed);
- adding multiples free variables;
- unlocking variables.

These methods skip multiple round-trips when multiple free variables have to be added, and their indices used to construct clauses. Variables should be locked only for a short period of time since `addVariable` calls sent by other SAT memory users will wait until variables are unlocked.

Figure 3 illustrates a sample scenario of using SAT memory (a `SatCnf` instance).[14] Firstly, the application creates a new `SatCnf` instance and fills it

---

[14] For the sake of clarity, we omitted the web kernel and some steps of Fig. 2.

with variables and clauses (by invoking the `addVariable` and `addClause` web calls). Then the application invokes the `solve` web call. When solving the SAT instance, each solver working on a specific subtask consults the SAT memory instance directly via web sockets.

5   Usage Example

In this section, we consider the integer factorization problem and its transformation to the SAT problem as a use case. For simplicity, we consider products of exactly two integer factors (>1) of the same length l. If both factors are primes, our transformation generates a SAT instance having the unique solution.

The input: the length l and $2l$ bits of the product.

The output: A SAT instance in the SAT memory.

When the SAT memory is filled, the `solve` web method of the first available portfolio-based SAT solver (found in the root web memory) is invoked to obtain the SAT assignment. The first $2l$ Boolean values of the assignment will correspond to the bits of the two factors in question.

5.1   The Karatsuba Algorithm

In order to asymptotically minimize the number of generated variables and clauses, we apply the Karatsuba multiplication algorithm, which is based on the recursive "divide and conquer" approach [14].

If $u = (u_{2n-1} \ldots u_1 u_0)$ and $v = (v_{2n-1} \ldots v_1 v_0)$ are $2n$-bit integers, they can be written as

$$u = 2^n U_1 + U_0 \text{ and } v = 2^n V_1 + V_0$$

(the most significant bits are on the left). Then

$$uv = (2^{2n} + 2^n)U_1 V_1 + 2^2(U_1 - U_0)(V_0 - V_1) + (2^n + 1)U_0 V_0. \quad (1)$$

The Karatsuba algorithm is applied recursively to each of the three multiplications of n-bit numbers from (1). Since the algorithm expects the even number of bits at each level, we start with u and v represented as 2^k-bit numbers (lacking leading zeroes are prepended).

5.2   Initializing Web Memory

In web memory, an m-bit integer will be represented as an ordered list of m literals: for a positive literal x_i, the i-th bit value will correspond to the x_i value (0 for `false` and 1 for `true`); for a negative literal $\neg x_i$, the i-th bit will correspond to the negation of x_i. Thus, one variable can be re-used as a positive or negative literal.

Since we are given the number of bits in each factor ($l = 2^k$ by the reasons explained above), we initialize a new SAT memory instance with $2l = 2^{k+1}$ free variables. Thus, factors u and v are represented as the literal lists $x_{l-1}, \ldots x_2, x_1$ and $x_{2l-1}, \ldots x_{l+1}, x_l$.

5.3   Generating the SAT Formula

The SAT formula generation process introduces additional integers (additional free variables are added when needed). Those additional integers result from existing integers by applying transformation functions.

Transformation functions are constructed as Boolean expressions that bind literals of the source and target integers. Boolean expressions are built from Boolean primitives And, Or, and Not, as well as from auxiliary Boolean Xor, Majority (of 3 elements), Implication, and Equivalence, which can be easily implemented through the Boolean primitives.

Here is the list of transformation functions used as the building blocks. $L_1, L_2, \ldots$ are lists of literals used to represent the corresponding source or target integers denoted as $I_1, I_2, \ldots$:

- L_1.`negation()` $\rightarrow$ L_2: transforms I_1 to $I_2 = -I_1$ represented as the two's complement in the $|L_1|$-bit notation. Technically, we inverse all bits of I_1 (by negating all literals of L_1) and add 1: the i-th bit of I_1 is added to the i-th carry bit by means of the half adder formula (from digital logic).
- L_1.`sum_with`(L_2) $\rightarrow$ L_3 (assume $|L_1| = |L_2|$): transforms I_1 and I_2 to $I_3 = I_1 + I_2$ in the $|L_1|$-bit two's complement notation. The overflow bit of I_3 (if any) is ignored. Technically, we use 1 half adder formula and $L_1 - 1$ adder formulas.
- L_1.`product_with`(L_2) $\rightarrow$ L_3 (assume $|L_1| = |L_2| = 2^k, |L_3| = 2 \cdot 2^k$): transforms two 2^k-bit integers I_1 and I_2 (in the 2^k-bit two's complement notation) to a 2^{k+1}-bit integer $I_3 = I_1 \cdot I_2$ in the 2^{k+1}-bit two's complement notation according to Eq. (1). Some technical nuances are:
  - representing the difference of 2 numbers by means of `sum_with` and `negation`;
  - determining the sign of the inner Karatsuba product $(U_1 - U_0)(V_0 - V_1)$ from Eq. (1);
  - propagating the sign bit from the 2^k-bit to the 2^{k+1}-bit two's complement notation.

By applying the transformation functions above we can construct a (non-CNF) SAT formula that binds the initial $2l$ free variables with the $2l$ literals of the product (the topmost transformation, obviously, will be `product_with` on two initial lists $x_{l-1}, \ldots x_2, x_1$ and $x_{2l-1}, \ldots x_{l+1}, x_l$). Our implementation of transformation functions introduces additional variables and re-uses literals for recurring formulas.

After constructing the formula, we convert it to CNF using the following patterns:

- re-phrasing auxiliary Boolean functions (such as Xor and Majority) using And, Or, and Not;
- applying De Morgan's laws in order to get rid of factored-out negations;
- introducing new variables and equivalences for inner conjunctions. For example, given the formula $(x_1 \vee (x_2 \& x_3 \& x_4))$, we replace $(x_2 \& x_3 \& x_4)$ with a new variable x_5, and add the equivalence $x_5 \equiv x_2 \& x_3 \& x_4$;

- introducing new variables for equivalences (from the previous pattern) having more than two literals on the right side, e.g., x_6 to represent $x_3 \& x_4$ (with the corresponding equivalence $x_6 \iff x_3 \& x_4$;
- constructing CNF clauses from 3-literal equivalences (such as $x_5 \iff x_2 \& x_6$ and $x_6 \iff x_3 \& x_4$ above) with the help of the truth table.

Afterward, we extend the CNF by appending a conjunction of literals corresponding to the product bits. The corresponding single-literal clause is added if the product bit is 1, and the literal is negated if the bit is 0.

In order to exclude the case when one the factors is 1, we add two clauses $(x_{l-1} \lor \ldots x_3 \lor x_2)$ and $(x_{2l-1} \lor \ldots x_{l+2} \lor x_{l+1})$, meaning that, for each factor, there must be at least one bit set to 1, not counting the right-most bit $(x_1$ or $x_l)$.

We exclude negative factors by adding two single-literal clauses $\neg x_{l-1}$ and $\neg x_{2l-1}$, meaning that the most-significant bit of each factor is 0 (it must be 0 for non-negative numbers in two's complement notation).

In order to specify the unique solution when the product consists of two primes, we use the condition $u - v \geq 0$. The clauses for it can be obtained in a similar manner as for the main SAT formula.

The transformation functions listed above (applied to integers represented as lists of literals) can be easily mapped to any OOP-based programming language. Access to web memory and SAT solvers (by means of web methods of the corresponding web I/O devices) is also OOP-based. Thus, SAT instances can be generated, placed into web memory, and then passed to a solver in a truly OOP way, without the need to think about the network. Furthermore, our building blocks can serve as a basis for building larger transformation functions.

The current version of the SAT generator (work-in-progress) is available at the IMCS GitHub page https://github.com/LUMII-Syslab/sat-generator.

6   Related Work

The invention of advanced heuristics, search space pruning, and intelligent pre-processing of SAT clauses have drastically increased the performance of SAT solvers intended to run on a single CPU. Such solvers are primarily based on the DPLL[15] variants CDCL[16] and VSIDS[17]. Much research has also been done in the parallelization direction, where the three main approaches are 1) running multiple sequential SAT solvers with different settings, 2) partitioning the search space into (disjoint) subtasks and running multiple solver instances on them, and 3) the portfolio-based approach, where different types of solvers are working in parallel, with the ability to diversify them and exchange learned clauses between them [4, 12].

---

[15] The Davis–Putnam–Logemann–Loveland algorithm.
[16] Conflict-driven clause-learning.
[17] Variable State Independent Decaying Sum.

In our approach, each SAT solver is viewed as a serial one (even if it internally uses parallelization). However, multiple solvers (of different types or the same) are also possible, and the web kernel (a part of webAppOS) allows integrating them to support different types of parallelization.

SAT memory is our innovative solution to provide distributed memory tailored to solving the SAT problem. In our implementation of the SAT memory, we use the centralized approach (as opposed to the distributed one) to deal with the coherence problem [17]. However, our bi-directional web sockets allow web memory clients to exchange clauses, a step towards a hybrid approach. Besides, that also allows us to avoid callbacks. The direct access to SAT memory resembles how shared character devices (from the /dev directory) are accessed in Linux and BSD systems.

Our APIs for solvers and the SAT memory resemble Portfolio Solver Interface used by HordeSAT, as well as MiniSAT's external interface [4]. However, we separate methods related to SAT solving from the ones used to access clauses in web memory. Besides, both our APIs (for solvers and the SAT memory) follow the pure OOP principles [23]. Furthermore, HordeSat uses the same `setSolverInterrupt` call for both pausing and canceling the search (MiniSAT interface does not have such capability). In contrast, we use distinct methods, since in the former case, the call stack has to be maintained, while, in the latter case, we can free all the resources used by the solver.

The integer factorization problem is one of the approaches used to generate hard SAT instances. ToughtSAT[18] is a collection of SAT generators, which includes a generator for SAT instances for the integer factorization problem. It has been used in SAT Competition 2019 [5]. Sadly, although the generator generates succinct SAT instances, it emits errors on some factors and generates SAT instances with a non-unique solution.

A more generic approach to SAT instance generation is to use SAT compilers. Picat-SAT, FznTiny, and MiniZinc-SAT are good representatives [13,20,24]. Although some SAT compilers use binary log encoding for integers, none of the known generic SAT compilers use the Karatsuba algorithm to represent integer products.

Our conversion to CNF utilizes the pattern of constructing CNF clauses used in the proof that SAT is reducible to 3-CNF-SAT [1].

7   Conclusion

We have proposed a software architecture where SAT solvers are shared in the distributed environment by means of the webAppOS web kernel. In our approach, any type of SAT solver can be used as a shared solver; the only requirement is to represent it as `SatSolver` subclass and implement the API (web methods) from Sect. 3.1 (usually, glue code is sufficient for that). Our design

---

[18] In 2022, it is available at https://github.com/joebebel/toughsat.git; older references point to https://toughsat.appspot.com/, which is no more available.

is suitable for a single shared SAT solver, as well as for multiple SAT solvers launched with different settings or on parallel subtasks.

The web kernel is a mediator between all software units mentioned in the paper. In the future, we plan to formalize the minimal set of web kernel APIs, which can be re-implemented in systems other than webAppOS.

Since SAT solvers are represented as independent webAppOS I/O devices, they can be either on-premise (e.g., installed on specific hardware) or cloud-based. That opens opportunities to commercial SAT solvers available as a service.

In our architecture, a novel component is shared SAT memory, which can be accessed either as a webAppOS virtual I/O device or directly via web sockets. While we have considered SAT memory for storing CNF clauses, the architecture can be generalized to support clauses in the disjunctive normal form (DNF) and algebraic normal form (ANF). Having multiple types of SAT memory, our architecture allows the developers to create web methods that use multiple SAT memories simultaneously (e.g., for data conversion).

We also envisage further extensions of SAT memory. For example, belief propagation and survey propagation-based SAT solvers need to store real weights (called "warnings") associated with SAT variables and clauses [8].

Acknowledgements. Research supported by the Latvian Council of Science, Project No. 2021/1-0479 "Combinatorial Optimization with Deep Neural Networks".

References

1. Aho, A.V., Hopcroft, J.E., Ullman, J.D.: The Design and Analysis of Computer Algorithms. Addison-Wesley Series in Computer Science and Information Processing. Addison-Wesley, Reading (1974)
2. Andrews, M., Whittaker, J.A.: How to Break Web Software: Functional and Security Testing of Web Applications and Web Services. Addison-Wesley Professional, Boston (2006)
3. Audemard, G., Simon, L.: On the glucose SAT solver. Int. J. Artif. Intell. Tools **27**(01), 1840001 (2018)
4. Balyo, T., Sanders, P., Sinz, C.: HordeSat: a massively parallel portfolio SAT solver, May 2015. https://doi.org/10.1007/978-3-319-24318-4_12
5. Bebel, J.: Harder SAT Instances from Factoring with Karatsuba and Espresso. In: Proceedings of SAT Race 2019. University of Helsinki (2019)
6. Biere, A., Heule, M., Maaren, H.V. (eds.): Handbook of Satisfiability. Frontiers in Artificial Intelligence and Applications, vol. 336, 2nd edn. IOS Press, Amsterdam; Washington, DC (2021). oCLC: on1250382566
7. Boulanger, J.L. (ed.): Formal Methods Applied to Complex Systems: Implementation of the B Method. Computer Engineering Series, ISTE; Wiley, London: Hoboken, New Jersey (2014)
8. Braunstein, A., Mezard, M., Zecchina, R.: Survey propagation: an algorithm for satisfiability. Random Struct. Algorithms **27**, 201–226 (2005)
9. Eggersglüss, S., Eggersglüß, S., Drechsler, R.: High Quality Test Pattern Generation and Boolean Satisfiability. Springer, New York (2012). https://doi.org/10.1007/978-1-4419-9976-4

10. Eén, N., Sörensson, N.: An extensible SAT-solver. In: Giunchiglia, E., Tacchella, A. (eds.) SAT 2003. LNCS, vol. 2919, pp. 502–518. Springer, Heidelberg (2004). https://doi.org/10.1007/978-3-540-24605-3_37

11. Folino, G., Pizzuti, C., Spezzano, G.: Parallel hybrid method for SAT that couples genetic algorithms and local search. IEEE Trans. Evol. Comput. **5**(4), 323–334 (2001)

12. Hamadi, Y., Jabbour, S., Sais, L.: ManySAT: a parallel SAT solver. JSAT **6**, 245–262 (2009)

13. Huang, J.: Universal booleanization of constraint models. In: Stuckey, P.J. (ed.) CP 2008. LNCS, vol. 5202, pp. 144–158. Springer, Heidelberg (2008). https://doi.org/10.1007/978-3-540-85958-1_10

14. Knuth, D.E.: The Art of Computer Programming, Volume 2: Seminumerical Algorithms, vol. 2, 3rd edn. Addison-Wesley, Reading (1997)

15. Kozlovičs, S.: The web computer and its operating system: a new approach for creating web applications. In: Proceedings of the 15th International Conference on Web Information Systems and Technologies (WEBIST 2019), Vienna, Austria, pp. 46–57. SCITEPRESS (2019)

16. Kozlovičs, S.: webAppOS: creating the illusion of a single computer for web application developers. In: Bozzon, A., Domínguez Mayo, F.J., Filipe, J. (eds.) WEBIST 2019. LNBIP, vol. 399, pp. 1–21. Springer, Cham (2020). https://doi.org/10.1007/978-3-030-61750-9_1

17. Li, K., Hudak, P.: Memory coherence in shared virtual memory systems. ACM Trans. Comput. Syst. **7**(4), 321–359 (1989)

18. Malik, S., Zhang, L.: Boolean satisfiability: from theoretical hardness to practical success. Commun. ACM **52**(8), 76–82 (2009)

19. Moskewicz, M., Madigan, C., Zhao, Y., Zhang, L., Malik, S.: Chaff: engineering an efficient SAT solver. In: Proceedings of the 38th Design Automation Conference (IEEE cat. No. 01CH37232), pp. 530–535 (2001)

20. Nethercote, N., Stuckey, P.J., Becket, R., Brand, S., Duck, G.J., Tack, G.: MiniZinc: towards a standard CP modelling language. In: Bessière, C. (ed.) CP 2007. LNCS, vol. 4741, pp. 529–543. Springer, Heidelberg (2007). https://doi.org/10.1007/978-3-540-74970-7_38

21. Ozolins, E., Freivalds, K., Draguns, A., Gaile, E., Zakovskis, R., Kozlovics, S.: Goal-aware neural SAT solver. In: Proceedings of the 2022 International Joint Conference on Neural Networks (IJCNN 2022) (2022)

22. Rintanen, J.: Planning as satisfiability: heuristics. Artif. Intell. **193**, 45–86 (2012)

23. West, D.: Object Thinking. Microsoft Professional. Microsoft, Redmond (2004)

24. Zhou, N.-F., Kjellerstrand, H.: The Picat-SAT compiler. In: Gavanelli, M., Reppy, J. (eds.) PADL 2016. LNCS, vol. 9585, pp. 48–62. Springer, Cham (2016). https://doi.org/10.1007/978-3-319-28228-2_4

Data, Data Science, and Computing for Digital Business and Intelligent Systems

Outlier Analysis for Telecom Fraud Detection

Viktoras Chadyšas$^{(\boxtimes)}$ [ID], Andrej Bugajev[ID], Rima Kriauzienė[ID], and Olegas Vasilecas[ID]

Vilnius Gediminas Technical University, 10223 Vilnius, Lithuania
{viktoras.chadysas,andrej.bugajev,rima.kriauziene,
olegas.vasilecas}@vilniustech.lt

Abstract. Every year, the number of telecommunication fraud cases increases dramatically, and companies providing such services lose billions of euros worldwide. It has been receiving more and more attention lately mobile virtual network operators (MVNOs) which operate on top of existing cellular infrastructures of the basic operators, and at the same time are able to offer cheaper call plans. This paper is aimed to identify suspicious customers with unusual behaviour, typical to potential fraudsters in MVNO. In this study, different univariate outlier detection methods are applied. Univariate outliers are obtained using call detail records (CDR) and payments records information which is aggregated by users. A special emphasis in this paper is put on the metrics designed for outlier detection in the context of suspicious customer labelling which may support the fraud experts in evaluating customers and revealing fraud. In this research, we identified specific attributes that could be applied for fraud detection. Threshold values were found for the attributes examined, which could be used to compile lists of suspicious users.

Keywords: Telecom fraud · Outlier detection · Unsupervised learning · Data mining

1 Introduction

Telecommunications service providers are constantly suffering significant financial losses due to various malicious activities against them. Having a comprehensive understanding of telephony fraud is a challenging task. There are many definitions of telecommunications fraud, but it is generally agreed that telecommunications fraud usually involves the theft of services or deliberate abuse of mobile networks [5].

In the field of telecommunications, fraud detection methods are mostly based on customer profiles, the part of the profile's information is derived from customers' behaviour. Behaviour-based fraud detection methods aim to identify users who behave abnormally. Solving such a task is performed analysis of customer behaviour [1,8] aimed at:

M. Ivanovic et al. (Eds.): Baltic DB&IS 2022, CCIS 1598, pp. 219–231, 2022.
https://doi.org/10.1007/978-3-031-09850-5_15

– define rules of conduct to identify the fraudulent customer;
– identify significant changes in fraudulent customer behaviour.

Different techniques are used:

– rules-based systems;
– supervised machine learning methods based on past fraud cases;
– unsupervised machine learning methods discovered for new fraudsters.

In rules-based fraud detection systems, fraud cases are defined by rules. They may consist of one or more conditions. When all the conditions are correct post warning. The terms of the rules may include different sources of data: call detail records, data of the customer or their behaviour during its real-time frame [12]. For example, the user can be suspected as a fraud if he made Y different calls during the X period, in different directions, which are defined by country direction code. Such a rule could detect fraud, but it could also detect false danger. Alerts, along with suspicious user data, should be collected while the data analyst should determine in each case whether fraud has taken place or not. The main disadvantages of rule-based systems are:

– fixed thresholds for the attributes included in the rule, which also needs to be adjusted over time;
– result of rules yes/no;
– there is no way to determine the interaction of attributes.

Traditionally, fraud rules are defined by an expert or data analyst, but with the emergence of new forms of fraud, there is a need to clarify the existing rules or even automate their creation. Namely, models based on machine learning methods are increasingly being used to detect fraud. Their main advantages:

– adapts to data and can adjust over time;
– thresholds for the values of a combination of all variables are used instead of a single variable;
– ability to present a probability of potentially suspicious fraud.

Most machine learning methods use labelled data, e.g. in the dataset, each record is marked with the appropriate class. In telecom fraud detection, appropriate classes would be fraudster and non-fraudster. Such methods are classified as supervised machine learning methods and routines used to solve classification or forecasting tasks. A huge problem for researching and developing a fraud detection system is the lack of labelled data. Labelling requires expertise and is a time-consuming process.

Unsupervised methods are commonly used in situations where there is no prior knowledge of users belonging to a particular class in a dataset. If we do not know which users are fraudsters and which are not, these methods can be used to identify groups of suspicious users, potentially fraudsters.

It is our goal to use unsupervised statistical methods to detect potential fraudsters. Existing studies also lack in providing the clear and accurate definition of telecom fraud. Thus, in the context of the mentioned research gaps, in this article we make the following contribution:

- we provide the approach for the usage of outlier analysis to identify specific attributes that should be given more attention;
- the metrics designed for outlier detection to detect fraudulent customers.

The remainder of the article is organized as follows. Section 2 presents an overview of telecom fraud and presents an in-depth analysis of existing studies relevant to the detection of telecom fraud to identify research gaps that need to be considered in this research. Section 3 provides detailed information on the methods for detecting univariate outliers and the design of metrics for this purpose. Section 4 shows our experimental results. Finally, Sect. 5 concludes the discussion with describe issues for the future research of fraud detection.

2   Telecom Fraud Detection

Since telecommunication frauds cause financial loss to telecommunications service providers, it is necessary and urgent to detect it. Research in telecommunications fraud detection is mainly focused on fraudulent activities in the field of mobile technology. Historically, fraud takes many different forms, examples of some common varieties of fraud in telecommunications, given in Table 1 [2]:

Table 1. Telecommunications fraud forms.

Fraud type	Description
Subscription	Someone signs up for service (e.g., a new phone, extra lines) with no intent to pay. In this case, all calls associated with the given fraudulent line are fraudulent but are consistent with the profile of the user
Intrusion	A legitimate account is compromised in some way by an intruder, who subsequently makes or sells calls on this account
Masquerading	Credit card numbers can be stolen and used to place calls masquerading as the cardholder

Telecommunications fraud is not static, new types of fraud appear regularly, and these schemes are evolving and trying to adapt to attempts to stop them. To detect telecommunications fraud, most current methods are based on labelling customers that are considered to be fraudsters. In addition, many researchers use machine learning techniques to detect fraudsters.

In [3] to identify fraudulent users, the supervised learning method neural network classification and the unsupervised learning method hierarchical clustering were used. Each of the above methods was applied separately to identify the most important features of the methods. Based on the experiments, an effective user profile, defined by generalized attributes, was identified, which helps to distinguish normal from malicious behaviour. Experiments using real data from a traditional telecom operator have shown that neural network classifiers can distinguish malicious users from traditional ones according to the user profile provided. At the same time, the authors emphasize that neural networks act as black boxes in terms of data analysis. Experiments were also performed with unlabelled data. Hierarchical clustering was used to identify user groups that would be identified as fraudsters. The results depended on the choice of distance measures. The Euclidean use of the distance measure in hierarchical clustering helped to differentiate different groups of users according to their behaviour, while using the correlation-based distance measure it was the group of malicious users that became clearer. Zheng and Liu [14] also examine ways to identify a group of users suspected of fraud using telecommunications data. The Multi-faceted Telecom Customer Behavior Analysis (MTCBA) framework for anomalous telecom customer behavior detection and clustering analysis is proposed. Because users of unusual, suspicious behavior are excluded from the data, the authors suggest first identifying a group of distinguished users using the hierarchical Locality Sensitive Hashing-Local Outlier Factor (LSH-LOF) algorithm of hierarchical clustering and then re-grouping users using the k-means method to identify a specific group of fraudulent users.

In [7] the authors examine one of the most common types of fraud in the telecommunications industry, which generates large traffic for profit-making purposes. In their view, it would be difficult to identify such fraudulent consumers as a distinct exception, and therefore suggests that a whole group of such consumers be sought. To address this challenge, it recommends a fraud detection system based on data clustering and subsequent classification methods. First, clustering techniques are used to identify homogeneous user segments, such as traditional users, business customers, call centres, or fraudulent users. Second, apply the decision tree classification method to the forecast based on the results obtained by marking the dataset.

Most of the scientific work on the detection of malicious activity in telecommunications is based on data from traditional operators and only a few works are aimed at MVNOs. The performance of the MVNO ecosystem has been analysed to understand various key aspects, including its architecture, customers in [10]. Analysis of big data, statistical modelling and machine learning were used for MVNO's main concerns related to data usage prediction, customer churn mitigation and fraudulent activity detection.

Finally, it could be summarised that, the most effective method for detecting malicious activity in telecommunications has not yet been found and that its search is still ongoing. The experiments are performed with a different set of attributes, without analysing too much how they were selected and which ones are most significant in detecting fraudulent activity. Even more, many methods are applied or tested using labelled data. It is often mentioned that data are labelled with the help of experts and that the data themselves are not provided for data protection reasons, so it is not possible to test other methods. In the meantime, we suggest using outliers detection methods, both for labelling data and to identify important attributes that may be relevant in detecting fraudulent activity in telecommunications.

3   Outliers Detection Methods

Outliers detection is one of the main data mining challenges to be addressed in various areas to identify inaccuracies in the collection of data, unusual data templates or anomalies in the data, for example including suspicious consumer behaviour. Outlier detection is employed to measure the "distance" between data objects to detect those objects that are grossly different from or inconsistent with the remaining data set.

An outlier is usually considered to be an unusual event or object whose properties do not correspond to most of the data set. In the scientific literature, outliers are often identified with anomalies, and even the same methods are used to detect them. Although these two terms have a similar meaning in the context of data analysis, the concept of an anomaly is more closely linked to unusual behaviour, which is being tried to conceal. Searching for anomalies is the process of identifying those that stand out objects that should not be in the data and their identification is important in identifying an example of fraud.

The choice of method usually determines which objects are identified as distinctive, which means that there is no objective way of knowing what an object that stands out is, and what's not. Decision-making, in this case, becomes subjective, influenced by the analysis performed goals or challenges.

Typical numerical values of individual variables in a data set are generally considered to be close to their mean or median. Meanwhile, with outliers, the values are greater away from the sample mean or median. This can be determined using statistical or data representation methods [6]:

- normal distribution standard deviation rule (z-criterion);
- modified normal distribution deviation rule (modified z-criterion);
- boxplot and Interquartile Range (IQR) method.

If the values $x_1, x_2, \ldots, x_n$ of the attribute X correspond to the normal distribution, for each observation x_n assigned values:

$$z_n = \frac{x_n - \overline{x}}{s} \qquad (1)$$

will correspond to the standard normal distribution $N(0,1)$. Here $\overline{x}$ is the mean and s is the standard deviation of the values. Generally, if $z > 3$ observation (x value) is an outlier. This rule is derived from the fact based on the characteristics of a normal distribution for which 99.87% of the data appear within the 3 standard range deviations from the mean. Unfortunately, three problems can be identified when using the mean as the central tendency indicator: firstly, it assumes that the distribution is normal (outliers included); secondly, the mean and standard deviation are strongly impacted by outliers; thirdly, this method is very unlikely to detect outliers in small samples [9].

Using the traditional z-criterion method to identify exclusions, z-values are calculated using an arithmetic mean that is sensitive to outliers and may therefore fail to find the outliers properly. Modification of the z-criterion was proposed by Iglewicz and Hoaglin [6] has adjusted the formula for calculating z-values:

$$z_n = \frac{0.6745 \cdot (x_n - \tilde{x})}{MAD} \tag{2}$$

where $\tilde{x}$ is the median of the values and MAD is the median of the absolute deviation, which is defined as:

$$MAD = median(|x_n - \tilde{x}|) \tag{3}$$

The authors of this method recommend that the values of the variable x be considered as outliers if their respective absolute z-values are greater than 3.5.

Conditional outliers for individual attributes can be determined by plotting the distribution of values for that attribute using a box plot [13]. In the box plot, the possible values of the outliers are marked with certain symbols and these are the values:

$$< (Q_1 - 1.5 \cdot IQR) \quad or \quad > (Q_3 + 1.5 \cdot IQR), \tag{4}$$

where $IQR = Q_3 - Q_1$, Q_1 and Q_3 are the first and third quartiles, respectively. This is not the most efficient method to determine the outliers of the attributes under consideration, but these plots may draw the investigator's attention to the fact that their data contains conditional outliers.

In [4] the rules

$$< (Q_1 - k \cdot IQR) \quad or \quad > (Q_3 + k \cdot IQR), \tag{5}$$

and their dependence on the selection of the k value and the amount of data for determining outliers were examined. Rules with $k = 3$ were named conservative to identify outliers in the data. They can also be applied when the distribution of values of the variable in question is not symmetric. There is no single common method for identifying all possible outliers, and the results may be affected by the specifics of the data under consideration. Experiments with the real dataset, their results and comments are provided in the next section.

4   Experimental Results

Our experiments are based on real data is taken from the mobile virtual network operator (MVNO) Lithuanian company Moremins. This company focuses its activities on customers migrating between countries, offering them cheaper international calls for which they pay by prepaid. Moremins dataset is not available to the public because of the restriction applied on it from Moremins company since the license was granted for research purposes only. The data is available to researchers in Moremins company and will be available for others after getting permission from the company [11]. The dataset contains 670 days of usage information the period covered is from 2020-01-01 to 2021-10-31. The data was derived by aggregating Call Detail Records (CDRs) and payments history information. Nearly 3 million phone calls and nearly 200000 payment records were

Table 2. Dataset description.

Attribute	Description	Object
X1	Total number of outgoing calls	Int64
X2	Avg. number of outgoing calls per day	Float64
X3	Number of phone numbers in outgoing calls	Int64
X4	Total duration of outgoing calls	Int64
X5	Avg. duration of outgoing calls	Float64
X6	Proportion of outgoing calls at night (20 h–8 h)	Float64
X7	Total number of non-answered calls	Int64
X8	The sum of costs of payments	Float64
X9	Avg. cost of payments per month	Float64
X10	Ratio of the X1 over the X3	Float64

examined and characterized. The aggregation of these data by users yielded 7960 vectors with values of 10 features of whole period behaviour. The attributes of the prepared dataset for the experiments are given in Table 2.

These are widely used attributes and proved to be effective by existing studies of fraud detection and that could be collected from available data.

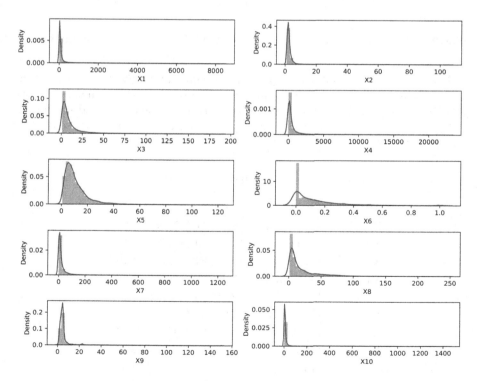

Fig. 1. The histograms of the values of each attribute.

One of the first steps is to check the normality of the data, as the choice of the method for determining outliers depends on it. Essentially, graphical methods provide a qualitative assessment of data normality. The most frequently used plot is the histograms Fig. 1 it indicates the symmetry and spread of the data. In addition, the most popular methods Kolmogorov-Smirnov and Shapiro-Wilk tests were performed to check the hypothesis of data normality. Both methods confirmed that the values of the analysed attributes did not correspond to the normal distribution. Outliers were identified for all selected attributes using the different methods described in Sect. 3. The obtained results are presented in the Fig. 2 and Table 3.

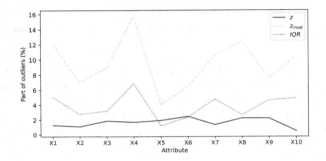

Fig. 2. Proportion of outliers (%) for different attributes using different methods.

The study found that the results using different methods for identifying outliers differed significantly in some cases. The results were influenced by the attributes analysed. The main reason for this is likely the different distributions of the values of the attributes under consideration and the methods sensitivity to their specifics.

Table 3. The quantities and percentage of outliers in the dataset.

Attribute	z	z_{mod}	IQR
X1	102 (1.28%)	964 (12.11%)	400 (5.03%)
X2	87 (1.09%)	557 (7.00%)	218 (2.74%)
X3	147 (1.85%)	712 (8.94%)	254 (3.19%)
X4	133 (1.67%)	1253 (15.74%)	545 (6.85%)
X5	151 (1.90%)	321 (4.03%)	95 (1.19%)
X6	194 (2.44%)	514 (6.46%)	186 (2.34%)
X7	106 (1.33%)	839 (10.54%)	377 (4.74%)
X8	176 (2.21%)	990 (12.44%)	211 (2.65%)
X9	174 (2.19%)	599 (7.53%)	368 (4.62%)
X10	39 (0.49%)	832 (10.45%)	389 (4.89%)

The z-criterion method (z) for finding outliers applies to normally distributed data, and this condition is not true for the data we are analysing. Using this method, a sufficiently small percentage of users was identified for each of the attributes as outliers. Modification of the z-criterion (z_{mod}), meanwhile, in contrast to z-criterion, identified very large amounts of outliers for many of the attributes. Thus, the IQR method was chosen to determine the specific limits (thresholds) of the outliers of the attributes under consideration. The Table 4 below sets out the outliers thresholds that can be used to create lists of suspicious users who are distinguished by their behaviour, e.g. the customers called more than 34 different numbers (X3), the customers with the higher than 0.6 proportion of outgoing calls at night (X6) and so on.

Table 4. Outliers thresholds were determined using the IQR method.

X1	X2	X3	X4	X5	X6	X7	X8	X9	X10
254.0	6.5	34.0	1659.0	39.7	0.6	75.0	73.5	10.0	28.5

This should help experts in identifying suspicious users. It would be good to know which of the attributes are the most significant, but to assess this we need already marked data that we don't normally have.

One of the aims of our experiments is to study the behaviour of telecommunications customers in various aspects to provide valuable information to telecommunications operators to detect fraudulent activity. Customers who stand out from the whole by their behaviour could be placed on a list of suspicious users. The problem is that it's not easy to check the effectiveness of methods until we know if there are fraudulent users in our data at all. We offer metrics that could be used to tag users as unfavourable and at the same time test and determine the effectiveness of the methods examined for outliers detection.

Let's define derivative metric - the ratio of the sum of costs of customers payments to the sum of minutes from all calls (activity):

$$M1 = \frac{X8}{X4}, \tag{6}$$

which helps to estimate the cost per minute of each user's calls data (used for the entire period). It is logical to assume that active users who talk a lot but pay little are unfavourable to the company. Because of such metric, the range of values is small, the inverse metric is more suitable for identification outliers:

$$M2 = \frac{X4}{X8} = \frac{1}{M1}. \tag{7}$$

Using both metrics, they were estimated for each customer individually, the box plots and histograms are presented in Fig. 3.

The value of the metric $M2$ was identified using the IQR method, at which point the user is considered to be distinguished and this is when $M2 > 141.91$.

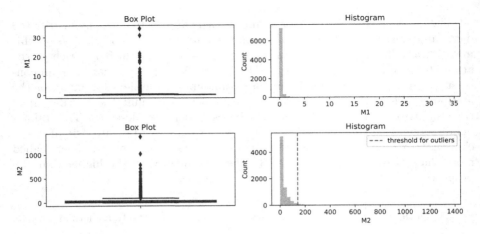

Fig. 3. Box plots and histograms of the calculated values of both metrics $M1$ and $M2$ for each customer.

It is also possible to estimate $M1$ the price per minute paid by stand-alone users, potentially unfavourable to the company, and this is when $M1 < 0.007$. 283 such customers were identified, who paid less than 0.007 Eur per minute of the call, which is 3.56% of all customers. Favourable and unfavourable customers are shown in Fig. 4.

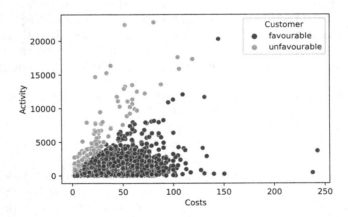

Fig. 4. A scatter plot showing the favourable and unfavourable customers.

We look for answers to the following key question: what are the most significant attributes of a customer to identify potentially fraudulent activity? To do this, we will analyse what proportion of users identified as outliers matched those labelled unfavourable users. Results, comparative value, presented in Fig. 5.

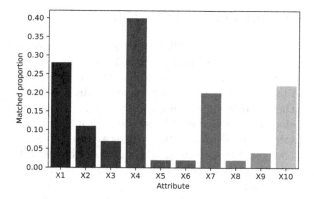

Fig. 5. Bar Chart of matched proportion.

We should pay more attention to the attributes: X1 (total number of outgoing calls), X4 (total duration of outgoing calls), X7 (total number of non-answered calls), and X10 (ratio of the total number of outgoing calls over the number of phone numbers in outgoing calls), because the matched proportions are the largest.

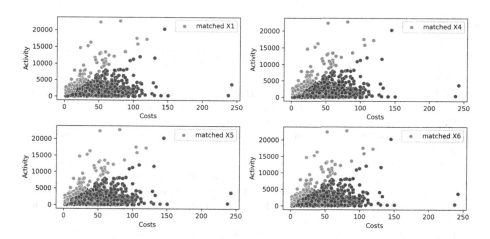

Fig. 6. Matches between unfavourable users and outliers according to different attributes.

Meanwhile, it would be difficult to identify suspicious users based on outliers from other attributes, at least in terms of how we labelled potentially unfavourable users. Examples of the use of identified outliers for two important and, conversely, two irrelevant attributes for unfavourable users are shown in Fig. 6.

5   Conclusion and Future Direction

The detection of fraud, even regardless of the field, has received increasing attention recently. The research deals with various methods aimed at detecting fraudsters as effectively as possible. Machine learning methods have been increasingly used to solve such tasks, but some require labelled data, while the effectiveness of others is difficult to measure. Typically, the detection of fraudulent activity in telecommunications is based on a profile of customer behaviour is created considering individual attributes. However, to create a profile of customer behaviour, we need to determine the most significant attributes. In this article, we examined the univariate outliers that could be used to suspect fraudulent customer behaviour. A metric has been proposed that can be used to tag unfavourable telecommunications customers to test and compare other methods' efficiency. Threshold values were found for the attributes examined, which could be used to compile lists of suspicious users. Experiments have shown that the most important attributes that need more attention in detecting fraudulent activity in telecommunications are total number and total duration of outgoing calls. Of course, it is necessary to continue the experiments in search of other attributes that would allow the detection of fraudsters as soon as possible. Hopefully, our study can will benefit both MVNO companies and the research community in the future.

References

1. Alves, R., et al.: Discovering telecom fraud situations through mining anomalous behavior patterns. In: Proceedings of the DMBA Workshop on the 12th ACM SIGKDD. Citeseer (2006)
2. Becker, R.A., Volinsky, C., Wilks, A.R.: Fraud detection in telecommunications: history and lessons learned. Technometrics **52**(1), 20–33 (2010)
3. Hilas, C.S., Mastorocostas, P.A.: An application of supervised and unsupervised learning approaches to telecommunications fraud detection. Knowl. Based Syst. **21**(7), 721–726 (2008)
4. Hoaglin, D.C., Iglewicz, B., Tukey, J.W.: Performance of some resistant rules for outlier labeling. J. Am. Statist. Assoc. **81**(396), 991–999 (1986)
5. Ibrahim, I.A., Mohammed, I., Saidu, B.: Fraud management system in detecting fraud in cellular telephone networks. Int. J. Innov. Res. Comput. Sci. Technol. (IJIRCST) **3**(3), 92–99 (2015)
6. Iglewicz, B., Hoaglin, D.C.: How to Detect and Handle Outliers, vol. 16. ASQ Press (1993)
7. Irarrázaval, M.E., Maldonado, S., Pérez, J., Vairetti, C.: Telecom traffic pumping analytics via explainable data science. Decis. Support Syst. **150**, 113559 (2021)
8. Kilinc, H.H.: A case study on fraudulent user behaviors in the telecommunication network. Electrica **21**(1), 74–84 (2021)
9. Leys, C., Ley, C., Klein, O., Bernard, P., Licata, L.: Detecting outliers: do not use standard deviation around the mean, use absolute deviation around the median. J. Exp. Soc. Psychol. **49**(4), 764–766 (2013)
10. Li, Y., et al.: Understanding the ecosystem and addressing the fundamental concerns of commercial MVNO. IEEE/ACM Trans. Netw. **28**(3), 1364–1377 (2020)

11. Moremins (2021). https://www.moremins.com/en
12. Rosset, S., Murad, U., Neumann, E., Idan, Y., Pinkas, G.: Discovery of fraud rules for telecommunications-challenges and solutions. In: Proceedings of the Fifth ACM SIGKDD International Conference on Knowledge Discovery and Data Mining, pp. 409–413 (1999)
13. Tukey, J.W., et al.: Exploratory data analysis, vol. 2. Reading, Mass (1977)
14. Zheng, F., Liu, Q.: Anomalous telecom customer behavior detection and clustering analysis based on ISP's operating data. IEEE Access **8**, 42734–42748 (2020)

ModViz: A Modular and Extensible Architecture for Drill-Down and Visualization of Complex Data

David Rademacher, Jacob Valdez, Endrit Memeti, Kunal Samant, Abhishek Santra, and Sharma Chakravarthy[✉]

IT Laboratory and CSE Department, UT Arlington, Arlington, USA
{david.rademacher,jacob.valdez2,endrit.memeti,kunalnitin.samant, abhishek.santra}@mavs.uta.edu, sharma@cse.uta.edu

Abstract. Analysis of data sets that may be changing often or in real-time, consists of at least three important synchronized components: **i)** figuring out what to infer (objectives), **ii)** analysis or computation of those objectives, and **iii)** understanding of the results which may require drill-down and/or visualization. There is considerable research on the first two of the above components whereas understanding actionable inferences through visualization has not been addressed properly. Visualization is an important step towards both understanding (especially by non-experts) and inferring the actions that need to be taken. As an example, for Covid-19, knowing regions (say, at the county or state level) that have seen a spike or are prone to a spike in the near future may warrant additional actions with respect to gatherings, business opening hours, etc. This paper focuses on a modular and extensible architecture for visualization of base as well as analyzed data.

This paper proposes a modular architecture of a dashboard for user interaction, visualization management, and support for complex analysis of base data. The contributions of this paper are: i) extensibility of the architecture providing flexibility to add additional analysis, visualizations, and user interactions without changing the workflow, ii) decoupling of the functional modules to ease and speed up development by different groups, and iii) supporting concurrent users and addressing efficiency issues for display response time. This paper uses Multilayer Networks (or MLNs) for analysis.

To showcase the above, we present the architecture of a visualization dashboard, termed CoWiz++ (for Covid Wizard), and elaborate on how web-based user interaction and display components are interfaced seamlessly with the back-end modules.

Keywords: Multilayer Networks · Modular and extensible architecture · Complex data analysis · Drill down and visualization · Covid-19 data analysis

M. Ivanovic et al. (Eds.): Baltic DB&IS 2022, CCIS 1598, pp. 232–250, 2022.
https://doi.org/10.1007/978-3-031-09850-5_16

1   Motivation

Since early 2020, when the Covid-19 cases were first reported in the US, the virus has spread to all 3141 US counties[1] in all states at different rates. As the hunt for a vaccine was launched, the number of cases has grown and leveled off based on the actions taken by different counties and states. Lack of a national policy and lack of synchronization between state and federal mandates have resulted in undesirable situations as compared to other coordinated efforts in other parts of the world.

From a data collection viewpoint, a number of sources provide features associated with a confirmed report, such as infected case, hospitalization, death, or recovery making this data set complex with diverse entity (person, county), feature (case, hospitalization, vaccination, ...), and relationship (similarity in cases, hospitalizations, vaccinations, ...) types.

Currently, many visualizations are used to plot the *peak, dip, and moving averages or colored maps* of Covid data, **without much analysis on the base data or inclusion of associated data** [1,5–7,11,12]. In other words, most of these focus on the visualization of base data using simple statistical computations. However, for a comprehensive understanding of the spread of the pandemic (or any data for that matter), there is a need to *analyse and compare the effects of different events (mask requirement, social distancing, etc.) and demographics, in multiple geographical regions across different time periods.*

Broadly, visualizations for a data set can be classified into:

I. Visualization of **Base Data:** There is very little *analysis* involved in this visualization. Visualization includes primarily statistical information. Attributes and visualization alternatives can be selected by the end-user. Temporal ranges, animation, and other visualization parameters can also be chosen. Some examples of this Category I objectives are:

(A1) Did the vaccination drive increase confidence among people to take more road trips?

(A2) In states with low per capita income, how testing progressed? Was there a surge in the number of cases?

(A3) Has the death rate reduced in countries where most of the population has received all vaccine doses? What about countries where the vaccination drive is slow?

II. Visualization of **analyzed data:** *Explicit analyses* are performed on base and associated data prior to visualization. Various alternate visualizations may be produced for the analysed results and drilled-down details of results.

Typically a model is used for analysis and objectives computed using that model. Some examples of this Category II objectives are:

---

[1] We focus on the USA as we have more accurate data for that although the pandemic is worldwide! Any country can be analyzed by swapping the data sets and with minor changes, such as prefectures in Japan instead of states.

(A4) In which regions was vaccination most effective? That is, how have geographical regions with maximum (and minimum) rise in cases shifted between the periods pre and post the beginning of the vaccination drive?

(A5) Which regions got significantly affected due to long weekends/holidays (such as, Thanksgiving, New Year Celebration, Spring Break, Labor Day, ...)? What precautions need to be taken for future events? The inverse can be computed which may be very helpful as well.

Currently available online dashboards/visualizations primarily address parts of category I discussed above. For example, JHU (Johns Hopkins University) dashboard [5] shows a lot of base data and shows some of them also on a US map with circles indicating the numbers to get a relative understanding. Similarly, the WHO (World Health Organization) dashboard [11] shows base data for the world and a clickable map to show some base data for that country. For Covid data, most dashboards focus either on reporting and/or visualizing daily cases on maps [1,2,11,12] or generating time series plots and statistical information [5–7].

However, for category II, there is a need to **model** the base data which is dependent on the semantics of the data set. As an example, for Covid data, analysis is based on counties/states. We need to model *entities and relationships* in order to *analyze* and understand the data set from *multiple perspectives*. The result needs to be *visualized* to maximize understanding. In this paper, we use the Covid-19 data set as well as related information, such as population, average per capita income, education level etc. The focus is on an interactive dashboard architecture that is **modular, flexible, provides good response time, and supports both categories I and II above.**

For the analysis part, this dashboard uses the widely-popular Entity-Relationship (ER) model and its conversion to **Multilayer Networks**[2] **or MLNs** [20]. MLNs can handle multiple entities, relationships and features. Informally, MLNs are layers of networks where *each layer is a simple graph and captures the semantics of a (or a subset of) feature of an entity type*. The layers can also be connected. Moreover, an efficient **decoupling-based approach** proposed and used in [25,26,31] is used to analyze specified objectives.

The contributions of this paper are:

– An **interactive web-based dashboard**[3] for visualizing base and analyzed data using parameters.
– A **modular** architecture to minimize interaction between the modules to facilitate **development and optimization** of the system by multiple groups with different skill sets.

---

[2] A Multilayer Network is a set of networks (each network termed a layer) where nodes within a layer are connected by intra-layer edges and nodes between two layers can be optionally connected using inter-layer edges.

[3] Dashboard [24]: https://itlab.uta.edu/cowiz/, Youtube Videos: https://youtu.be/4vJ56FYBSCg, https://youtu.be/V_w0QeyIB5s. **Readers are encouraged to play with the dashboard and watch the videos.**

- **Extensibility** of each module to add analysis, visualization, interaction/display and/or optimization alternatives with minimal effort.
- **Multiple visualizations** of base and analyzed results.
- Use of **multilayer network for modeling** and performing analysis underneath.
- Guaranteeing **consistency** while providing good response time for **a large number of concurrent users**.

This paper is organized as follows. Section 2 discusses related work. Section 3 details the architecture of the dashboard in terms of its modules.

Section 4 presents base and objective-based analysis visualizations for the Covid-19 data set. Conclusions are in Sect. 5.

2   Related Work

Currently available online dashboards address category I and focus on reporting and visualizing daily cases on maps [1,2,11,12] or time series plots and statistical modeling [5–7]. They are more focused on visualizing the base daily data. In contrast, drill-down of analysis of results is critical especially for complex data which has both structure and semantics. For example, it is not sufficient to know the identities of objects in a *community* (e.g., similar counties), but also additional details of the objects (e.g., population, per capita income etc.) Similarly, for a *centrality hub* or a *frequent substructure*. As MLNs are being used as the data model, it is imperative to know the objects across layers and their intra- and inter-connections [19]. From a computation/efficiency perspective, minimal information is used for analysis and the drill-down phase is used to expand upon to the desired extent. Existing MLN algorithms, especially the decoupling-based ones, make it easier to perform drill-down without any additional mappings back and forth for recreating the structure [25,31]. The schema generation also separates information needed for drill-down (Relations) and information needed for analysis (MLNs) from the same Enhanced Entity Relationship (EER) diagram [20].

Visualization is not new and there exists a wide variety of tools for visualizing both base data, results, and drilled-down information in multiple ways [1,5,7]. Our focus, in this paper, is to make use of available tools in the best way possible and not propose new ones. For example, we have experimented with a wide variety of tools including, maps, individual graph and community visualization, animation of features in different ways, hovering to highlight data, and real-time data fetching and display, based on user input from a menu. The main contribution is our architecture with a common back end to drive different user interaction and visualization front ends. We have also paid attention to efficiency at the back end by caching pre-generated results and use of an efficient data structure for lookup.

Community detection algorithms have been extended to MLNs for identifying tightly knit groups of nodes based on different feature combinations

[17,18,22,32]. Algorithms based on matrix factorization [16], cluster expansion [21], Bayesian probabilistic models [33], regression [15] and spectral optimization of the modularity function based on the supra-adjacency representation [35] have been developed. Further, methods have been developed to determine *centrality measures* to identify highly influential entities [29,34]. However, all these approaches *analyze a MLN by reducing it to a simple graph* either by aggregating all (or a subset of) layers or by considering the entire MLN as a whole, thus leading to loss of semantics as the entity and feature type information is lost.

3   Modular Dashboard Architecture

As part of research on big data analytics (using graphs and multilayer networks), the need for drill-down and visualization of results for understanding and ground truth verification has been emphasized. The results of *aggregate analysis* as compared to statistics, require more details (or drill-down). For example when a community of counties are computed or centrality nodes (cities) are identified, it is important to understand the related information such as population density, per capita income, education level, etc. This was further exacerbated by the fact that the data sets we deal with have multiple types of entities, features, and relationships. So, drill-down and visualization of analyzed data along with additional details became pronounced.

To clearly understand Covid data analysis results, it was important not only to drill-down, but also to visualize the data set and analysis results in multiple ways combining different aspects of the data set. For example, it was useful to visualize new cases in multiple states on a daily/weekly basis to see how they were changing. This could be done for multiple features, such as deaths, hospitalizations, etc. We also wanted to visualize similar regions in the country that had same/similar increase/decrease in new cases over the same time period. This would be very useful in understanding the effects of certain measures taken (e.g., masking, lockdown, social distancing) in different parts of the country. This essentially involved processing the same data under the categories I and II indicated above. This is also true for other data sets.

As we tried to develop a dashboard for Covid-19 visualization, we realized that the skill sets needed for analysis was significantly *different* from those needed for visualization/user-interaction. Analysis required a much deeper understanding of the knowledge discovery process including modeling of the data, coming up with objectives and computing them efficiently. On the other hand, visualization required a deeper understanding of the packages that can be used based on what and how we wanted to display. The client module needed yet another different set of skills in terms of layout, menu design, Java Script, HTML and CSS. It seemed natural that these could be developed by different individuals or groups with appropriate skills if the dashboard can be **modularized along these functional components**. This primarily motivated our architecture shown in Fig. 1.

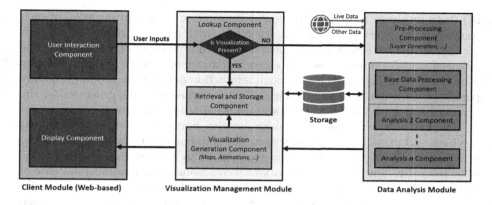

Fig. 1. Modular `CoWiz++` dashboard architecture

The second thing we noticed was that most of the currently available visualization dashboards seem to be *application and analysis specific*. That is, if the data set description and application objectives change over a period of time, then the entire system has to be re-built. Although there is likely to be a separation between the client and back end module, having a single back end module seemed to defeat extensibility in addition to modularity. This would create bottlenecks for progress making the development process quite inefficient. So, the requirement of **extensibility at the module level** was born out of this observation. This will also allow applying **different optimization strategies at the module level**.

Finally, **ability to visualize the same data in multiple ways** is extremely important from an understanding perspective. For example, one may want to visualize Covid cases/deaths/hospitalizations as a temporally animated graph for different states. One may also want to see the same data to make decisions by comparing geographical regions using MLN analysis [27]. Multiple visualizations and analysis capability in CoWiz++ follows directly from the extensibility aspect of the architecture. Currently, we support two visualization (one from each category above) as part of the visualization management module and multiple analysis (base and MLN) in the analysis module. We plan on adding more to each category.

3.1   Components of the Modular Architecture

Our proposed architecture and its components shown in Fig. 1 have been designed to support the above observations: modularity with *minimal interaction* between the modules and extensibility within *each module*. Data is transferred between modules using file handles for efficiency as all modules are running on the same machine. These two, when incorporated properly, facilitate re-use of code within each module and the development of modules independently (by different groups) from one another for different applications. This is one of the major contributions of this paper, where we introduce 3 decoupled modules, each optimized for a specific functionality: **i) a web-based client, ii) visualization management**, and

iii) data analysis modules. This architecture permits the optimization of each component, independently by separate groups with appropriate skill sets resulting in a flexible, extensible and efficient dashboard. In this paper, we show how the different modules interact and how a mix and match of analysis and visualization can be achieved. Also, note the minimal interaction between the modules (mainly parameters, file handles, etc.) As large number of files are used/generated by the two back end modules, a persistent storage is needed to store them.

There is a need for a closer synchronization between the client module and the back end visualization management module. For this to work correctly, the first step was to identify a web framework that can support these two modules, synergistically. The other considerations were: seamless communication, ease of use, availability of detailed documentation and strong open-source community for future development and extensions. Support for web deployment for increased portability was important.

Table 1. Web framework alternative and feature comparison

	Minimalistic	Language	Plotly compatibility	Documentation available	Flexibility and control
Flask [4]	**Yes**	**Python**	**Yes**	**Extensive**	**High**
Django [3]	No	Python	Limited	Extensive	Low
Vaadin [9]	No	Java	No	Limited	Low

Table 1 lists the features of the widely used web frameworks that we considered. The **python-based web framework Flask** was chosen over Django and Vaadin, mainly due to its minimalistic, interactive, flexible and extensible characteristics. Flask satisfied all our requirements as shown in the table. Moreover, visualization tools like Plotly are supported exhaustively by Flask, which is not supported by others. Most importantly, as compared to others, it gives maximum flexibility and control due to granular tuning for customisation and makes no assumptions about how data is stored, thus becoming a viable choice for a wider spectrum of applications. Below, we describe each module emphasizing the modularity and extensibility aspects.

This modular approach allows **independent parallel collaboration** in **development, debugging and optimization** of every component. Any new user interaction component, data source, data model/structure, analysis algorithm and visualization technique can be added easily to a specific module, thus supporting **efficient extensibility**. Every module has various capabilities (compartmentalized through packages or sub-modules) which are **flexibly** utilised based on the requirements of the application. And most importantly, this **robust underlying system** can be readily used for different applications without major modifications. The following sections will talk in detail about these modules, in specific to the interactive COVID-19 data analysis and visualization. In Sect. 4, we show all these modules, together, seamlessly fulfill the goal - from accepting user inputs to analysing to displaying the results visually.

3.2   Interaction and Display (Client Module)

Each analysis and visualization uses a specific set of inputs given by the user. The client module is responsible for presenting an unambiguous, clear, and simple user interface for collecting those parameters. Once the parameters and display types are identified, this module can be implemented independently and the collected parameters are passed. The inputs can be in the form of ranges (dates, latitude-longitude, times, ...), lists and sets (features, items, ...) or filtering options. The various elements of this component are supported using HTML and CSS.

The other task of this module is to display the visualization generated by the other two modules, for the input parameters, typically in the form of an html file that is displayed using the *iframe component* which lets you load external URL elements (including other web pages) in your project within an iframe. An inline frame (iframe) is a HTML element that loads another HTML page within the document. In some cases, interaction with the HTML canvas element may be required to generate and display the visualization to enhance efficiency. In addition to displaying visualizations, this component is also responsible for tickers and other relevant information (part of display type.) For example, the visualization of top 10 Covid-19 news articles and the latest cumulative number of cases and deaths is achieved through *scrollable or moving tickers*, implemented using *JavaScript and AJAX scripts* and the *marquee component*. Note, this is based on the input and is done in real-time.

3.3   Visualization Management Module (Dashboard Back End)

Functionally, this is an important module, detailed in Fig. 2, that handles several tasks: **i) visualization generation** – using either base data, or computed results – from the analysis module, **ii) reusing the generated visualization** using an efficient data structure[4], and **iii) looking up whether the visualization exists** for a given set of parameters and display type to *avoid re-generation and speedup response-time*. As can be seen in Fig. 2, there are two separate visualization generation components, a hash and cache component for quick lookup and storage. Additional visualization generation modules can be easily added. This module interacts with the other two modules and the storage.

---

[4] Currently, an in-memory hash table is used for quick lookup. If this hash table size exceeds available memory, this can be changed to a disk-based alternative (extendible hash or B+ tree) **without affecting any other module**. In this case, disk-based, pre-fetching and/or other buffer management strategies can be used to improve response time. Separate hash tables are used for different visualizations for scalability. Also, hash tables are written as binary objects and reloaded avoiding reconstruction time.

Since analysis and generation of the visualization accounts for most of the response time, we have used two known techniques for improving response time: **i) materialization of previous analysis results** – widely used in DBMSs to trade off computation with space and **ii) efficient hash-based lookup** to identify whether a **materialized visualization exists**. The first check in this module is to find the presence of the display file generated earlier. As there are hundreds of thousands of possible user input combinations, avoiding collisions in hashing is important. If the display is present, it is used. If not, the parameters are sent to the analysis module to generate computed results so this module can generate the visualization after that. **This approach has shown significant improvement and has reduced the average response time from 15 s to 3 s (80% improvement)** for map visualizations (instrumented and averaged over several interactions.) This module uses packages from Python, R and Tableau to provide diverse types of interactive graphical visualizations. Two visualizations are currently supported by this module and are discussed briefly below. Also, note that the display as well as the ticker information is based on user input. Currently, after multiple user interactions from 20+ countries (as per Google analytics), 4000+ analysis result files and 1000+ map visualization files are present. The dashboard has been operational and publicly available for more than a year (getting more than 4500 hits from 20+ countries.) Due to the extensible architecture, we have been able to add new data (e.g., on vaccinations) with very little effort and with different developers.

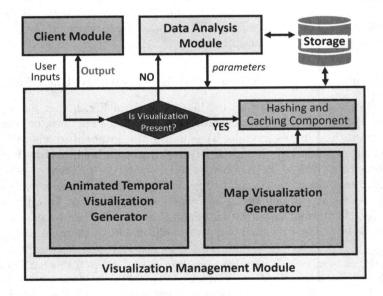

Fig. 2. Visualization management module details

Support for Multiple Concurrent Users: The flask app generates a separate thread for each concurrent user. In order to maintain consistency in the backend in the presence of multiple concurrent users, concepts of *multi-threading* have been used. *Critical sections* have been identified and *write-write* conflicting threads (that is, multiple threads with *same* parameters for which *visualization does not exist*) have been properly synchronized so that the *consistency of generated visualization is guaranteed.*

Animated Temporal Visualizations: This is an example of visualization used for category I objectives discussed earlier. Based on the temporal requirements of (**A1**)–(**A3**), the change in 2 selected features for up to 5 US states are compared by generating *2 side-by-side synchronized animated timeline plots* with a scrollable bar that the users can drag in either direction across the entire timeline. In the plots, the *per day* (or *per period*) values are synchronously plotted for each feature corresponding to the states (or countries) selected. In each plot the y-axis corresponds to one of the feature's values and x-axis to the timeline. The visualizations for these objectives are shown in Figs. 6, 7 and 8 in Sect. 4.

Two implementation alternatives help showcase the extensibility of the system. Initially, the visualizations were generated using Python's popular *Plotly library and R language*, where two separate plots were displayed side-by-side by embedding in a single plotly subplot, to implement the *synchronised animated timeline with a slider*. This visualization was *stored* as an *html file*, and *sent over the network* to the client module for display. However, this alternative had *two drawbacks* - (**i**) The embedding of two feature-wise plots in the plotly subplot to enable the synchronization requirement led to *large processing time*, and (**ii**) The generated and stored html visualization files were *large* (approx. 20+ MB for 5 states with just 3 months of data points), thus taking a hit at the network I/O and page loading time. These issues led to a *high response time*.

To address these issues, we applied an optimization technique where *generation of the temporal visualizations have been shifted to the client side*. In this case, based on the user inputs (states and features) received in Data Analysis Module (Sect. 3.4), the required data points to be plotted are *fetched* from the data set and *stored* as an object. The visualization module sends over this generated object to the Client module. On the client side, these data points are used by the *customized* JavaScript classes, that have been written for interacting with the *native HTML canvas element*, to generate the required side-by-side line graphs with a synchronized timeline. This **optimization strategy** removed the overhead processing time to generate the plotly plots and the network I/O and loading time for receiving and displaying the heavy html files. Thus, **improving the average response time by about two orders of magnitude (from 5 min to less than 5 s for 5 states and 2 features).** This also showcases that due to the modular and extensibility feature of the architecture, separate optimizations can be applied for different visualization needs. Moreover, apart from US states, support has been extended to **Indian States and World Countries**, as well. This support can be easily extended to additional countries, subject to data availability, due to the **parameterized approach followed in the module implementations**.

Map-Based Visualizations: As part of the requirements of category II analysis objectives **(A4)** and **(A5)**, communities are generated, where the counties are clustered based on similar change in a feature (in this case, similar change in *new cases*). Each county in the community is displayed on a colored US map based on the *severity* of changes in Covid cases reported in its assigned community which corresponds to a range - from SPIKE (as red) to BIG DIP (as **green**). The FIPS (Federal Processing Information Standards) codes of the US counties present in the community allocation file generated by Data Analysis Module (Sect. 3.4) are used by the *choropleth_mapbox() function of Python's plotly* library to generate colored counties on the US map with *pan and zoom capability* enabled. Moreover, the census information available as part of this file is used to generate the *hover text* for counties. The generated US map for a community file is stored as an *html file*. This visualization for objectives **(A4)** and **(A5)** is shown in Figs. 9 and 10 in Sect. 4, respectively.

3.4   Data Analysis Module (Dashboard Back-End)

The analysis module is another key module of the architecture. This module contains all aspects of a particular analysis using the same base data. We have chosen to showcase the multilayer analysis for this dashboard. This can be any other analysis, such as relational database analysis using SQL or multi-dimensional analysis supported by data warehouses. In fact, multiple analysis modules can co-exist and feed the results into the same visualization management module.

It supports several components that are important for different aspects of data analysis: *i) extraction of relevant data* from external sources, *ii) pre-processing* of extracted (or downloaded) data, and *iii) generation of results* for both base and analysis alternatives. It is more or less agnostic to visualization except to generate information needed for visualization, but does not even know how they are visualized. All three components are extensible in their own right and only rely on the user input passed from client module through the visualization management module. This module interacts with the persistent storage for both input data and output generated. This module generates output for visualization. Of course, base data preparation is much simpler than the other one.

Extraction/Downloading and Pre-processing Component: Components of this module are responsible for the real-time extraction of data from identified web sources (e.g., New York Times, WHO, CDC), update of data that changes periodically – once a day/week/month (e.g., Covid data in our dashboard) using *cron jobs*. For example, when date ranges are input by the user as part of the menu, that information is used to extract information *only for those periods*, pre-processed (cleaned, filtered, sorted/ranked), and prepared for visualization. All pre-processing of data extracted from real-time sources as well as base data used for analysis are done in this component. Examples from the current dashboard are - **(i) Period Specific Top 10 Covid-19 Articles**: For category II,

2 periods are provided. From the set of New York Times articles, a subset of top 10 most relevant Covid-19 news articles for the *latest* period specified by the user are filtered using keywords, sorted in reverse chronological order and the top-k are chosen for display, and **(ii) Latest Cumulative Case and Death Count for Selected US States and/or Countries**: For category I, the latest total number of cases and deaths for the user specified US states (along with, US and World) are filtered out from the consistent clean WHO and CDC extractions.

Complex Analysis Component(s): Any analysis for the two categories discussed earlier is supported by this module. It can be *as simple as* fetching only required base data points or generating moving averages to be plotted to *as complex as* generating required models (graphs, MLNs, ...) and detecting network communities, centralities, patterns, frequent structures and so on.

For **(A1)**–**(A3)** in category I, just the *fetching and storing* of data points for the selected states and features is required. However, the category II involves modeling, computation of objectives, and drill-down before visualization. For understanding the *effect of vaccination drives and holiday breaks and on Covid cases in the US*, the formulated objectives **(A4)** and **(A5)** (stated earlier) are to be analyzed on the Covid data set using the Multilayer Network (MLN) model[5].

For **(A4)** and **(A5)**, *geographical regions* need to be analyzed across two periods for similar Covid spread. MLN layers are created using US counties as nodes and connecting them if the change of feature (e.g., new cases (shown in Fig. 3), deaths, hospitalizations etc.) across the two periods is similar (using slabs of percentages.) Community detection algorithms (e.g., Louvain [13], Infomap [14], etc.) on the generated individual MLN layers for detecting communities that will correspond to geographical regions showing similar change in the feature. Any user-selected feature can be used for this purpose. The communities generated are categorized based on the severity of

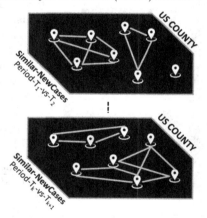

Fig. 3. MLN for category II Obj.

change in Covid cases - from spike in cases (>100% increase) to big dip (100% decrease). This generated *community allocation file* is enriched by adding the US census data like *population density per sq. mile, median household and percentage of high school graduates* for each county. The results of **(A4)** and **(A5)** are shown in Sect. 4.

---

[5] Any analysis approach and associated model can be used. We are using the Multilayer Network (MLN) model proposed in [25,28] for this dashboard. This also validates our assertion of the applicability of MLN model for complex analysis of real-world applications.

The analysis module only needs to know the information used by the visualization management module and not the actual visualization *type*. This information is known to the client module for each type of user interaction and is passed on to other modules.

4   User-Interaction and Visualization of COVID-19 Data

Fig. 4. Input panel for category I objectives *(with inputs for Fig. 6 visualization)*

Fig. 5. Input panel for cat. II obj. *(with inputs for Fig. 10 (b) viz.)*

The CoWiZ++ dashboard is hosted on an Nginx Web Server 1.20.1 on Linux machine. It is supported on all major web browsers. For the best user experience, screen sizes above 1200 pixels are recommended.

The homepage of the current dashboard supports the two different types of analyses and visualizations. Figures 4 and 5 show sample user-interaction screens (with input), for Categories I and II, respectively. Category I objectives are currently supported for *World Countries*, the *US States* and the *India States*. Category II objectives are supported for *US counties*.

Here we discuss how the current dashboard has been used to address the analysis objectives from (**A1**) to (**A5**) based on *different periods*.

Vaccination vs. Road Trips in US States (**A1**): For *understanding correlation between vaccination and people taking road trips outside their homes*, the user-interaction component shown in Fig. 4 is used. Figure 6 shows the completely rendered *snapshot* of the animated timeline depicting the correspondence between the *number of new vaccinations* and *number of new trips* undertaken by people in two of the *largest US states by population density* - **California and Texas**, till April 2021. The plots reveal something interesting. **In Texas, new trips rose disproportionately to the vaccine whereas in California, that is not the case.** This conforms to our understanding of the way these two states have handled Covid. *Note the difference in scale between the two animations.*

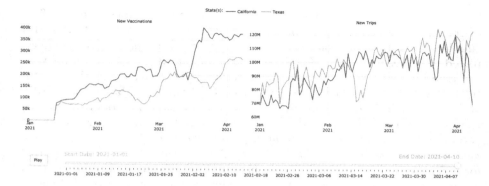

Fig. 6. (A1) Vaccinations vs. road travel trend in 2 populous US states California and Texas

New Covid Cases vs. Testing in US States (A2): Testing for Covid is important according to CDC and should be continued independently of the new cases. For understanding whether this is the case, we considered **West Virginia** as the input for the paper, one of the **low per capita income** states. Figure 7 shows these animated plots side-by-side till April 2021. For an unknown reason, testing seems to follow new cases instead of staying constant. This seems to give the impression that **the ones that are being tested are mainly the ones coming with symptoms whereas general population is not likely being tested**. For a state-level decision maker, this can be useful as an important piece of information discovered through the visualization tool.

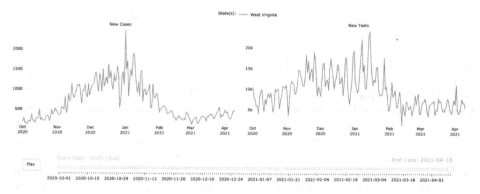

Fig. 7. (A2) New cases vs. new tests in low per capita income US state West Virginia

Fully Vaccinated Population vs. New Deaths in World Countries (A3): Medical bodies across the globe have advised getting a large percentage of the population fully vaccinated at a faster rate in order to avoid serious Covid cases, and potentially achieve herd immunity. In order to understand this correlation, the snapshot in Fig. 8 till June 2021 has been presented to illustrate the effect of getting a higher percentage of the population fully vaccinated. **Israel and the US** are two of the countries, where most of the people are **fully vaccinated (59.35% and 40.86%,** respectively, as of June 3, 2021.) Over time, with the rising vaccinations, the new Covid deaths have decreased in these countries. However, **in India where just 3.19% of the population was fully vaccinated until then, the number of new deaths had been on a rise and was more than the other better vaccinated nations.** Moreover, it is observed from *India's vaccination slope that the rate of second vaccine dose had also decreased since mid-May 2021.* Similar animations can be re-produced for different countries through the dashboard. Such **disparity in vaccination rates among countries is a cause of concern and a major roadblock in attaining global herd immunity against Covid-19** [10].

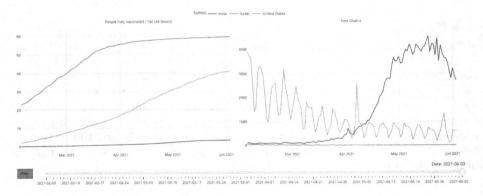

Fig. 8. (A3) Percentage of people fully vaccinated vs. new deaths in India, Israel, and USA

Vaccination Drive Effect in the US **(A4):** Here we visualize how the geographical regions with decline in daily confirmed cases shift in month-apart 3-day periods pre and post the *Vaccination Drive*. The vaccination drive in the US began from **December 14, 2020** [8]. For the *pre* vaccination drive layer, the 3-day intervals considered were Sep 20 to Sep 22 vs. Oct 21 to Oct 23 in 2020. For the *post* vaccination drive layer, the 3-day intervals were Jan 20 to Jan 22 vs. Feb 21 to Feb 23 in 2021. The *community* (groups of counties) results have been drilled-down from the individual layers and the ones displaying a downward trend have been visualized in Fig. 9. This visualization clearly shows how the **vaccination drive became one of the reasons that led to controlling the spread of COVID across US.** This fact is also verified from independent sources that say how the administration of the vaccine has led to a *decline in severe cases, hospitalizations and deaths* in the US (and many other countries) even with newer variants around [23,30].

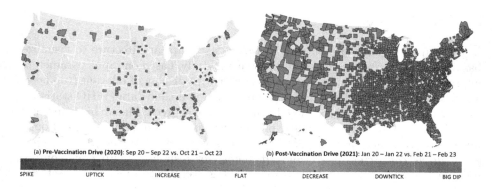

(a) Pre-Vaccination Drive (2020): Sep 20 – Sep 22 vs. Oct 21 – Oct 23   (b) Post-Vaccination Drive (2021): Jan 20 – Jan 22 vs. Feb 21 – Feb 23

SPIKE   UPTICK   INCREASE   FLAT   DECREASE   DOWNTICK   BIG DIP

Fig. 9. (A4) BIG DIP due to vaccination drive in the US (Color figure online)

<u>2022 New Year Holiday Break Effect in the US</u> **(A5)**: For this category II visualization, we use the dashboard front-end shown in Fig. 5 to first find out the geographical regions where a rise in daily confirmed cases was observed between two consecutive 5-day intervals *prior to the 2022 new year holiday break* - Dec 13 to Dec 17 vs. Dec 18 to Dec 22. Similar consecutive 5-day periods were chosen *post the 2022 new year holiday break* - Jan 5 to Jan 9 vs. Jan 10 to Jan 14. The drill-down results have been visualized in Fig. 10 that show how **after the new year holiday break there was a spike in the number of daily cases in counties across the US as compared to pre winter holiday break.** For example, the *San Diego County in California showed a surge of more than 300% in the number of new cases post the new year break*, as illustrated in the zoomed in display in Fig. 10 (b). Various reports attributed this massive surge to the widespread travel to popular tourist destinations during the break leading to **crowds and non-adherence to social distancing norms** at the time when the Omicron Covid variant was becoming dominant!

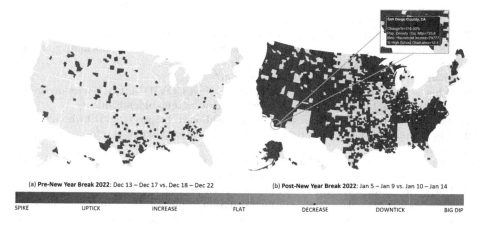

(a) **Pre-New Year Break 2022**: Dec 13 – Dec 17 vs. Dec 18 – Dec 22   (b) **Post-New Year Break 2022**: Jan 5 – Jan 9 vs. Jan 10 – Jan 14

SPIKE   UPTICK   INCREASE   FLAT   DECREASE   DOWNTICK   BIG DIP

Fig. 10. (A5) SPIKE in cases due to the 2022 new year holiday break (Color figure online)

5   Conclusions

In this paper, we have presented a modular dashboard architecture to visualize base data and complex *analysis* results meaningfully, based on input parameters interactively. In addition, we have enhanced it with display of relevant (top news articles from NYT for the period of interest) and real-time data (WHO statistics as they become available) extracted from multiple sources. The architecture and modularity, based on functionality, provide *flexibility* (of development and optimization), *extensibility* (of visualizations, analysis, and data sets), *consistency for multiple concurrent users*, and *efficiency* (for response time). Each component within a module is parameterized making it easier to replace data sets for similar visualization or change visualization for same data set.

Future work includes adding additional base data, other analysis options, and hierarchical visualizations for country and further into states. Other extensions to support multiple users efficiently and good throughput for large number of users are underway.

Acknowledgements. This work has been partly supported by NSF Grant CCF-1955798 and CNS-2120393.

References

1. The centre for disease control COVID dashboard. https://covid.cdc.gov/covid-data-tracker/
2. COVID-19 surveillance dashboard by Univ. of Virginia. https://nssac.bii.virginia.edu/covid-19/dashboard/
3. Django web framework. https://www.djangoproject.com/
4. Flask web framework. https://palletsprojects.com/p/flask/
5. Johns Hopkins University COVID dashboard. https://www.arcgis.com/apps/opsdashboard/index.html#/bda7594740fd40299423467b48e9ecf6
6. The New York Times COVID dashboard. https://www.nytimes.com/interactive/2020/us/coronavirus-us-cases.html
7. The University of Washington COVID dashboard. https://hgis.uw.edu/virus/
8. US administers 1st doses of Pfizer coronavirus vaccine. https://abcnews.go.com/US/story?id=74703018
9. Vaadin web framework. https://vaadin.com/
10. What would it take to vaccinate the world against COVID? https://www.nytimes.com/2021/05/15/world/americas/covid-vaccine-patent-biden.html
11. The World Health Organization COVID dashboard. https://covid19.who.int/
12. Worldometer COVID statistics. https://www.worldometers.info/coronavirus/country/us/
13. Blondel, V.D., Guillaume, J.-L., Lambiotte, R., Lefebvre, E.: Fast unfolding of community hierarchies in large networks. CoRR, abs/0803.0476 (2008)
14. Bohlin, L., Edler, D., Lancichinetti, A., Rosvall, M.: Community detection and visualization of networks with the map equation framework. In: Ding, Y., Rousseau, R., Wolfram, D. (eds.) Measuring Scholarly Impact, pp. 3–34. Springer, Cham (2014). https://doi.org/10.1007/978-3-319-10377-8_1

15. Cai, D., Shao, Z., He, X., Yan, X., Han, J.: Mining hidden community in heterogeneous social networks. In: Proceedings of the 3rd International Workshop on Link Discovery, pp. 58–65. ACM (2005)
16. Dong, X., Frossard, P., Vandergheynst, P., Nefedov, N.: Clustering with multi-layer graphs: a spectral perspective. IEEE Trans. Sig. Process. **60**(11), 5820–5831 (2012)
17. Fortunato, S., Castellano, C.: Community structure in graphs. In: Encyclopedia of Complexity and Systems Science, pp. 1141–1163 (2009)
18. Kim, J., Lee, J.-G.: Community detection in multi-layer graphs: a survey. SIGMOD Rec. **44**(3), 37–48 (2015)
19. Kivelä, M., Arenas, A., Barthelemy, M., Gleeson, J.P., Moreno, Y., Porter, M.A.: Multilayer networks. CoRR, abs/1309.7233 (2013)
20. Komar, K.S., Santra, A., Bhowmick, S., Chakravarthy, S.: EER→MLN: EER approach for modeling, mapping, and analyzing complex data using multilayer networks (MLNs). In: Dobbie, G., Frank, U., Kappel, G., Liddle, S.W., Mayr, H.C. (eds.) ER 2020. LNCS, vol. 12400, pp. 555–572. Springer, Cham (2020). https://doi.org/10.1007/978-3-030-62522-1_41
21. Li, H., Nie, Z., Lee, W.-C., Giles, L., Wen, J.-R.: Scalable community discovery on textual data with relations. In: Proceedings of the 17th ACM Conference on Information and Knowledge Management, pp. 1203–1212. ACM (2008)
22. Magnani, M., Hanteer, O., Interdonato, R., Rossi, L., Tagarelli, A.: Community detection in multiplex networks. ACM Comput. Surv. **54**(3), 38:1–38:35 (2021)
23. Rinott, E.: Reduction in COVID-19 patients requiring mechanical ventilation following implementation of a national COVID-19 vaccination program–Israel, December 2020-February 2021. MMWR Morb. Mortal. Weekly Rep. **70**, 326–328 (2021)
24. Samant, K., Memeti, E., Santra, A., Karim, E., Chakravarthy, S.: Cowiz: interactive COVID-19 visualization based on multilayer network analysis. In: ICDE (2021). https://itlab.uta.edu/cowiz/. https://www.youtube.com/watch?v=4vJ56FYBSCg
25. Santra, A., Bhowmick, S., Chakravarthy, S.: Efficient community re-creation in multilayer networks using Boolean operations. In: International Conference on Computational Science, Zurich, Switzerland, pp. 58–67 (2017)
26. Santra, A., Bhowmick, S., Chakravarthy, S.: HUBify: efficient estimation of central entities across multiplex layer compositions. In: IEEE ICDM Workshops (2017)
27. Santra, A.: Analysis of complex data sets using multilayer networks: a decoupling-based framework. Ph.D. thesis, The University of Texas at Arlington, July 2020
28. Santra, A., Komar, K.S., Bhowmick, S., Chakravarthy, S.: A new community definition for multilayer networks and a novel approach for its efficient computation. arXiv preprint arXiv:2004.09625 (2020)
29. Solé-Ribalta, A., De Domenico, M., Gómez, S., Arenas, A.: Centrality rankings in multiplex networks. In: Proceedings of the 2014 ACM Conference on Web Science, pp. 149–155. ACM (2014)
30. Thebault, R.: Four reasons experts say coronavirus cases are dropping in the United States. https://www.washingtonpost.com/health/2021/02/14/why-coronavirus-cases-are-dropping/
31. Vu, X.-S., Santra, A., Chakravarthy, S., Jiang, L.: Generic multilayer network data analysis with the fusion of content and structure. In: CICLing 2019, La Rochelle, France (2019)
32. Xin, Z.: Community detection in social networks. Ph.D. thesis, University of California, Davis (2018)

33. Xu, Z., Ke, Y., Wang, Y., Cheng, H., Cheng, J.: A model-based approach to attributed graph clustering. In: Proceedings of the 2012 ACM SIGMOD International Conference on Management of Data, pp. 505–516. ACM (2012)

34. Zhan, Q., Zhang, J., Wang, S., Yu, P.S., Xie, J.: Influence maximization across partially aligned heterogenous social networks. In: Cao, T., Lim, E.-P., Zhou, Z.-H., Ho, T.-B., Cheung, D., Motoda, H. (eds.) PAKDD 2015. LNCS (LNAI), vol. 9077, pp. 58–69. Springer, Cham (2015). https://doi.org/10.1007/978-3-319-18038-0_5

35. Zhang, H., Wang, C.-D., Lai, J.-H., Yu, P.S.: Modularity in complex multilayer networks with multiple aspects: a static perspective. Appl. Inform. 4 (2017). Article number: 7. https://doi.org/10.1186/s40535-017-0035-4

Efficient Computation of All-Window Length Correlations

Adam Charane[(✉)] [ID], Matteo Ceccarello [ID], Anton Dignös [ID],
and Johann Gamper [ID]

Free University of Bozen-Bolzano, Dominikanerplatz/piazza Dominican 3,
39100 Bozen-Bolzano, Italy
adam.charane@stud-inf.unibz.it, matteo.ceccarello@unibz.it,
{dignoes,gamper}@inf.unibz.it

Abstract. The interactive exploration of time series is an important task in data analysis. In this paper, we concentrate on the investigation of linear correlations between time series. Since the correlation of time series might change over time, we consider the analysis of all possible subsequences of two time series. Such an approach allows identifying, at different levels of window length, periods over which two time series correlate and periods over which they do not correlate. We provide a solution to compute the correlations over all window lengths in $O(n^2)$ time, which is the size of the output and hence the best we can achieve. Furthermore, we propose a visualization of the result in the form of a heatmap, which provides a compact overview on the structure of the correlations amenable for a data analyst. An experimental evaluation shows that the tool is efficient to allow for interactive data exploration.

Keywords: Time series · Correlation analysis · All-window length

1 Introduction

Time series data is a set of ordered observations about some phenomena or process, and they are naturally generated in many domains [2,3]. The ever-increasing volume of such data makes their analysis extremely challenging, at least for the following reasons. First, very long time series are computationally expensive to process. Furthermore, time series are often multi-variate, i.e., each observation consists of more than one measurement.

A basic task in the analysis of multi-variate time series is to study the relationships between different signals with the aim to understand whether any two signals exhibit the same or different behavior [6,7,10]. This can, for example, be explored by computing the Pearson correlation coefficient. A high correlation might indicate that either the two signals are redundant, and hence one can be

---

This work was supported by the European Regional Development Fund - Investment for Growth and Jobs Programme 2014–2020 in the context of the PREMISE project (FESR1164).

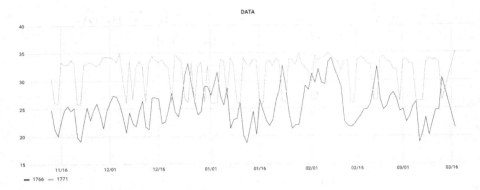

Fig. 1. Two time series which have different correlations at a small scale

removed, or that both are governed by the same process. However, correlations might occur at different scales. That is, even if there is no global correlation over the entire time series, there might be subsequences over short periods that are highly correlated or anti-correlated. Hence, focusing only on global properties of time series might hide interesting phenomena over short periods of time [8,12]. As an example, consider the two time series shown in Fig. 1. Both cover a period of about four months of temperature data collected from an industrial device in the context of the PREMISE project. The overall correlation of the two time series is -0.078, indicating that there is essentially no correlation between the two. However, if we zoom into the details, we observe that the two time series exhibit a similar behavior over the first month, followed by a period over which they are anti-correlated. Indeed, we have a correlation of 0.73 over the first month and -0.62 over the second month. This might be useful information for a data analyst to understand the behavior of the device.

Identifying periods with significantly different correlations is a useful, yet challenging task in time series analytics. A data analysts might set a window length w and compute the pairwise correlations for all subsequences of length w of the two given time series. However, what is a good window length w is initially unknown. Trying several values of w over a wide range is a viable option to investigate both global and local behaviors, however it is computationally very expensive.

In this paper, we propose an efficient method to quickly provide an overview to data analysts about the linear correlation of two signals in a multi-variate time series. Given two signals, we compute their correlation over all possible subsequences, thus providing information about their relationships at all different granularity levels, from a global view down to the local behavior over very short time periods. Such an analysis comes with two major challenges: (1) a high computational cost and (2) the need for an effective presentation of the correlation information for a data analyst. To tackle the first challenge, we reduce the number of computations by exploiting the overlap between neighboring subsequences of the time series. This is achieved by pre-computing and updating sufficient statistics that allow for an efficient computation of the correlations and improves the algorithmic complexity by a linear factor (Sect. 4). We also use parallelization to further speed up the computation using multiple CPUs. For the second challenge, we propose a visual representation as a heatmap amenable for data analysts. It encodes the correlations between all pairs of corresponding subsequences, organized along the two dimensions: the starting time point and the duration of the subsequences (Sect. 5).

The rest of this paper is organized as follows. Section 2 discusses related work and similar approaches in the literature. Section 3 provides basic definitions and the formalization of the problem. In Sect. 4, we present our proposed method and its implementation. Section 5 shows the representation of the correlation information in the form of a heatmap. In Sect. 6 we provide the results of an experimental evaluation.

2   Related Work

To the best of our knowledge, no previous works have studied the same problem, namely the pairwise correlations of all aligned subsequences of two signals, for all possible window lengths. The most similar work in previous research to our method is the Matrix Profile [13], which computes the distance between all pairs of subsequences of a certain length in a given time series. That is, the matrix profile compares subsequences of a fixed length by taking, for each position in the time series, the subsequence at that position and comparing it to all other subsequences in the time series. In our approach, we compare two different time series, by computing all possible pairs of corresponding subsequences from the two time series which start at the same position and have the same length. This difference makes the two approaches serve different purposes. The Matrix Profile looks for fixed size patterns such as discords [5,13] and motifs [8]. Our approach aims at computing the correlation between all subsequences over all possible lengths in order to facilitate the identification of periods over which the two signals behave the same or differently.

The authors of DCS (Detection of Correlated Streams) [1] use similar ideas to find highly correlated signals in a database. The correlation is not directly computed on the signals. Instead, a window size is fixed and correlations are computed in a sliding fashion. Whenever a window shows a correlation that exceeds a given threshold, a counter is increased. The decision about whether two signals are correlated or not is based on the value of the counter, i.e., how many subsequences have a correlation higher than the threshold. The usage of rolling statistics for computing correlations is similar to our method, however, the window is fixed, and the final goal is to quickly (in an interactive time) find correlated signals in a database.

Another work with some similarities to our method is AWLCO (All-Window Length Co-Occurence) [11], but it has been proposed for different measures and a different type of data. AWLCO computes co-occurrences in an item-set for all possible window lengths in a string. The authors use the inclusion-exclusion principle to reduce the complexity to linear time.

Later in the use case section, we will use visualization to get some insight about periods of interest. In the same direction, and since plotting the raw data streams obscures large-scale trends due to small-scale noise, the authors of ASAP [9] smooth the signals as a pre-processing step before plotting the data. The idea is to use moving average windows, but a small window or large window will produce, respectively, under-smoothed or over-smoothed plots. To choose the right window, the authors introduce two metrics, roughness and preservation. The roughness measures how smooth the signal is, whereas the preservation uses Kurtosis to measure how the global trend is being preserved.

3   Problem Statement

In this section, we introduce the definitions used throughout the paper, and we formalize the research problem.

Definition 1 (Time Series). *A time series S of length n is a sequence of real numbers s_i for $i \in [1, 2, \dots, n]$.*

Definition 2 (Pearson Correlation). *The Pearson correlation coefficient of two vectors S and R is defined as*

$$\rho_{S,R} = \frac{\mathbb{E}[(S - \mu_S)(R - \mu_R)]}{\sigma_S \sigma_R},$$

where $\mathbb{E}(Z)$, μ_Z, and σ_Z are, respectively, the expectation, mean, and standard deviation of a vector Z in R^n.

The Pearson correlation is defined for any two real-valued vectors of the same size. Since we are interested in analyzing the behavior of two time series for any period of time, we compute the correlation between subsequences of the two series. We denote subsequences in terms of starting position and window length.

Definition 3 (Subsequence). *Given a time series S of length n, $S_{i,w}$ is the subsequence of S starting from index i and having length w (i.e., ending at $i + w - 1$), where $i \in [1 .. n - 1]$, $w \in [2 .. n]$, and $i + w - 1 \leq n$.*

The research problem tackled in this paper is to compute the Pearson correlation coefficient between all pairs of corresponding subsequences of two different time series, where both subsequences start at the same position and have the same length, as specified in the following definition.

Definition 4 (All-Window length correlations set). *Given two time series S and R of equal length n, the all-window length correlations set is defined as $\{\rho_{S_{i,w}, R_{i,w}} \mid i \in [1 .. n - 1] \wedge w \in [2 .. n] \wedge i + w - 1 \leq n\}$.*

The All-Window length correlations set can be trivially computed in $O(n^3)$ time by considering all the valid pairs of starting positions i and window lengths w, and computing the corresponding correlation coefficient (which takes $O(n)$ time). We deem this algorithm *naïve*. While straightforward, this approach is non-optimal, in that the size of the output is $O(n^2)$. In the following section, we present an approach that matches the time complexity to the output size of the problem.

4   Computing All-Window Length Correlations Set

In this section, we present a method for computing the All-Window Length Correlations Set. First, we describe how overlapping and caching can be used to speed up the computation. Then, we propose three memory layouts in which data can be stored, and they support a parallelization of the computation. Finally, we discuss how to deploy the computation in a resource-constrained setting by using dimensionality reduction using Piecewise Aggregate Approximation (PAA) [4] when the dimension of time series is large.

4.1   Incremental Computation

The Pearson correlation coefficient can be computed for any two vectors in linear time with respect to the dimension of the vectors. In our case, we have to compute it for all possible window lengths. With signals of dimension n, there are $n-1$ possible lengths and starting positions. Therefore, the All-Window Length Correlations Set contains $\frac{n \times (n-1)}{2}$ elements. This is also a lower bound for the computation time for any exact algorithm. Since each correlation coefficient requires linear time, computing the entire correlation set naively requires $\mathcal{O}(n^3)$ time. In the following, we show how to reduce this complexity to $\mathcal{O}(n^2)$ time using an incremental approach.

Consider two subsequences $S_{i,w}$ and $R_{i,w}$. We rewrite the Pearson correlation in the following form, following Sakurai et al. [10]:

$$\rho_{S_{i,w},R_{i,w}} = \frac{\mathbb{E}[(S_{i,w} - \mu_{S_{i,w}})(R_{i,w} - \mu_{R_{i,w}})]}{\sigma_{S_{i,w}} \sigma_{R_{i,w}}} \tag{1}$$

$$= \frac{n \sum_{j=i}^{i+w-1} s_j r_j - \sum_{j=i}^{i+w-1} s_j \sum_{j=i}^{i+w-1} r_j}{\sqrt{n \sum_{j=i}^{i+w-1} s_j^2 - (\sum_{j=i}^{i+w-1} s_j)^2} \sqrt{n \sum_{j=i}^{i+w-1} r_j^2 - (\sum_{j=1}^{i+w-1} r_j)^2}} \tag{2}$$

Define now the following five quantities:

- $S_{\Sigma}^{(i,w)} = \sum_{j=i}^{i+w-1} s_i$
- $R_{\Sigma}^{(i,w)} = \sum_{j=i}^{i+w-1} r_i$
- $S_{\Sigma^2}^{(i,w)} = \sum_{j=i}^{i+w-1} s_i^2$

- $R_{\Sigma^2}^{(i,w)} = \sum_{j=i}^{i+w-1} r_i^2$
- $SR_{\Sigma}^{(w,)} = \sum_{j=i}^{i+w-1} s_i r_i$

They allow us to express the Pearson correlation coefficient as

$$\rho_{S_{i,w}, R_{i,w}} = \frac{n SR_{\Sigma}^{(i,w)} - S_{\Sigma}^{(i,w)} \cdot R_{\Sigma}^{(i,w)}}{\sqrt{n S_{\Sigma^2}^{(i,w)}} \cdot \sqrt{n R_{\Sigma^2}^{(i,w)}}} \tag{3}$$

Now, assume that we have already computed $S_{\Sigma}^{(i,w)}$. Then, we can compute in constant time both $S_{\Sigma}^{(i+1,w)}$ and $S_{\Sigma}^{(i,w+1)}$ using the following incremental update rules:

$$S_{\Sigma}^{(i+1,w)} = S_{\Sigma}^{(i,w)} + s_{i+w} - s_i \tag{4}$$

$$S_{\Sigma}^{(i,w+1)} = S_{\Sigma}^{(i,w)} + s_{i+w} \tag{5}$$

For the other quantities $R_{\Sigma}^{(i,w)}$, $S_{\Sigma^2}^{(i,w)}$, $R_{\Sigma^2}^{(i,w)}$, and $SR_{\Sigma}^{(i,w)}$, we can define similar update rules.

Based on the above update rules, our solution to compute the All-Window Length Correlations Set is shown in Algorithm 1 and works as follows. First, from the input time series, we initialize $S_{\Sigma}^{(1,2)}$, $R_{\Sigma}^{(1,2)}$, $S_{\Sigma^2}^{(1,2)}$, $R_{\Sigma^2}^{(1,2)}$, and $SR_{\Sigma}^{(1,2)}$, which requires only constant time. Then, we compute in a dynamic programming fashion the correlation between pairs of subsequences for any window length $w \in [2, n]$ and starting position $i \in [1, n - w]$ by using Equation (3) and updating the five quantities using the corresponding update rule. The output is a one-dimensional array containing the computed correlations. Different kinds of traversals of the output matrix are possible, which will be discussed in the next section.

Theorem 1. *Given two time series S and R of length n, Algorithm 1 requires time $O(n^2)$ to compute the All-Window Lengths Correlation Set.*

Proof. There are $\binom{n}{2}$ correlations to compute, and each one requires constant time by the use of the update rules. Therefore, the algorithm requires $O(n^2)$ time overall. $\square$

This reduces the time complexity by a linear factor from $\mathcal{O}(n^3)$ to $\mathcal{O}(n^2)$. Observe that this running time is optimal, in that it is the same order of the size of the output.

Notice also that the same statistics could be used to compute the Euclidean distance and z-normalized Euclidean distance (as an alternative metric to the Pearson correlation), since the mean and standard deviation can be extracted in constant time, too.

Algorithm 1: Incremental algorithm for computing the All-Window lengths Correlations set

---

Input : Two time series S and R of length n

Output : Array of length $\frac{n \times (n-1)}{2}$

---

for $i \leftarrow 1$ to n do

  | if $i = 1$ then

  | | $S_{\Sigma}^{(1,2)} \leftarrow s_1 + s_2$; $\quad R_{\Sigma}^{(1,2)} \leftarrow r_1 + r_2$;

  | | $S_{\Sigma 2}^{(1,2)} \leftarrow s_1^2 + s_2^2$; $\quad R_{\Sigma 2}^{(1,2)} \leftarrow r_1^2 + r_2^2$;

  | | $SR_{\Sigma}^{(1,2)} \leftarrow s_1 r_1 + s_2 r_2$;

  | else

  | | $S_{\Sigma}^{(i,2)} \leftarrow S_{\Sigma}^{(i-1,2)} + s_{i+1} - s_{i-1}$; $\quad R_{\Sigma}^{(i,2)} \leftarrow R_{\Sigma}^{(i-1,2)} + r_{i+1} - r_{i-1}$;

  | | $S_{\Sigma 2}^{(i,2)} \leftarrow S_{\Sigma 2}^{(i-1,2)} + s_{i+1}^2 - s_{i-1}^2$; $\quad R_{\Sigma 2}^{(i,2)} \leftarrow R_{\Sigma 2}^{(i-1,2)} + r_{i+1}^2 - r_{i-1}^2$;

  | | $SR_{\Sigma}^{(i,2)} \leftarrow SR_{\Sigma}^{(i-1,2)} + s_{i+1} r_{i+1} - s_{i-1} r_{i-1}$;

  | end

  | $\rho_{S_{i,2}, R_{i,2}} \leftarrow \dfrac{n SR_{\Sigma}^{(i,2)} - S_{\Sigma}^{(i,2)} R_{\Sigma}^{(i,2)}}{\sqrt{S_{\Sigma 2}^{(i,2)}} \sqrt{R_{\Sigma 2}^{(i,2)}}}$;

  | for $w \leftarrow 3$ to $n - i$ do

  | | $S_{\Sigma}^{(i,w)} \leftarrow S_{\Sigma}^{(i,w-1)} + s_{i+w}$; $\quad R_{\Sigma}^{(i,w)} \leftarrow R_{\Sigma}^{(i,w-1)} + r_{i+w}$;

  | | $S_{\Sigma 2}^{(i,w)} \leftarrow S_{\Sigma 2}^{(i,w-1)} + s_{i+w}^2$; $\quad R_{\Sigma 2}^{(i,w)} \leftarrow R_{\Sigma 2}^{(i,w-1)} + r_{i+w}^2$;

  | | $SR_{\Sigma}^{(i,w)} \leftarrow SR_{\Sigma}^{(i,w-1)} + s_{i+w} r_{i+w}$;

  | | $\rho_{S_{i,w}, R_{i,w}} \leftarrow \dfrac{n SR_{\Sigma}^{(i,w)} - S_{\Sigma}^{(i,w)} R_{\Sigma}^{(i,w)}}{\sqrt{S_{\Sigma 2}^{(i,w)}} \sqrt{R_{\Sigma 2}^{(i,w)}}}$;

  | end

end

4.2 Memory Layout

We store the output of Algorithm 1 in a one-dimensional array. There are different ways how to layout the correlation values in the array, which all have a different impact on the use of the cache and the visualization of the correlation coefficients in a heatmap (cf. Sect. 5). Figure 2 shows three different layouts we consider in this paper. On the horizontal axis we have the starting position of the subsequences and on the vertical axis the length of the subsequences (i.e., window length). Hence, columns correspond to different starting positions (starting from 1) and rows correspond to different window lengths (starting from 2). The numbers in the cells report the index in the output array, where the corresponding correlation coefficient is stored. The sequence of these numbers indicates the order in which the correlation coefficients are calculated.

Figure 2a shows the *anti-diagnoal layout*. Given a starting position i and a window length w, the index l in the array where the correlation of the two corresponding subsequences is stored and can be retrieved in constant time is the following:

$$l = i - 1 + \frac{(i + w - 3) \times (i + w - 2)}{2} \qquad \text{(Anti-diagonal indexer)}$$

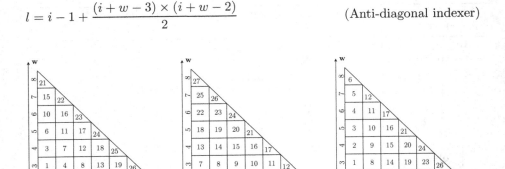

(a) Anti-Diagonal   (b) Horizontal   (c) Vertical

Fig. 2. Linearization of the matrix for the different memory layouts for two time series of dimension 8.

Another approach is to use a *horizontal layout* and compute the correlation coefficients in horizontal order, i.e., we fix a window length and compute the correlations for all starting positions (cf. Fig. 2b). For this layout the mapping from the starting position i and the window length w to the position in the array is determined as

$$l = (w - 2) \times n - \frac{(w - 2) \times (w - 1)}{2} + i - 1 \qquad \text{(Horizontal indexer)}$$

A third representation is a *vertical layout* (cf. Fig. 2c). Instead of fixing the window length, the starting position is fixed first, and then the window size is increased. The relationship between the starting position i and the window length w with the index in the output array is

$$l = (i - 1) \times (n - 1) - \frac{(i - 1) \times (i - 2)}{2} + w - 2 \qquad \text{(Vertical indexer)}$$

The choice of the best layout depends on the application. If the goal is to show the correlation results in a heatmap (as we will do in Sect. 5), the horizontal layout (indexer) computes and stores the correlation coefficients in a way that is ready for consumption by image-producing software. This layout, however, is not very cache friendly: computing each correlation along the rows entails reading values from both the end and the start of the sliding window, which for large windows might incur in cache misses.

In the experimental evaluation (Sect. 6) we compare the three memory layouts. For each memory layout we arrange the iterations of Algorithm 1 so that it follows the same pattern as the output layout.

4.3   Parallelization

To further speed up the computation of the All-Window Length Correlations Set, we describe next how to parallelize our algorithm. Consider again the layouts in Fig. 2. If we first compute either the first row or the first column, then the computation of the remaining correlations in each column (resp. row and diagonal) is independent of the others. For instance, once in the horizontal layout in Fig. 2b the first row is computed, we can compute each column independently of the others. We can thus easily parallelize these computations across several threads.

One issue when parallelizing this computation is load balancing. Consider again Fig. 2: the columns to the right have far fewer values than the columns on the left. To balance the workload across different threads, then, we must take care of assigning columns to threads in such a way that each thread has approximately the same number of elements, overall.

The memory layouts presented in Fig. 2 have different indexers to the array storing the correlations. For the anti-diagonal layout, for instance, consecutive values in an anti-diagonal are consecutive in the array, and consecutive anti-diagonals are also represented consecutively in the array (as indicated by the numbers in the cells). The same is true for the other memory layouts. By distributing the computations of consecutive anti-diagonals over threads, each thread can make use of the cache memory resulting in speed-ups.

Suppose we want to distribute the computation using the anti-diagonal layout shown in Fig. 2a over two threads. An optimal scheduling would assign the first five anti-diagonals to one thread and the last two to the other. Notice that the first thread will have to compute fifteen correlations, whereas the second will compute thirteen. In general, given the length of a time series n and the number of threads k, we want each thread to have a number of columns (row or anti-diagonal depending on the memory layout), where the total number of correlations is approximately $\frac{n \times (n-1)}{2k}$. This can be formulated as a minimization problem:

Problem 1 (Scheduler). Given a time series of length n and k threads, find $k-1$ (intermediate) break points b_i for $i \in [1 .. k-1]$, such that

$$\sum_{j=0}^{k-1} |T_j - \frac{n \times (n-1)}{2k}|$$

is minimized, where $T_j = \sum_{t=b_j+1}^{b_{j+1}} t$ is the number of correlations assigned to the thread j. The first and the last break point are fixed, respectively, to $b_0 = 0$ and $b_k = n-1$.

To solve the above scheduling problem for the anti-diagonal memory layout, we use a greedy approach described in Algorithm 2. The same algorithm can be used for the other memory layouts with slight modifications: the anti-diagonals start by having 1 correlation to compute and end with $n-1$, whereas the horizontal and vertical layouts start with $n-1$ correlations for the first rows and columns, respectively, and end with 1 correlation.

Algorithm 2: Greedy algorithm for assigning anti-diagonals to threads

---

Input   : n - Length of the time series
            k - Number of threads
Output : Array of indices, each two consecutive indices map computations to
            one thread.

$B \leftarrow [0]$;
$b \leftarrow 0$;
expected $\leftarrow \frac{n \times (n-1)}{2k}$;
$T_{\text{current}} \leftarrow 0$;
$T_{\text{prev}} \leftarrow 0$;
for $i \leftarrow 1$ **to** $n - 1$ **do**
   | $T_{\text{prev}} \leftarrow T_{\text{current}}$;
   | $T_{\text{current}} \leftarrow T_{\text{current}} + i$;
   | $b \leftarrow b + 1$;
   | **if** $T_{current} >= expected$ **then**
   | | **if** $T_{current} - expected < expected - T_{prev}$ **then**
   | | | B.append(b);
   | | | $T_{\text{current}} \leftarrow 0$;
   | | **else**
   | | | B.append($b - 1$);
   | | | $T_{\text{current}} \leftarrow i$;
   | | **end**
   | **end**
end
B.append($n - 1$);

4.4   Dimensionality Reduction

For long time series, the quadratic running time of Algorithm 1 might be too high for real-time data analysis. However, if the correlation coefficients are visualized in a heatmap, the size of the All-Window Lengths Correlation Set might be larger than the number of available pixels for the visualization. Therefore, there is no need to compute all the correlation values at the granularity of the data, since the results cannot be readily visualized.

In this case, we first apply Piecewise Average Approximation (PAA) to the raw time series with an appropriate window length. The window length is chosen such that the length of the compressed time series corresponds to the number of available horizontal or vertical pixels for the visualization of the heatmap such that the number of computed correlation coefficients corresponds to the number of pixels in the plot. This has the effect of both reducing the size of the output to a user-defined maximum and of limiting the computation time. We want to stress that using PAA might introduce some errors. That is, the dimensionality reduction might create phantom (i.e., non-existing) correlations or hide existing ones, however the error is bounded [4].

5 Visualization of Correlations in a Heatmap

One of the major issues that data analysts encounter most of the time when dealing with time series is the size of the window length to use for the analysis. To address this issue, we will make use of the computed correlations between two time series in the above section, and provide a visual tool to assist data analysts in the form of a heatmap to interpret the correlations. The idea is no matter at what time or how long this behavior lasts, we should be able to detect it as we are computing all the possible correlations between the two signals. The heatmap plots the results on a 2-D plane, where on one axis the starting position changes, whereas on the second one, the window length changes.

Our proposed solution was implemented as a web application using the open source framework Dash Plotly[1], where the user can load time series, plot them with the possibility of normalizing, since sometimes the gap of scale between signals is so big, that some signals do not appear at all if they are plotted in their raw format.

Figure 3 shows an example of the interactive web application with some real-world data. The upper image shows the time series loaded with Min-Max scaling being applied. The lower image is the heatmap of correlations.

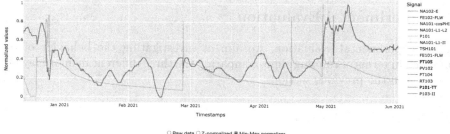

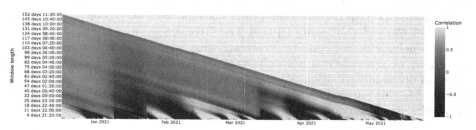

Fig. 3. Web application of the Heatmap in interactive mode

Notice how easy it is to spot on the heatmap when correlations change. Overall the two signals are not correlated, as the window of size 152 days has

---

[1] https://dash.plotly.com/.

a color intensity representing a Pearson coefficient of value almost 0. However, there are small regions where the correlation goes close to 1, indicating some change happened in one or both of the signals that made them behave almost in the same way. There are also plenty of anti-diagonal lines that have the same color. Even that they have different window sizes, but they all end at the same timestamp, which points to an important change in the signals at that time. At the bottom of the heatmap (i.e., small window sizes), the correlations are not stable. The extreme case is with a window of size 2, for which the correlation can only be 1 or −1. These small perturbations get smoothed with larger window sizes.

Figure 4 shows an example using synthetic data. We use two sine waves A and B with some random noise. The two sine waves are perfectly in sync and thus have a high (positive) correlation between 0 and 70 and between 150 and 240. Between 70 and 150 we flip the sine wave B to make it anti-correlated, i.e., with a high negative correlation. We can see in the heatmap that the phenomena is well visible using the anti-diagonal lines. If we look at the correlation values for the entire time series, i.e., top-left, we would conclude that the two time series have no correlation, i.e., a correlation value close to 0. Using the heatmap we identify three "triangles" that exactly map to the three periods of high positive correlation, high negative correlation, and again high positive correlation.

6   Experimental Evaluation

In the experimental evaluation, we aim at investigating the behavior of our approach in terms of running time, comparing the three different memory layouts proposed in the previous section.

6.1   Experimental Setup

Our algorithm and data-structures have been implemented with C++14, and the experiments have been executed on a machine with 16 GB of memory and an Intel® Core™ i7-4720HQ CPU @ 2.60 GHz × 8.

As benchmarks, we consider synthetic time series of different lengths. In particular, we generate random walks with offsets distributed according to the standard normal distribution. We remark that the complexity of the algorithms described in this paper does not depend on the distribution of the data. Hence, the results we obtain on these benchmarks generalize to any distribution.

6.2   Comparison with Baseline Solution

We first focus on the performance on small inputs, such as the ones that might be obtained with PAA in the context of our use case. Table 1 reports the running time of our algorithm compared with the naïve algorithm. We can clearly see that the naïve algorithm exhibits a cubic complexity, making it impractical even on such small inputs: for a time series of length 1 600 it requires over 12 s

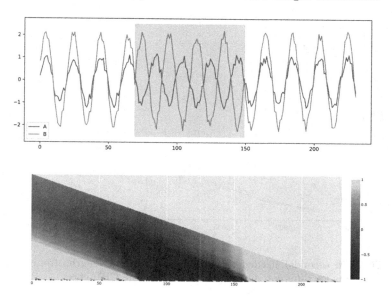

Fig. 4. Example using two synthetic time series

to compute all correlations. Our incremental algorithm, instead, computes the solution within a time limit that is compatible with interactive usage, in the range of the tens of milliseconds, confirming its usefulness in a data-exploration setting.

Table 1. Running time (in milliseconds) of our approach and the naïve algorithm.

Algorithm	Size				
	100	200	400	800	1 600
Naïve	8.12	36.00	215.19	1 583.93	12 632.13
Anti-diagonal	0.45	1.34	2.70	9.68	38.98
Horizontal	0.55	1.54	3.28	11.68	46.74
Vertical	0.41	1.21	2.65	9.46	38.20

6.3 Scalability in the Input Size

To test the scalability of our algorithm, we consider time series of up to ≈ 52 000 points. Figure 5 reports the results of this experiment for all three memory layouts presented in Sect. 4.2. The green line reports the performance of the naïve algorithm on inputs up to 1 600 points.

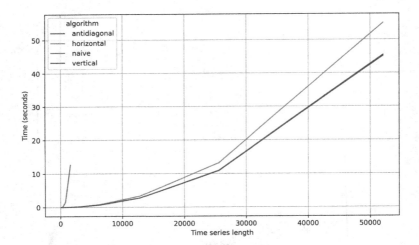

Fig. 5. Time (in seconds) needed to compute all window lengths from all possible starting positions for different time series sizes using one CPU core.

First, we observe that the running time is quadratic with respect to the input size, as expected, for all three layouts. The best performing layout is the anti-diagonal, followed closely by the vertical layout. The horizontal layout is ≈ 20% times slower than the other two.

These differences in performance can be explained by different cache behaviors of the algorithms. In particular, to update the running statistics needed to compute the correlations, the horizontal layout may incur in four cache misses: one for the new value to be added to each statistic and one for the old value to be subtracted, for both time series. The other two approaches, instead, incur in up to one cache miss for each of the two time series, leading to better performance.

6.4   Parallel Execution

To show the impact of parallelization on the algorithms we evaluate the approach described in Sect. 4.3. We use two time series of length 40 000 and vary the number of threads k from 2 to 8. The results in terms of speedup as compared to the single threaded executions are shown in Fig. 6. The speedup for the anti-diagonal algorithm using two, four, and eight threads is 1.6, 2.3, and 3.3, respectively. For the other algorithm we have similar speedups, i.e., 1.6, 2.6, and 3.6 for the vertical algorithm and 1.7, 2.8, and 4 for the horizontal algorithm.

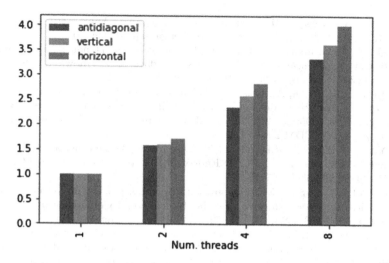

Fig. 6. Speedup of parallel execution as compared to the single threaded execution.

7   Conclusions

In this paper, we studied the all-window lengths correlations set problem, which is a useful primitive in the data exploration phase for a set of time series data. The naïve solution of this problem requires time $O(n^3)$, which is impractical even for moderately sized datasets. To address this issue, we investigate incremental algorithms that reuse computations, obtaining a $O(n^2)$ running time, which matches the size of the output and is therefore optimal. We use this primitive to efficiently (i.e., within interactive time constraints) build a heatmap visualization of the structure of correlations between subsequences of two given time series. Such visualization allows the data analyst to uncover, at a glance, patterns in the data that might otherwise go unnoticed.

Future works points in different directions. It would be interesting to make the analysis tool interactive with the possibility to zoom in and out to analyze and visualize the data at different granularity levels. Another direction is to extend the analysis tool to consider not only a pair of time series but sets of more than two time series.

References

1. Alseghayer, R., Petrov, D., Chrysanthis, P.K., Sharaf, M., Labrinidis, A.: Detection of highly correlated live data streams. In: Proceedings of the International Workshop on Real-Time Business Intelligence and Analytics, BIRTE 2017. Association for Computing Machinery, New York (2017). https://doi.org/10.1145/3129292.3129298
2. Esling, P., Agon, C.: Time-series data mining. ACM Comput. Surv. **45**(1), 1–34 (2012). https://doi.org/10.1145/2379776.2379788

3. Fu, T.C.: A review on time series data mining. Eng. Appl. Artif. Intell. **24**(1), 164–181 (2011). https://doi.org/10.1016/j.engappai.2010.09.007

4. Keogh, E., Chakrabarti, K., Pazzani, M., Mehrotra, S.: Dimensionality reduction for fast similarity search in large time series databases. Knowl. Inf. Syst. **3**(3), 263–286 (2001). https://doi.org/10.1007/pl00011669

5. Keogh, E., Lin, J., Fu, A.: Hot sax: efficiently finding the most unusual time series subsequence. In: Proceedings of the Fifth IEEE International Conference on Data Mining, ICDM 2005, pp. 226–233. IEEE Computer Society, USA (2005). https://doi.org/10.1109/ICDM.2005.79

6. Li, Y., U, L.H., Yiu, M.L., Gong, Z.: Discovering longest-lasting correlation in sequence databases. Proc. VLDB Endow. **6**(14), 1666–1677 (2013). https://doi.org/10.14778/2556549.2556552

7. Papadimitriou, S., Sun, J., Faloutsos, C.: Streaming pattern discovery in multiple time-series. In: Proceedings of the 31st International Conference on Very Large Data Bases, VLDB 2005, pp. 697–708. VLDB Endowment (2005)

8. Patel, P., Keogh, E.J., Lin, J., Lonardi, S.: Mining motifs in massive time series databases. In: Proceedings of the 2002 IEEE International Conference on Data Mining (ICDM 2002), 9–12 December 2002, Maebashi City, Japan, pp. 370–377. IEEE Computer Society (2002). https://doi.org/10.1109/ICDM.2002.1183925

9. Rong, K., Bailis, P.: ASAP: prioritizing attention via time series smoothing. Proc. VLDB Endow. **10**(11), 1358–1369 (2017). https://doi.org/10.14778/3137628.3137645

10. Sakurai, Y., Papadimitriou, S., Faloutsos, C.: Braid: stream mining through group lag correlations. In: Proceedings of the 2005 ACM SIGMOD International Conference on Management of Data, SIGMOD 2005, pp. 599–610. Association for Computing Machinery, New York (2005). https://doi.org/10.1145/1066157.1066226

11. Sobel, J., Bertram, N., Ding, C., Nargesian, F., Gildea, D.: AWLCO: all-window length co-occurrence. In: 32nd Annual Symposium on Combinatorial Pattern Matching (CPM 2021). Leibniz International Proceedings in Informatics (LIPIcs), vol. 191, pp. 24:1–24:21. Schloss Dagstuhl - Leibniz-Zentrum für Informatik, Dagstuhl, Germany (2021). https://doi.org/10.4230/LIPIcs.CPM.2021.24. https://drops.dagstuhl.de/opus/volltexte/2021/13975

12. Ye, L., Keogh, E.: Time series shapelets: a new primitive for data mining. In: Proceedings of the 15th ACM SIGKDD International Conference on Knowledge Discovery and Data Mining, KDD 2009, pp. 947–956. Association for Computing Machinery, New York (2009). https://doi.org/10.1145/1557019.1557122

13. Yeh, C.C.M., et al.: Matrix profile i: all pairs similarity joins for time series: a unifying view that includes motifs, discords and shapelets. In: 2016 IEEE 16th International Conference on Data Mining (ICDM), pp. 1317–1322 (2016). https://doi.org/10.1109/ICDM.2016.0179

Author Index

Printed in the United States
by Baker & Taylor Publisher Services